Jim Northcott was previously head of PSI's programme of longer-term studies, where he designed and managed the highly acclaimed *Britain in 2010* project and wrote the resulting best-selling report. His many other publications include the follow-up study to *Britain in 2010: The Future of Britain and Europe*. He has worked for the Economist Intelligence Unit, was a Director of Economic Consultants Limited, and is an award-winning documentary film director. Jim is a member of the Royal Institute of International Affairs, a fellow of the Royal Geographic Society and a founder member of the UK and European Futures Groups.

ate you. ... I
, but also the
imilar studies

acques Delors

Neil Kinnock

rmation, and
seful book to

·f

tt

well.

ernard Cazes

Britain's Future:
Issues and Choices

Jim Northcott

POLICY STUDIES INSTITUTE, LONDON

UNIVERSITY OF WESTMINSTER

PSI is a wholly owned subsidiary of the University of Westminster

The statements and opinions contained in this book are solely the responsibility of the author, and not those of the Policy Studies Institute.

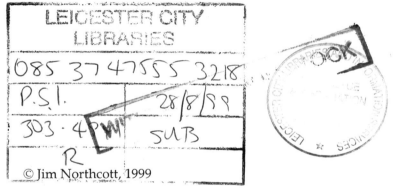

ISBN 0 85374 755 5
PSI Report number 860

Edited and typeset by Oxford Publishing Services, Oxford
Printed and bound by Polestar Wheatons Ltd, Exeter

For further information please contact
Policy Studies Institute, 100 Park Village East, London NW1 3SR
Tel: (44) 171 468 0468 Fax: (44) 171 388 0914 Email: pubs@psi.org.uk

Contents

Charts and Maps

Acronyms and Abbreviations

ACS	Association of Caribbean States
APEC	Asia-Pacific Economic Cooperation Conference
ASEAN	Association of South East Asian Nations
AWACS	airborne warning and control system
BMA	British Medical Association
BP	British Petroleum
BUPA	British United Provident Association
CERN	Conseil européen pour la recherche nucléaire (European Organization for Nuclear Research); now called European Laboratory for Particle Physics
CFC	chlorofluorocarbon
CFE	Conventional Forces in Europe
CHI	Commission for Health Improvement
CIA	Central Intelligence Agency (USA)
CIS	Confederation of Independent States
EBM	evidence-based medicine
EFTA	European Free Trade Association
EMU	European Monetary Union
ERM	Exchange Rate Mechanism
EU	European Union
FBI	Federal Bureau of Investigation
FTAA	Free Trade Agreement for the Americas
G8	Group of Eight (leading industrial nations)
GATT	General Agreement on Tariffs and Trade
GDP	gross domestic product
GNP	gross national product
IMF	International Monetary Fund
IPCC	Intergovernmental Panel on Climate Change
IT	information technology
MAD	mutually assured destruction
MFA	Multi-Fibre Arrangement
NAFTA	North American Free Trade Association
NAIRU	nonaccelerating inflation rate of unemployment

NATO	North Atlantic Treaty Organisation
NHS	National Health Service
NI	national insurance
NICE	National Institute for Clinical Excellence
OECD	Organisation for Economic Cooperation and Development
PFI	Private Finance Initiative
PSBR	public sector borrowing requirement
R&D	research and development
SADC	Southern African Development Community
SALT	Strategic Arms Limitation Talks
SERPS	state earnings related pensions scheme
START	Strategic Arms Reduction Talks
TESSA	Tax-Exempt Special Savings Account
TINA	There Is No Alternative
UNDP	United Nations Development Programme
UNSCOM	UN commission charged with identifying and eliminating Iraq's weapons of mass destruction
USAID	United States Agency for International Development
VAT	value added tax

1 Introduction

The next century will bring new issues needing new policies, and the time to work on them is now. The reason for this is that we can *shape* the future, by thinking clearly and acting early. For the future is not fixed and immutable; it is largely the result of a succession of choices made along the way. By analysing likely future developments and the factors affecting them we can identify ways we can act *now* to minimise the risks and amplify the opportunities that lie ahead. Foresight can give choice; if we ensure that the policies of today are also consistent with the needs of tomorrow, we have the chance to make the future better than it would have been otherwise. In that sense *the future is what we make it.*

In the *Britain in 2010* project[1] the Policy Studies Institute used its multi-disciplinary research team to make a systematic analysis of likely developments in Britain over a period two decades ahead. This was followed by *The Future of Britain and Europe*[2] which sketched out the implications of these same developments for the future of Europe and of Britain's place in it. The purpose of the present book is to take this analysis a stage further by examining the policy choices that expected future developments present: if this is the way things are going, *what can we actually do about it?*

The book focuses on seven of the most important developments that will affect Britain in the first half of the twenty-first century:

- an ageing population,
- growing inequality,
- persistent unemployment,
- an increasingly global economy,
- an ever more threatened environment,
- rising world population, and
- the new security needs of the post-cold war world.

Britain's future is closely tied up with Europe and the rest of the world, and in each of the seven areas that will be important for Britain there are international aspects to be considered. For example, ageing population is bringing problems not only for Britain, but also for all the other countries in

Europe, most of which are responding in ways quite different from Britain. Increasing inequality is a problem Britain shares with the United States, because it is the result of policies being pursued mainly in these two countries. The problems of high unemployment and slow economic growth are shared by many countries and are being caused in part by developments in the global economy; a key part in the solution of these problems will therefore lie in reform of the EU and the international economic organisations. With the environment some problems, such as climate change, are essentially global in their impact and can only be dealt with by worldwide joint action. With world population, it is predominantly in the least developed countries that the increases are greatest and it is the future of these which is most at risk if population grows at rates too fast to be supported; but if it does, Britain will be affected also. And with security, it is developments in other countries that will determine what form future threats will take and what defence capabilities will be needed for dealing with them. In each of the seven areas, therefore, it is unrealistic to consider the future of Britain in isolation; on the contrary, it is essential to examine the way ahead for Britain in the wider context of developments in Europe and the rest of the world.

The following seven chapters take each of the seven areas in turn, outlining the likely developments, analysing the issues that will arise from them, and setting out the policies for addressing them.

Chapter 2 is about the implications of an ageing population – by 2040 the number of people of working age available to support each person over 65 will fall by nearly a half. This will bring problems in providing pensions, and also in health care – people aged 65–74 cost the National Health Service (NHS) four times as much per head as people aged 5–64, and people aged 85 and over cost 16 times as much. Will we still be able to 'afford' the welfare state? Chapter 2 examines the form and scale of future problems for health care and pensions, assesses the merits of alternative new policies, and sets out the requirements for health and security in old age in the decades ahead.

Chapter 3 is about the increase in inequality. Since 1979, the income gap between the richest 10 per cent and the poorest has more than doubled and the number of people living on welfare benefits has gone up by a half. One-third of the nation's children now live in poverty and, if recent trends continued, by the year 2010 Britain would be as unequal as Brazil. Hardship is widespread already and social cohesion will be in jeopardy in the future. There is nothing inevitable about this – it has not been happening in other European countries. This chapter analyses the causes of increasing inequality in Britain, and outlines the policies needed to reverse this dangerous trend.

Chapter 4 is about unemployment. This has risen to previously unthinkable levels – the real level is now about 5 million people. The cost of not having full employment currently amounts to more than £8 billion a year in additional government expenditure and more than £16 billion a year in lost government revenues – equivalent to more than one-fifth of the yield of income tax. It is *not* inevitable that mass unemployment will continue indefinitely. This chapter explains how a return to full employment is feasible – with difficulty, and over a period – and elaborates the combination of policies needed to bring it about.

Chapter 5 is about the challenges of the global economy. The world economy is increasingly working as a single market system; world trade is rising twice as fast as output and by the year 2010 imports to Britain will be equivalent to two-thirds of total consumer spending. Globalisation brings new opportunities for Britain, but also new risks, for example in the form of massive international financial movements. On the day Britain was forced out of the ERM (Exchange Rate Mechanism), turnover on the London market was greater than the total value of imports and exports over the *whole year*, and more than ten times as great as the total value of the foreign exchange reserves. This increasing international interdependence makes it all the more important to improve Britain's uneven economic performance, while imposing constraints on the means available to any government for bringing this about. This chapter assesses the policy options available and explains what needs to be done to secure faster economic growth and deal with the pressures of the global market.

Chapter 6 is about some of the most important long-term environmental issues, such as pollution and congestion, and the range of policies needed to secure a better, sustainable environment. It focuses in particular on the most threatening and intractable problem of all – global climate change. To prevent it there will be a need ultimately to reduce world emissions of carbon dioxide (from burning oil, gas and coal) by 60 per cent. Britain is the world's seventh largest emitter of carbon dioxide, and the implied reduction for Britain will be even greater. This will present formidable problems and the need for a range of policies to reduce energy consumption and make greater use of renewables – at present Britain gets far less of its energy from renewable sources than any other country in the European Union.

Chapter 7 is about world population, which is currently growing by more than 80 million people (another Britain and a third) *each year*. If 1990 fertility rates continued, world population would quadruple between 1990 and the middle of the next century – making it impossible to grow enough food for all the extra people. Even with substantial reductions in fertility rates, world population is expected to nearly double by the middle of the next century, implying severe pressure on resources, a growing North–South gap and increasing immigration pressures on Europe. This chapter examines the factors affecting Third-World development and outlines the policies that offer the best hope of meeting basic human needs and bringing down fertility rates to more manageable levels.

Chapter 8 is about national security. The cold war is over and there is no possibility of it being restarted. The main threat to Britain's security in the future lies not in possible invasion by the Russians, or anyone else, but in the danger of nuclear proliferation – the remaining, insecurely held, Russian stockpile of 3500 nuclear warheads represents more than 100 times the total explosive power of all the munitions used in the Second World War. In future, Britain will need a military capability, not for repelling all-out attack by a superpower, but for intervening effectively in civil and regional wars such as those in Bosnia and the Gulf, and for taking its share in UN peace-keeping operations. This chapter explains how Britain's defence policy has for the past decade been frozen in a scaled-down cold war posture, involving the spending of billions of pounds a year on weapons systems that will never be needed, while not providing sufficient capability for the kinds of operations that *will* be needed. It argues that defence policies geared to meeting future needs rather than past ones will give Britain more effective power and influence in the world and at the same time make possible a substantial peace dividend.

Finally, chapter 9 brings together some of the common factors in the previous analysis and outlines some of the general conclusions which arise from it. An important aspect of many of the developments expected, and of many of the possible responses to them, is *the market*. The chapter analyses why market forces, left to themselves, will not be able to meet the needs of the future. They do not take account of externalities, they bring ever increasing inequality, and they bring mounting economic instability. It follows from this that the operation of the market will need to be modified to provide a practical way forward for the decades ahead. There *are* alternatives to *laissez-faire*, they *will* work better than leaving things to blind market forces, and they *do* need to be adopted if we are to meet the challenges head.

It follows from this analysis that the essentially *laissez-faire* approach to the market adopted by the previous government would offer little prospect of meeting the needs of the future. However, the New Labour government is following a 'Third Way', which aims to be distinctively different from either the *laissez-faire* capitalism of the right or the planned economy of the left, in that it seeks to rely mainly on the market system – but regulated in order better to meet social objectives. It professes a more pragmatic approach, getting away from old dogmas and going for whatever works best.

The chapter examines the ways these principles are being given expression in the policies of the New Labour government and assesses how far they represent a new approach that is different and relevant to future needs. It concludes that New Labour has already made a valuable fresh start in many areas; but its overall effectiveness is still critically constrained by the same attitudes to the market that underlay the failures of the previous government. It will need to shed this conservative inheritance if it is to achieve its radical objectives.

In order to keep the book to a readable length it has been necessary to focus on only seven of the most significant longer term issues facing Britain. Even with these, it has been necessary to compress the evidence and argument, and to leave out the many details, qualifications, reservations and discussions of counter-arguments that would be appropriate to a book on a single subject. However, a list of references (indicated by index numbers in the text) is given at the back of the book to indicate the sources of the facts and figures cited; and a list is also given of sources of particular interest for further reading.

2 Ageing population

Will we be able to afford a free health service and adequate pensions?

By the year 2041, the proportion of people in Britain who are over retirement age will be up by a half, and the proportion of working age to support them will be down by a tenth. This will have serious consequences for the provision of pensions, health-care and welfare services.

In these more difficult circumstances, will we be able to 'afford' the welfare state? Should we envisage relying more on various kinds of market-based private provision? Or will other kinds of changes be preferable?

Changes in population age distribution

Total population in Britain is expected to rise by only a further 6 per cent before levelling off at about 62 million around 2026.[3] This is not expected to create any major problems – some inner city areas will continue to have high population densities, but not noticeably more so than at present.

What *is* likely to create problems is the expected change in the *age distribution* of the population. Over the period from 1991 to 2041, the proportion of young people (below 20 years of age) is expected to fall from 26.6 per cent of the total to 23.4 per cent; the proportion of people aged 65 and over is expected to rise from 15.8 per cent to 24.5 per cent; and the proportion of very old people aged 80 and over is expected to rise from 3.8 to 7.8 per cent.[3]

The fall in the proportion of people under 20 years of age should not initially give rise to many difficulties. Indeed, the falling numbers should make it easier to provide the improvements that will be needed in education and training (see Chapter 4). The rise in the number of old people, however, will inevitably give rise to problems in health care and pensions.

Impact on health care

People aged 65–74 cost the NHS four times as much per head as people aged 5–64. People aged 75–84 cost eight times as much, and people aged 85 or more cost 16 times as much[4] – and there will be twice as many of them.[3] So NHS costs are bound to go up.

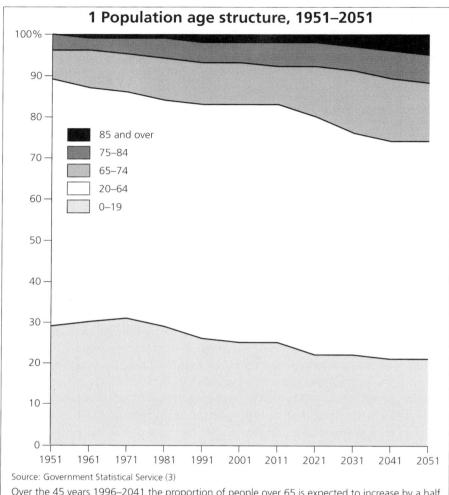

1 Population age structure, 1951–2051

Legend:
- 85 and over
- 75–84
- 65–74
- 20–64
- 0–19

Source: Government Statistical Service (3)

Over the 45 years 1996–2041 the proportion of people over 65 is expected to increase by a half and the proportion over 80 to double – giving rise to problems for health care and pensions. However, in the previous 45 years it has been found possible to accommodate even larger increases in the proportions of both – suggesting the problems should not be insurmountable.

But it is not only the costs of the NHS itself that will be affected. Between 1991 and 2031 the total number of people aged 60 and over who are disabled is expected to increase by 50 per cent and the number disabled severely enough to need regular or continuous care is expected to increase by 78 per cent.[5] The great majority of these disabled people will be cared for *outside*

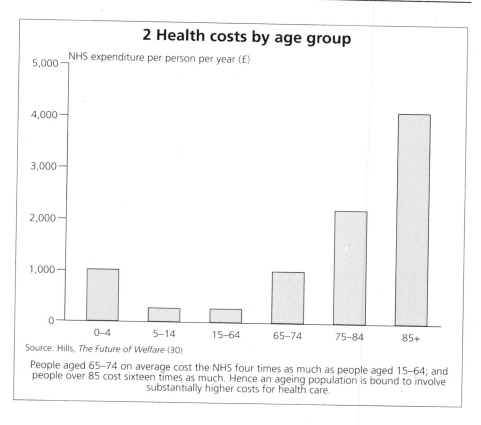

2 Health costs by age group

NHS expenditure per person per year (£)

Source: Hills, *The Future of Welfare* (30)

People aged 65–74 on average cost the NHS four times as much as people aged 15–64; and people over 85 cost sixteen times as much. Hence an ageing population is bound to involve substantially higher costs for health care.

the NHS. At present, for every elderly person cared for in an NHS hospital bed, three are being cared for in a nursing home, five are in a residential home, nine are receiving home help in their own home from the local council – and no less than 27 are being looked after in their own home by relatives and friends.[6–9]

Thus, an ageing population implies increased pressures, not only on family doctors and acute hospitals, but also on nursing homes and residential homes, on the services provided by local councils to help disabled people to carry on living in their own homes and on the army of informal carers who at present carry the greatest part of the load – at present an estimated 1.5 million people put in more than 20 hours a week (and a further 5 million smaller amounts of time)[8–9] looking after relatives and friends. They are unpaid but, if they *were* paid at the same average hourly rates as private sector domiciliary care providers, they would cost about £20 billion a year,[10–11] the equivalent of more than half the cost of the NHS.

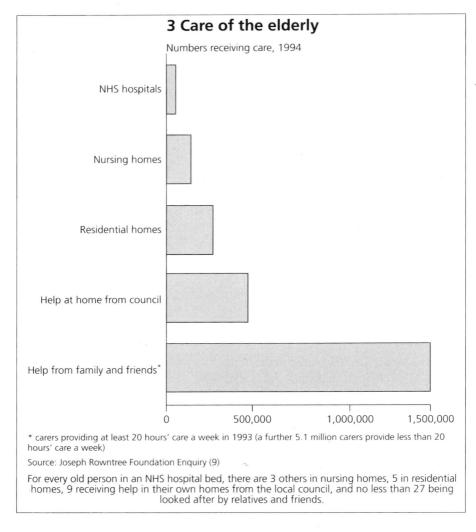

3 Care of the elderly

Numbers receiving care, 1994

NHS hospitals	
Nursing homes	
Residential homes	
Help at home from council	
Help from family and friends*	

0   500,000   1,000,000   1,500,000

* carers providing at least 20 hours' care a week in 1993 (a further 5.1 million carers provide less than 20 hours' care a week)

Source: Joseph Rowntree Foundation Enquiry (9)

For every old person in an NHS hospital bed, there are 3 others in nursing homes, 5 in residential homes, 9 receiving help in their own homes from the local council, and no less than 27 being looked after by relatives and friends.

Despite the contribution they make to keeping down the costs of the formal health and welfare services, these informal carers often feel that they get less support than they need from the formal 'Community Care' system,[12] and it is likely that the supply of them will diminish in the future. Some 30 per cent of the carers are spouses, and with rising divorce rates there may in future be fewer of them available. And 63 per cent are women, and with more women in jobs there may in future be fewer willing and able to give them up to look after elderly relatives.

These long-term changes in population age structure, together with social changes such as the rise in divorce and the changing attitudes of women towards jobs and caring for elderly relatives, are bound to put increasing pressures both on the NHS and on the various kinds of care provided in the community. Accordingly, it has been argued that in the future we will no longer be able to 'afford' a welfare state that provides everyone with care from the cradle to the grave and that we should instead move to a more market-based approach – for example by setting up an internal market in the NHS, by introducing more charges for health and welfare services and by making greater use of the private sector.

Changes along these lines, it is claimed, would reduce bureaucracy, improve efficiency, enhance flexibility, increase individual self-reliance, widen personal choice, and – the key point – reverse the rise in public expenditure and thus open up the possibility of cuts in taxation.

The previous government made a start with changes in this direction. Does the evidence so far suggest that this is the best way to meet the needs of the future?

The internal market

An 'internal market' system has been set up for family doctors and hospitals within the NHS. By giving fundholding family doctors the power to shop around for specialist services for their patients, and a direct financial incentive to get the best value for their money, it was hoped that hospital service providers would have to become more efficient in response to the purchasing power of their doctor customers, that fundholding family doctors would use their purchasing power to get better value for their patients, and that patients would be able to get better service by switching to the doctors who were performing most successfully in the new market.

However, the results have been less satisfactory than hoped. A report in 1993 by the independent Audit Commission[13] found that the scheme had failed to deliver the promised benefits and should be phased out, and its further report in 1996[14] found that savings were more than offset by extra costs and that, while the best managed practices had a major impact, the vast majority had carried out only minor changes and 'the great majority of their purchasing is for the same services, in the same quantities, delivered in the same way by the same providers (hospitals) and with few measurable extra benefits to patients.'

Where there *have* been gains for the patients of fundholding doctors is in getting quicker access to consultants. A survey by the British Medical Association (BMA) found that 73 out of 173 acute hospitals were offering patients of fundholders faster admission or other services not available to other patients. However, the effect was not that *average* waiting times were reduced, but that the fundholders' patients got *shorter* waiting times at the expense of other patients who had *longer* waiting times. Thus the main effect of fundholding has been to introduce a two-tier service, with speed of treatment depending not on the medical requirements of the patient but on the contractual arrangements of the doctor.

For hospitals, the internal market has taken the form of independent hospital trusts to compete with one another for the funding of health authorities and GP fundholders. It was hoped that this competition would invigorate management and over a period would improve efficiency and reduce costs through more of the available resources going to the more effective units.

One effect of the new arrangements has been to generate a lot of new information, particularly on performance, revealing wide differences in the costs of different hospitals and in the success of different treatments. The new information has made possible the development of 'evidence-based medicine' (EBM), which concentrates on the treatments research has shown to be the most effective. The director of research and development on the NHS executive estimates that it should be possible to save at least £1 billion a year by cutting out the use of drugs or surgical procedures that are unnecessary or do not work.[15]

Unfortunately, operating the internal market involves far more than just collecting and analysing useful information. It also involves drawing up thousands of complex contracts each year and costing, billing, paying and accounting for millions of individual items. It involves a mountain of paper and a hugely expanded bureaucracy to process it all. One of the great merits of the NHS used to be its low administration costs. However, since the reforms, NHS management costs have risen from 6 per cent to 10.5 per cent of spending – an increase of about £1.8 billion a year[16] – without evidence yet of corresponding benefits from increased efficiency.

There was a 400 per cent increase in NHS managers over the five years from 1989 to 1994,[17] and this has gone with increasing pressures, declining morale and worsening shortages of other NHS staff. The number of nurses emerging from training fell from 37,000 in 1983 to 14,000 in 1995/6 and is forecast to fall further to only 9000 in 1997/8.[18] More than a quarter of all Accident and Emergency junior hospital doctor posts are unfilled, and one junior doctor in four leaves medicine within three years of qualifying. A

BMA survey of family doctors found 90 per cent reporting greater stress as a result of the NHS reforms, 70 per cent saying this adversely affected patient care, 35 per cent saying it led them to drink more heavily and 21 per cent saying that they even contemplated suicide. The BMA has predicted an acute shortage of doctors by 2010 unless there is a substantial increase in recruitment and training.[19]

Accordingly, the internal market is now being substantially modified. The preferential treatment of fundholding doctors is being replaced by a system of primary care groups embracing *all* the doctors in general practice in an area, thus making hospitals more responsive to patients' needs, but without a two-tier system of provision. Paperwork is being reduced by replacing annual contracts with three-year ones. And greater emphasis is being placed on improving efficiency through cooperation rather than competition, with the intention being to steer more resources to the treatments and teams that work best and cost least through NICE (the National Institute for Clinical Excellence) and CHI (the Commission for Health Improvement).

Health service charges

Charges for prescriptions were first introduced in 1950. They led to the immediate resignation of Aneurin Bevan from the cabinet, and have been a subject of controversy ever since. Between 1979 and 1997 the previous government raised them from 20p to £5.65 – a ninefold increase after allowing for inflation – and in 1998 the present government raised them again, although by less than the rate of inflation, pending a comprehensive review of spending. While this is still only about 60 per cent of the average *cost* of a prescription, for some prescriptions it is actually *more* than the cost. While part of the aim was supposed to be to cut out unnecessary prescribing, among the effects has been some *over*-prescribing by doctors hoping to save their patients the added cost of repeat prescriptions, and fraud estimated at £30 million a year from people falsely claiming exemption.

Over a number of years dental charges have been increased to the point where for most people they now cover the full cost of treatment. At the same time, the fees paid to dentists have been repeatedly squeezed to the point where it has become unattractive or impossible for many dentists to remain within the NHS. The result has been a large-scale departure of dentists into private practice, to the point where the NHS service has almost disappeared in some areas and over the country as a whole only a little over half of all adults are now registered with NHS dentists. Higher charges and the end of free check-ups have discouraged people on small incomes from going to the dentist regularly. This may have increased the risk of more serious dental problems and has been blamed for the rise in deaths from oral cancer.[20]

The introduction of health charges in Britain has not yet gone very far. For example, the £300 million a year from prescription charges represents less than 1 per cent of the NHS budget, and total revenue from all charges represents only about 4 per cent. But, even at their present level, they are open to the objections that they discourage checks and treatments that may avoid more serious troubles later, and for people on small incomes they can involve hardship or a failure to get the help they need. The new government has no plans to end the charges, but has given an undertaking not to raise them in future by more than the rate of inflation.

In addition to charges for services provided by the NHS itself, new charges have been introduced and existing ones increased for some of the services, such as home care, day care and meals-on-wheels, which are provided by local councils to help people with disabilities to manage in their own homes. While the charges are means-tested and anyway cover only about 9 per cent of the total cost of these services,[9] they can nonetheless be a considerable worry and burden to people living on small incomes.

Privatisation

Private health-care insurance in Britain has risen by 140 per cent since 1979 and now covers about 11 per cent of the population.[21] Some private treatment is in private hospitals, and some is in private beds in NHS hospitals. NHS private patient revenue has risen fivefold since 1979, and the NHS has become the leading provider of acute private health care, accounting for more than 16 per cent of the total market.[22] NHS trusts with tight budgets are under pressure to increase their private earnings further, and some of them are actively promoting private health insurance policies.

Some private treatment is by doctors wholly in private practice, but most is by NHS doctors who work part-time in private practice. Most NHS consultants also undertake private work, earning an average of £37,000 a year on top of their NHS salaries.[23] Consultants faced with increasing difficulties in the health service are under pressure to expand their private work.

A recent report[24] on the state of health services in Britain has put forward the suggestion that, in view of the difficulty in finding the extra public money that will be needed in the future, it would be worth considering limiting the role of the NHS to the provision of a core group of essential health services, leaving people to pay privately for any additional ones. Further proposals include what the BMA has described as 'creeping privatisation' in the form of contracting out to private commercial companies particular services, such as pathology or X-rays, or even running whole hospitals.[25]

These proposals are open to the objections that for cash-constrained NHS trusts and profit-seeking commercial companies there may be conflicts between their commercial interests and the needs of their patients, and for hard-pressed consultants there may be conflicts between the interests of their private patients and their NHS ones.

Another kind of privatisation, initiated by the previous government but used on a larger scale by the present one, is PFI (the Private Finance Initiative) under which commercial companies finance, build and own new hospitals, and then lease them back to the NHS. This enables new hospitals to be built now without immediate expenditure of more public money, but involves higher public spending in later years to lease them back from their private owners. It also involves higher total costs than normal public investment because of the higher cost of raising money commercially and the need to provide for profits on the private investments.

A further kind of privatisation has been the systematic shift of long-term care for the elderly from the public services to private ones. Between 1979 and 1994 the number of elderly people cared for in long-stay beds in NHS hospitals was cut by a third, while the number in private or voluntary nursing homes was more than trebled.[9] Similarly, the number of elderly people cared for in local authority residential homes was cut by 39 per cent, while the number in private or voluntary homes was increased by 218 per cent.[9]

One effect of these changes is that large numbers of elderly people have been shifted from NHS beds, which are provided free, to private ones, which are subject to means tests on both income and capital. Nursing costs in old age, if prolonged, can be considerable; accordingly, people who had supposed that, after many years of paying taxes and national insurance (NI) contributions, their nursing needs in old age would be covered, now feel let down when they find that they may be faced with bills so large that they will quickly run through all their liquid savings and in many cases that they will also have to sell the home they had hoped to pass on to their children. The effect is to provide new worries, a new disincentive to saving, and a new obstacle to wealth 'trickling down' from one generation to the next. The government has set up a Royal Commission to try to find a solution to this problem.

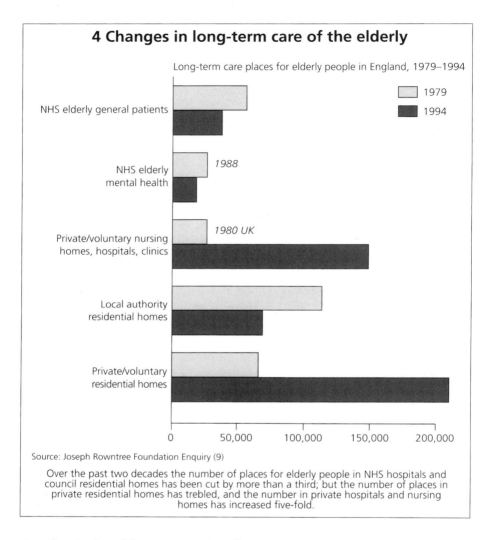

4 Changes in long-term care of the elderly

Long-term care places for elderly people in England, 1979–1994

☐ 1979
■ 1994

- NHS elderly general patients
- NHS elderly mental health — *1988*
- Private/voluntary nursing homes, hospitals, clinics — *1980 UK*
- Local authority residential homes
- Private/voluntary residential homes

0   50,000   100,000   150,000   200,000

Source: Joseph Rowntree Foundation Enquiry (9)

Over the past two decades the number of places for elderly people in NHS hospitals and council residential homes has been cut by more than a third; but the number of places in private residential homes has trebled, and the number in private hospitals and nursing homes has increased five-fold.

A private health-care system?

Some people see the internal market, increasing charges and greater use of the private sector as steps towards introducing a fully private health-care system. There would, however, be serious problems with this.

Health care can be very expensive. Ordinary travel insurance policies commonly provide health cover for up to £1 million or more – just for the risks from one holiday. The full cost of all possible health needs over a lifetime could be so great that very, very few people would be rich enough to be able to cover it from their own resources. Half the households in the country have savings (other than houses and pensions) of less than £450[26] — which, in the event of an acute health crisis, could easily go in less than a week. Accordingly, the only practicable way to cover all health risks is through insurance. But private insurance has a number of limitations.

Because private health insurance is expensive, at present the majority of policies are paid for not by individuals but by companies on behalf of their employees. The drawback with this is that it is *companies* that determine the kind of policies taken out, including the extent of coverage and the terms of eligibility – which are likely to include loss of entitlement in the event of changing jobs or being made redundant.

Since any scheme based on company contributions would leave many people out, it would be necessary for those not covered to make their own individual arrangements. Some people, not fully aware of the risks, might choose not to; and some, with low incomes, might be unable to afford the premiums. To provide universal coverage, it would therefore be necessary to make taking out private insurance compulsory for all who could afford it and to provide government support for those who could not.

It is a principle of commercial insurance that premiums vary with risk. Insurance companies perceive people who are already in poor health, and so in particular need of health-care cover, as bad risks. Faced with higher than average premiums – which they would mostly be unable to afford – they too would need to have their contributions topped up by the government.

Also, at present, different policies provide different kinds of cover. Most do not cover accidents and emergencies and hardly any cover chronic sickness in old age – although these can involve the highest costs and are therefore the most important eventualities to have cover for. It would therefore be necessary to stipulate that all policies included in the compulsory scheme provided cover for all contingencies – which would make the premiums much higher than they are for most present private policies.

Total costs would tend to be substantially higher than they would be for a comparable public service. An independent study[27] has shown that, in conventional business value-added terms, NHS hospital trusts are already twice as efficient as the private sector BUPA hospitals, and twice as efficient also as Tesco and Trust House Forte. The premiums in a private health insurance system would have to cover not only the actual costs of the health services provided, but also the additional costs of designing and promoting policies, collecting premiums and checking and paying out claims, as well as the profits for the companies to make it worth their while.

There would also be the problem experienced in countries with commercial insurance-based health-care systems, and in the private sector in Britain, that there is a tendency for particularly expensive procedures and drugs, unnecessary tests and over-long hospital stays to be prescribed when the health-care providers can present all their claims to an insurance company for payment. This has made it difficult to prevent a steady escalation of costs.

Thus, if it were to provide coverage for everyone, a market-based health-care system:

- would not bring full competition, because all the insurance companies would have to offer the same comprehensive cover;
- would not give free choice, because participation would have to be compulsory;
- would not be wholly private, because some government top-up would still be necessary; and
- would not be cheap, because administration costs would inevitably be much higher than in a public system.

The future of the National Health Service

Thus, the moves towards a market-based health-care system have brought more problems than advantages, and a fully private system would have even worse drawbacks. A comprehensive service, publicly funded and free at the point of need, like the NHS, is not only the fairest way of providing health care, it is also much the most efficient and economical. And, it is hugely popular. Accordingly, the present government has declared its intention to build up the NHS as the best way of providing good health care for all in the future.

There remains, however, the crucial question of how to pay for it. By how much are the costs likely to rise, and will we be able to afford them?

Certainly, an ageing population may be expected to bring rising health-care costs – though not necessarily to the extent that the demographic projections imply. It may turn out that people will not only live longer but also stay fit and healthy for longer, so that the years of high health risk are deferred rather than extended. However, the evidence for this is not encouraging. A study of six countries found that in all of them life expectancy had risen, but in only one of them (France) had this been accompanied by a similar rise in *healthy* life expectancy. In Britain, it found that the steady rise

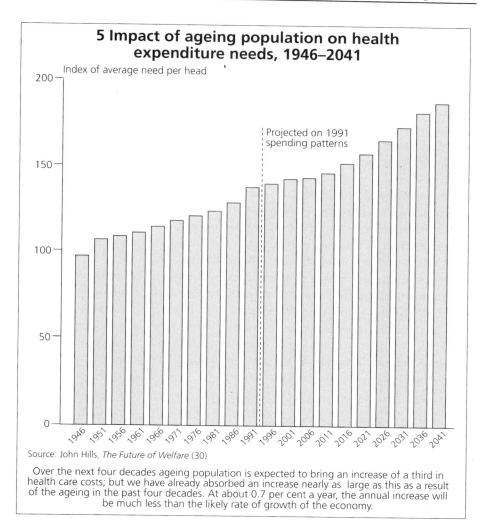

5 Impact of ageing population on health expenditure needs, 1946–2041

Index of average need per head

Projected on 1991 spending patterns

Source: John Hills, *The Future of Welfare* (30)

Over the next four decades ageing population is expected to bring an increase of a third in health care costs; but we have already absorbed an increase nearly as large as this as a result of the ageing in the past four decades. At about 0.7 per cent a year, the annual increase will be much less than the likely rate of growth of the economy.

in total life expectancy between 1976 and 1991 was not accompanied by a rise in the expectancy of life without incapacity.[28] Another study in Britain of age-specific causes of death found that in some ways the health of the elderly was improving, but in other ways getting worse; the overall effect was that between 1976 and 1992 life expectancy at age 65 increased by about two years, but *healthy* life expectancy by only about one.[29] So, it will be prudent to assume that with people living longer the health costs associated with old age will be higher, not just later.

Estimates of increases in health costs attributable to an ageing population have been made by John Hills in *The Future of Welfare*.[30] These show that the effect of ageing on costs is significant – but not new. The increase due to ageing expected over the 15 years 1996–2011 is in fact *less* than the increase already experienced over the 10 years 1986–96. After 2011, the expected rise gets steeper, and over the whole 40-year period, 2001–41, the total increase in costs attributable to an ageing population is expected to be around 30 per cent. This increase is substantial – but no more so than the increase *already* experienced as a result of an ageing population in the previous 40 years.

An increase of about 30 per cent spread over a period of 40 years represents an average increase of less than 0.7 per cent a year – about one-third of the average rate of growth in the economy in recent years. *In itself*, therefore, there is no reason to suppose that an ageing population will give rise to increases in costs too great to be affordable.

However, there are other factors that also tend to push up health-care costs. One is rising public expectations. Another is the tendency for health-care costs to rise faster than other costs. This is partly because most health care is labour intensive and offers less scope for automation to raise productivity than, for example, manufacturing. And, it is partly because medical science is always advancing, making possible treatments for conditions that were previously difficult or impossible to treat. Initially, these new techniques usually involve very expensive new drugs, very expensive new equipment, and very expensively acquired new expertise, and so tend to bring higher costs.

However, new drugs tend to become cheaper once research costs have been recovered and large production volumes reached; new surgical procedures tend to become easier and cheaper when more experience is gained with them; some new drugs can make expensive surgery avoidable, or make recovery from it quicker; and some new surgical techniques are more effective and less expensive than what was done before – making possible earlier discharge or treatment as a day-patient. So, advances in science and technique can in time also lead to *lower* costs.

Even so, it will be prudent to assume that health-care costs will continue to rise faster than prices in general. Over the period 1979 to 1996, NHS costs rose on average by about 1.8 per cent a year in excess of the general inflation rate. In future years, with a much lower rate of general inflation, it may be expected that the excess increase will be substantially lower. If allowance is made for increases of up to 1.5 per cent a year as a result of higher costs, this will imply, over the 40-year period, 2001–41, a total increase of about 81 per cent – more than double the increase due to an ageing population.

It will also be desirable to end all NHS charges. And it will be especially important to remove anxiety about very expensive care costs in old age, by making the costs of nursing homes and residential homes free (apart from a means-tested charge for accommodation costs), by removing charges for home care services and by giving more support to informal carers – which will cost an estimated £3 billion a year.[9]

Underspending in recent years has left the NHS severely stretched – as the chairman of the BMA put it, 'in danger of sinking like the *Titanic*'.[31] However, the substantial increase in public spending on health already announced for 1999/2000, 2000/1 and 2001/2[31] should be enough to make up the backlog by the turn of the century. Thereafter, over the 40-year period 2001–41 the total picture of the various increases involved may be roughly as follows:

Effects of ageing population	+30%
Effects of differential rise in costs	+81%
Removal of charges	+4%
Free nursing, residential care and home care	+9%
Total increase in real costs over 40 years	+167%
(the above increases multiplied by one another)	

A potential increase of 167 per cent should not be too large to accommodate; for it will be spread over a period of 40 years, and the average increase per year will be only about 2.5 per cent. This is less than the annual rate of economic growth it is reasonable to aim for in the future (see Chapter 8), and less than the growth rate already achieved in the period before 1979.

However, if the economy were to grow at an average of less than 2.2 per cent a year, or if health and welfare spending grew by more than the amount postulated, it would imply that the NHS was taking a larger share of total GDP (gross domestic product). This would be important – but not necessarily undesirable. In nearly all countries, spending on health as a percentage of GDP has tended to rise as people take an increasing part of rising prosperity in the form of better health care. Between 1960 and 1990, health spending as a percentage of GDP roughly doubled in most industrial countries, but, thanks partly to the relative efficiency of the NHS, rose by only half as much in Britain, where it currently represents a smaller proportion of GDP than in most other comparable countries.[31] Some increase

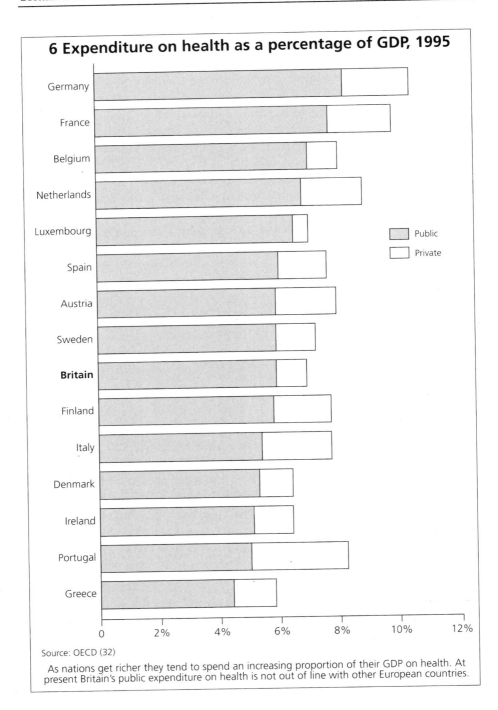

6 Expenditure on health as a percentage of GDP, 1995

Germany
France
Belgium
Netherlands
Luxembourg
Spain
Austria
Sweden
Britain
Finland
Italy
Denmark
Ireland
Portugal
Greece

Public
Private

0   2%   4%   6%   8%   10%   12%

Source: OECD (32)

As nations get richer they tend to spend an increasing proportion of their GDP on health. At present Britain's public expenditure on health is not out of line with other European countries.

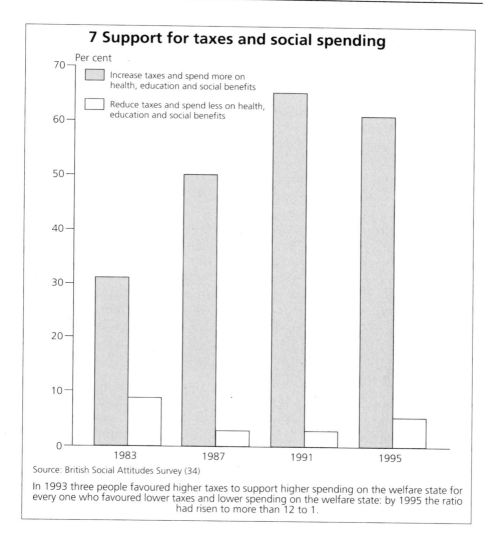

7 Support for taxes and social spending

Per cent

☐ Increase taxes and spend more on
health, education and social benefits

☐ Reduce taxes and spend less on health,
education and social benefits

1983   1987   1991   1995

Source: British Social Attitudes Survey (34)

In 1993 three people favoured higher taxes to support higher spending on the welfare state for every one who favoured lower taxes and lower spending on the welfare state: by 1995 the ratio had risen to more than 12 to 1.

in health spending's share of GDP would do no more than bring Britain into line with what other countries are doing already.

However, spending a higher percentage of GDP on health could well imply higher taxes. It has often been assumed that this would be impossible because higher taxes are unpopular. But, in the latest British Social Attitudes Survey,[34] when people were asked whether taxes should be raised to make possible increased spending on health, 74 per cent said they thought that it would be best for the country in general if they were, and 65 per cent said they thought it would be best for themselves and their families. The overwhelming majority in favour of 'tax and spend' extends across all ages, across all demographic and socioeconomic groups, across all three main parties, and across all income groups – indeed it is marginally *higher* among those with high incomes than those with low.

Similarly with elderly care services: in a survey in which people were asked who should pay when elderly people need long-term nursing or residential care, 81 per cent said society as a whole; only 7 per cent said individuals should use their personal liquid savings and a mere 3 per cent said that they should if necessary have to sell their home as well, as they do at present.

There is little doubt that health and care for the elderly are areas in which higher spending would be popular, and higher taxes to pay for them accepted – provided, of course, that there was conviction the extra taxes were in fact used to provide better services. So, although there are problems associated with general hypothecation (earmarking particular taxes for particular public spending), this would seem to be one area in which a certain amount of loose hypothecation – linking some increases in tax with greater spending on health and social care – might be helpful.

Pressures on pensions

An ageing population is also putting new pressures on pensions. The proportion of people older than the 'normal' retirement age of 65 will increase by more than a fifth over three decades and by more than a half over five decades, while the proportion in the economically active age groups of 20–64 will fall. This means that the 'elderly support ratio' (the number of people in the active age groups for each person of pensionable age) is expected to drop from 3.7 people per person of pensionable age in 1991 to only 2.9 by 2021 and 2.1 by 2041.

Does this mean we can no longer 'afford' adequate state pensions and will need to rely increasingly on private pensions? Since the original Beveridge scheme was introduced after the war there have been a number of changes made to update and improve it; then, there have been measures to cut it back and to rely more on occupational and private personal pensions; and, more recently, there have been proposals to supplement it with schemes for individual second pensions.

Changes in national insurance

National insurance was started in Britain after the war as a result of the Beveridge proposals. The idea was for an intergenerational compact under which the present generation of those at work would pay for the pensions of their parents' generation, and in due course their own pensions would be paid for by payments from their children's generation. It took the form of contributions from all those at work, their employers and the government to pay for a flat-rate pension to cover the basic living needs of all those above a fixed retirement age.

However, the basic pension turned out to be too low to cover basic needs and, in 1974, the government raised it by more than a quarter and provided for it and other benefits to go up automatically each year in line with national earnings. It also introduced a new state earnings related pensions scheme (SERPS), under which people paid additional contributions out of higher earnings in order to get, after 20 years, a second pension equivalent to 25 per cent of their previous earnings.

If the basic pension had continued to be raised in line with average earnings, it would now be more than one-third higher and enough to keep pensioners above the means-tested income support level;[35] if the SERPS scheme had continued unchanged it would by now be providing a reasonable second pension for those not covered by occupational schemes.

Instead, it was decided to cut back the national insurance scheme. In 1980, the provision for the basic NI pension to go up automatically each year in step with national average earnings was ended; instead, it has been raised only in line with inflation, as has the value of the means-tested income support for pensioners with no other source of income. This has meant that the incomes of those dependent on the basic pension and income support have been frozen in real terms while other incomes have been rising, thus contributing to the growth in inequality. And not everyone has been getting even the low level provided by income support. The Department of Social Security estimates that more than half a million people entitled to income support do not in fact claim it because they are put off by the means-test procedures.

Because of the ending of the earnings link, the value of the basic NI pension has already fallen to below 15 per cent of average male earnings and, if earnings grow by 2 per cent a year, by 2030 it will have fallen to only 7.5 per cent – by which time there may well be suggestions that it should be abandoned altogether as too small to be relevant.[30]

While the basic pension has been left to wither gradually away, SERPS, the earnings-related scheme, has been actively, some would say scandalously, cut back. In 1986, the previous government arbitrarily halved the benefits to be paid out under the scheme and, in 1995, halved them again.[36] The result has been to turn a scheme that had offered attractive benefits to contributors into one offering much poorer value; it has also had, as was intended, the effect of encouraging people to turn instead to occupational and personal pension schemes.

Occupational pensions

Many public sector and leading private sector companies have set up good occupational pension schemes to provide a second pension for their employees, and the better ones offer genuinely better benefits than SERPS in its present form. However, compared with SERPS in its original form, occupational schemes can have a number of important disadvantages.

The first is that more than half the working population are not covered by them, particularly people working for small and medium sized companies and people on below average earnings. They do not usually cover casual, short-term or part-time workers, nor do they cover people who are self-employed or unemployed, or women taking time away from paid employment to bring up children.

Benefits are seldom indexed to cover inflation after retirement, and they are normally defined in a way that is unfavourable to people made redundant, which is nowadays common, or changing jobs of their own accord, which is expected to become increasingly common in the future.

If the pension fund performs disappointingly, or the employer runs into difficulties, there is no binding legal commitment for the employer to keep to its commitments;[37] while, if performance exceeds expectations, it is common for the employer to use the benefit for itself in the form of a 'holiday' on its contributions. Thus, although the employees have most at stake in the scheme, it is the employers that have effective control of the assets and tend to use them in their own interests – in extreme cases, as with Maxwell, to the great cost of the employees who had entrusted their future pensions to the scheme.

A recent survey[38] of occupational schemes in smaller companies found that 60 per cent were now offering 'money purchase' schemes, which mostly involved lower contributions, but offered no guaranteed level of income on retirement. Hunter Devine, chairman of the Association of Consulting

Actuaries, which carried out the survey, said its findings 'raise the spectre of a huge underfunding of retirement provision in the years ahead ... this must draw into question the adequacy of the resulting pensions for perhaps a majority of our people'.[38]

Finally, although occupational pension schemes are 'private', they still involve considerable cost to the taxpayer because employee contributions to occupational pension schemes are free of income tax. For someone paying tax at the basic rate of 23 per cent, this means that 23 per cent of the contribution is covered by a tax relief and is in effect paid for by the exchequer. Contributions by employers are also tax deductible. In 1996/7, these concessions cost the exchequer £7 billion.[39] This considerable public subsidy does not 'show' in the budget statement, but is nonetheless real in the sense that, without it, taxes could be that much lower, or public expenditure on pensions or other things could be higher.

Thus, although many occupational pension schemes afford good provision for retirement, many others do not; and they involve risks from incompetence, misadventure or fraud, they penalise job mobility, they draw heavy subsidy from public funds, and for many people they are simply not available. Accordingly, they are by no means a fully satisfactory solution to the need for an adequate second pension for all in the twenty-first century.

Personal pensions

Since 1988, a third kind of pension has been available – these are personal pensions that take the form of an individual contract between the person wanting the pension and the insurance company providing it. They have some important potential advantages: there is a wide choice of policies and providers; people can take their personal pension policy with them when they change jobs; and the government is not a party to the contract, so there is no risk of a cut-seeking government adversely changing the terms of the contract at some later date. However, there are also a number of important limitations and disadvantages.

They are costly, so many people cannot afford them or do not take out adequate cover to provide for their future needs and they do not normally provide protection if payments have to be interrupted as a result of sickness, disability, redundancy or a move to a less well paid job. In practice, more than one-third of policyholders drop out within three years[40] – usually with heavy financial penalties.[41]

They do not guarantee any specified level of pension on retirement because they are arranged on a 'money purchase' basis: contributions are put into a fund invested in the stock market where, hopefully, they grow in value over the years; when the time comes to retire, the accumulated capital is used to buy an annuity to provide the policy-holder with a pension during the years of retirement. This means that the level of eventual pension is the outcome of a triple lottery: the extent of the rise in the stock market, the skill of the fund manager, and the price at which an annuity can be bought at the other end.

First, over a period that may be as long as 40 years, there is considerable uncertainty about the size of the rise in stock market prices – and hence the size of the pension it may buy. Second, whatever the *average* rise in the market, the performance of *individual* funds varies greatly – a survey of personal pension plans by *Money Management*[42] found that over 20 years the return from the worst fund was only about half the return from the best one. Third, the value of the annuity that can be bought with the accumulated fund will depend crucially on the situation at the particular date when it is bought: whether the stock market is at a peak or in a trough, the prevailing rate of interest, and the health and personal circumstances of the prospective pensioner. Even for the same person at the same time, the difference between the annuities offered by the best and the worst companies can be as much as 40 per cent.[43] The combined effect of these three uncertainties is to provide not a guaranteed level of income for retirement but a high-risk gamble on the stock market. The only thing that can be predicted with certainty is the need for regular payments.

There are also risks of a different kind. Personal pension plans are extremely complex. It is difficult for anyone who is not an actuary or a pensions expert to know whether a particular scheme offers good value and, in particular, whether a particular scheme offers better value than existing provisions in SERPS or an employer's occupational pension scheme. At the same time, the people who sell personal pension schemes tend to be very knowledgeable, persuasive and under pressure to sell their products – for they are paid on commission. Thus, when pension sellers meet their potential customers it is by no means on 'a level playing field'; people may be talked into signing up for schemes that are not advantageous for them. Unfortunately, this is not something that in theory *could* happen, but something that in practice *does* happen – not occasionally, but *usually*.

The accountants, KPMG Peat Marwick,[44] carried out a survey for the Securities and Investment Board of people who had been persuaded to move from occupational schemes to personal pension plans. They found that only 9 per cent of clients had their pension transfer handled satis-factorily, and no less than 91 per cent had done so on the basis of suspect advice or insufficient information. It is estimated that as many as 2.4 million people may have been talked into disadvantageous schemes[45] at a total cost that may reach £11 billion.[45] It is intended that the victims will be compensated; but it took five years before the extent of the abuse was revealed; and, four years after that, less than one-quarter of the 'priority' cases have had their assessments for compensation completed.[46] The 'priority' cases appear to account for only about 10 per cent of the total, which leaves 93 per cent of all cases still unsettled.

A further problem arises over the charges made to cover commissions, promotion, administration, investment management costs and profits. Typi-cally, charges absorb about 25 per cent of the value of contributions,[35,47] and with some funds absorb even more.[42] Moreover, many funds are 'front-end-loaded', which means that the first two years' contributions go on commission (so that investment in the fund does not even start until the third year); and after that there are annual charges, which are regularly increased.[42] The 25 per cent absorbed in charges compares with the 1.2 per cent it costs to administer the basic NI pension.[35]

Finally, it should not be supposed that personal pension plans involve no cost to the taxpayer. On the contrary, as with occupational schemes, contri-butions attract relief from income tax and, in addition, the government offered substantial tax rebates to encourage people to leave SERPS. These tax concessions cost the taxpayer a total of £20 billion[48] – an amount equivalent to two-thirds of total annual government spending on the basic NI pension.

Thus personal pension plans involve a huge gamble on future stock market movements, a high risk of abuse, high charges and high public subsidies. They do not provide a guaranteed level of pension on retirement and they do not provide for changes in people's circumstances. Accordingly, they cannot be regarded as a practical means of providing an adequate second pension for everyone.

Proposals for new kinds of funded schemes

In response to the inadequacies of current national insurance provisions, and the various drawbacks to occupational and personal pensions schemes, a number of proposals for national second pension schemes have been put forward by the Commission on Social Justice (Sir Gordon Borrie),[49] the

Commission on Wealth Creation and Social Cohesion (Ralf Dahrendorf),[50] the Institute of Community Studies (Frank Field)[51] and the Retirement Income Inquiry (Sir John Anson).[52] In addition, the previous government put forward proposals for national insurance to be phased out altogether; and the present government has been considering the possibility of supplementing national insurance with a new kind of stakeholder pension to provide a second pension for everyone not already covered in other ways.

These various proposals differ from one another in a number of important ways, but share in common the proposition that what is needed is a national scheme for second pensions on a *funded* basis – contributions from everyone at work paid into a fund where they would be invested and the accumulated capital used to provide pensions when the time came for retirement.

Funding is seen as likely to make people more willing to pay the high contributions required for decent pensions, since they would be paid into individual accounts earmarked strictly for the provision of their own pensions, and would therefore be safe from the future depredations of profit-seeking Maxwells or cut-seeking governments.

The supposed merit of a funded approach is that it is seen as a way of getting over the problems of an ageing population. If we make contributions year after year, we will be paying for our own pensions in advance; by saving now and in future years we can put enough aside to see us through the more difficult times ahead. Funding is thus seen as a prudent and efficacious way of dealing with an ageing population in the future. It is not.

As a means of overcoming the problems of an ageing population, funding is simply fudging. Going over to a funded basis will not work for two reasons. First, the goods and services of the real economy cannot be 'saved up' – the consumption of future pensioners will have to be met out of whatever is produced *then*, not now. And second, a shift to funding means that the present generation will have to pay twice over, once under the present 'pay-as-you-go' system for its parents' pensions, and again, through funding, for its own – which will be unfair and politically unacceptable. So, far from alleviating the problems of an ageing population, it will greatly *accentuate* them, by requiring during the transition period much greater increases in contributions than would have been necessary anyway.

If you, as an *individual*, take out a new contract for a funded pension, you pay your contributions over the years and, when retirement day comes, you have a legal right to take out 'your' money, together with any profits or interest it has earned in the meanwhile, to get a pension which you have already paid for. Through your contract you have, in effect, been able to defer some of your consumption during the years you were working, in order to be able to enjoy it instead after you have retired.

But, *over the economy as a whole*, it does not work like that. If everyone started to make contributions towards a funded pension, their consumption of goods and services would be reduced, bringing about (if nothing else changed) a deflationary shift in the economy and a fall in national output below what would otherwise have been produced. But, unlike money, unconsumed goods and services cannot be put aside and saved for later. In the real economy, almost all goods and services that are produced have to be consumed soon after production or not at all – physical goods and real-time services cannot be put away now in the deep-freeze or bank and taken out again years later to be enjoyed in retirement. The *money* with which to buy cars, cameras, food, foreign holidays and the rest can be put aside to use later, but for the most part the things themselves cannot. Thus, the consumption forgone as a result of having to pay contributions into a funded scheme involves a loss in the present without any compensating gain in the future.

The awkward fact of the matter is that, because real goods and services cannot be carried forward, the real consumption of future pensioners will have to be met out of *the goods and services produced at the time*. This applies equally whether the financial arrangements underlying money pension entitlements are funded or provided on a pay-as-you-go basis. Funding is fudging in the sense that the paper payments in the earlier years do nothing to increase the real resources available in the later years – they merely give an extra boost to deflation earlier and to inflation later. Moving pensions over to a funded basis would bring no escape from the hard fact that rising numbers of old people will put real pressure on real resources – although not on sufficient a scale to bring serious difficulties until the 2030s and 2040s.

The second problem with going over from a pay-as-you-go system to a funded one, is the problem of actually making the change from the one to the other. Under pay-as-you-go, the present generation at work is paying contributions to pay for the pensions already being enjoyed by the generation ahead, and expects its own pensions to be paid for by the contributions of the generation behind. If we changed over to a funded system, the present generation at work would be expected to pay contributions into a fund to pay for its own pensions and *at the same time* to carry on paying for the pensions of the generation ahead who are already retired. The present generation would thus have to *pay twice over*.

This is unfair to the present generation and the present generation

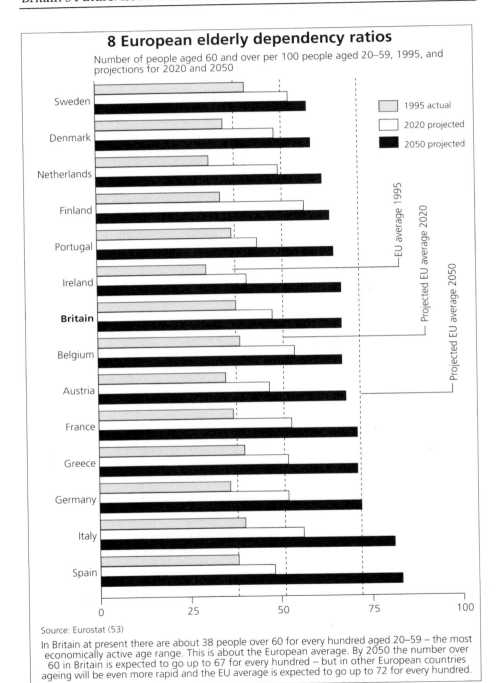

8 European elderly dependency ratios

Number of people aged 60 and over per 100 people aged 20–59, 1995, and projections for 2020 and 2050

Legend:
- 1995 actual
- 2020 projected
- 2050 projected

Source: Eurostat (53)

In Britain at present there are about 38 people over 60 for every hundred aged 20–59 – the most economically active age range. This is about the European average. By 2050 the number over 60 in Britain is expected to go up to 67 for every hundred – but in other European countries ageing will be even more rapid and the EU average is expected to go up to 72 for every hundred.

accounts for the majority of the electorate. Because changing over from pay-as-you-go to a funded basis involves this double burden, implying *much* higher contributions for a generation already believed to be feeling it is paying quite enough, it would involve formidable political difficulties, even at the best of times; with an ageing population looming, now does not seem to be the best of times.

It is significant that other European countries show little inclination to emulate Britain's proposed move to a funded basis. Most of them have had sharper falls in fertility than Britain, and so face greater difficulties ahead as the result of an ageing population.[53] Since most of them have much more generous levels of state pensions than Britain, their potential problems would seem far worse. Yet, they are not contemplating going over from pay-as-you-go to a funded basis because they recognise the double burden and see that a shift to funded schemes would make their problems, not easier, but more difficult.

Pensions for the twenty-first century

There is, unfortunately, no escaping the fact that an ageing population will bring difficulties with pensions. Since the needs of future pensioners will have to be met from the resources available at the time, and these will be finite, it follows that if in the future there will be more old people, something will have to give: either lower pensions than otherwise for those in retirement; higher contributions from those still at work; a higher normal age of retirement; or some combination of these.

There are obvious difficulties with each of these. It would be unfair to expect older people to bear the full cost of happening to belong to a generation with a demographic bulge; it would seem reasonable to expect the generation behind to take on *part* of the burden in the form of higher contributions and for the retired generation to accept the need for pensions somewhat lower than would have been possible with a more uniform age distribution. Very likely, the least painful way will be to take advantage of people's longer life expectancy and put the main weight on a higher than previous normal age of retirement.

In any case, the problem is still a quarter of a century away, so there will be plenty of time to debate the alternatives and map out the implications of whatever way is chosen. Meanwhile, because real resources cannot be 'saved' for that far ahead, there is not much that can be done to provide for it *now*, so it is somewhat disingenuous to use the problem of an ageing population in the future as an argument for raising contributions or cutting benefits at the present.

What *can* be done, and *should* be done, is to devise a pension system that meets the needs of the present and the decades immediately ahead, and does it so well that it will be robust enough to take the strains of an ageing population when they come.

It will need to take account of the many changes that have occurred in Britain in the half century since Beveridge, for instance: rising average living standards and changing and more varied life styles and aspirations; more common divorce, remarriage and cohabitation without marriage; women more often in jobs and more independent in attitudes; more frequent changes in jobs and earnings, more self-employment and casual and part-time work; higher unemployment (at least at present); and a wider spread of actual and desired ages of retirement. A new scheme will not merely need to take account of the changes of the past half a century, but to be flexible enough to accommodate the largely unforeseeable changes in the *next* half century.

National insurance, in its present form, will not meet the needs of the future. Its structure is too rigid, reflecting the social and economic patterns of 50 years ago. The basic pension is too low to live on, and is getting lower relative to other incomes; and it has to be supplemented by means-tested income support. And, SERPS, cut by three-quarters, does not now provide adequate benefits.

Occupational schemes exclude half the working population, impede job mobility and do not always provide adequate benefits. They are becoming increasingly inappropriate in the present world where people are having to change jobs with increasing frequency because of redundancy and the growth of short-term contracts and casual work. They will become even less appropriate in future, when more people will change jobs because they *want* to, because they are adaptable and wish to take opportunities to improve their prospects.

Personal pension schemes have been the biggest rip-off for decades. It will probably be a long while before people again trust the commercial companies that have given them such a poor deal. New kinds of individual stakeholder pensions may provide safeguards against the worst abuses, but it will be difficult to reconcile hard commercial imperatives with varied personal circumstances, competition and profitability for companies with fair and comprehensive coverage of people. With commercial schemes in the past, it has proved impossible to prevent charges being high, results uncertain and abuses frequent. Even if these problems could be reduced, and contracts made clear, fair and straightforward, it is hardly likely that a legal contract setting rigid terms for up to 40 years ahead is going to be able to provide the flexibility needed to cover all the unpredictable changes in personal and national circumstances that may lie ahead.

To meet the new needs of the present, and to offer a prospect of meeting the changing needs of the future as well, the pensions system will need to be fair, flexible, personal, economical, affordable in contributions, reliable in benefits, and all-inclusive in coverage. There is no way that commercial systems, on their own, could come even remotely near to meeting all these conditions. Attempts through government regulation and support to enable them to meet them at least in some degree are likely to prove messy, inefficient, expensive and unsatisfactory. This is an area where state provision is not only the most practical and efficient way of meeting the needs of the future, it is almost certainly the *only* way.

The new national pensions scheme for the next century will need to be very different from the national insurance scheme of the last. It will need to be *modern* in the sense that it fits current social and economic patterns and likely future ones, rather than those of a previous era.

It will need to be inclusive, covering everyone. That will mean getting contributions from everyone when they are at work, and also allowing credits for times when contributions cannot be paid because, for example, of time spent in education, training, looking after young children, sickness, disability or unemployment. This will require major government inputs; but it will make more sense to use government support to cover the contributions of those who *cannot* pay, rather than, as at present, in providing massive public subsidies to commercial schemes that would not be viable without them.

It will need to be *reliable in benefits* in providing everyone, as of right, with at least a basic pension adequate to live off; and for those making larger contributions out of higher earnings, larger pensions to reflect the larger contributions.

It will need to be *individualised* in the sense that everyone will make individual contributions to qualify for individual benefits, irrespective of marital or employment status – with women, for example, included in their own right, not just as appendages to their husbands.

It will need to be *flexible*, allowing for changes in personal and national circumstances, and also for variations in individual preferences, for example for higher/lower contributions in return for higher/lower levels of pension in retirement; for earlier/later retirement ages; for provisions for adjustment of entitlements for people who want to change the age at which they decide to give up work, or who want to go over to part-time working, or who want to phase-in their retirement over a period of years.

It will need to be *transparent*, with each individual given regular statements of prospective future contributions and entitlements, so that they cannot be defrauded of their rights by unilateral government action, as happened with the SERPS scheme.

And it will need to be conceived and run in a way that is *efficient* and imaginative. A single public scheme based on universal contributions and benefits should have inherently far lower costs than a multiplicity of separate competing commercial schemes; and it should aim to be versatile enough to cover almost all needs and circumstances. However, it will be important to keep the scheme's managers on their toes by encouraging competition from alternative providers if they are able to give better value in some areas, or meet particular needs not covered by the scheme.

Some people may object to such a scheme on the grounds that it is too ambitious. However, it will need to be to meet the more demanding expectations of the next century.

Others may object to it on the grounds that it will be very expensive. It will be. But, if people want financial security in old age, they will have to pay for it, whether through a public scheme or through private ones. A well designed modern public scheme could provide more and cost less than private alternatives, and so give better value for money.

It will not need to be introduced all at once; it could be built up over a period of years. A system of funded stakeholder second pensions would involve a large and immediate increase in contributions, but an increase in benefit entitlements that would build up only very gradually over a large number of years. A new state scheme, financed on a pay-as-you-go basis need involve only a gradual build-up in contributions, but could give an early payoff with benefits starting to increase right away in line with higher contributions. An ambitious new system of national pensions would be the best way of meeting the needs of the next century; and it should also be the most likely way of capturing the public imagination meanwhile.

3 Social Division

Can we reverse the trend towards increasing inequality and growing poverty?

Another longer term development of great importance is the increase in inequality. Since 1979 the income gap between the richest 10 per cent and the poorest 10 per cent has more than doubled. If this trend continued, by the year 2010 incomes in Britain would be as unequal as in Brazil and social divisions could become explosive. The underlying causes of this growing inequality lie in a widening spread in earnings, changes in social security and taxation, and rising unemployment. And these in turn are mainly the result of past public policies which need to be reversed.

Increasing inequality

The inequalities that existed in Britain before the war were greatly reduced by the changes made during the war and by the setting up of the welfare state after it. In the 1960s and 1970s, rising national prosperity was broadly shared between different income groups,[30] and this helped cement the high degree of social cohesion for which the country was renowned.

After 1979, however, there were major changes in public policies, which have resulted in dramatic increases in inequality. Between 1979 and 1994/5:

- average incomes increased by 42 per cent, incomes of the richest tenth increased by 68 per cent, but incomes of the poorest tenth actually *fell* by 8 per cent;[54]
- the total share of the richest tenth increased from 21 per cent of total income to 27 per cent, while the share of the poorest tenth fell from 4 per cent to only 2.2 per cent;[54] and
- the gap between rich and poor almost doubled, with the average income of the richest tenth rising from 4¼ times the average of the poorest tenth to more than 8 times.[54]

Changes in the distribution of *expenditure* have been less than the changes in *income*, because people with higher incomes find it easier to save

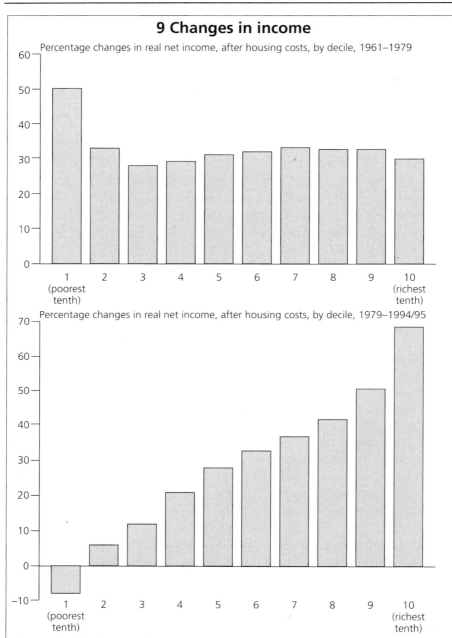

9 Changes in income

Percentage changes in real net income, after housing costs, by decile, 1961–1979

(Decile 1 = poorest tenth; Decile 10 = richest tenth)

Percentage changes in real net income, after housing costs, by decile, 1979–1994/95

(Decile 1 = poorest tenth; Decile 10 = richest tenth)

Source: John Mills, *The Future of Welfare* (30) and Department of Social Security (54)

Between 1961 and 1979 incomes at all levels rose at a similar rate, except for the bottom tenth whose incomes rose faster than the others. Between 1979 and 1994/95, in contrast, higher incomes rose much faster than lower ones, with the richest tenth's rising by 68 per cent and the poorest tenth's actually *falling* by 8 per cent.

while people with lower incomes more often need to spend beyond their incomes – for example while adjusting to a sharp fall in income after the loss of a job. However, even with expenditure, the shift to greater inequality has been marked – between 1979 and 1994/5 the spending of the highest spending tenth increased four times as fast as that of the lowest spending tenth.[54]

Of course, the composition of the income groups is not static – each year some individuals move from one group to another. However, recent research[56] showed that over a four-year period about half of all households remained in the same income tenth in which they had started, and most of those that moved went up or down only to the next band or the one beyond. Very few moved from being poor to being rich. The fact that there is constant movement means that far fewer than 10 per cent of households remain permanently in the poorest income group – but also that far *more* than 10 per cent experience life at this income level at one time or another, and far more still worry about the possibility of doing so.

The most widely used way of expressing the degree of inequality in a country in a single figure is the Gini coefficient. On this measure, between 1961 and 1979, variations were small (between .245 and .276), but between 1979 and 1991 it rose by 42 per cent (from .257 to .365).[57] On an alternative, and arguably better, measure – half the squared coefficient of variation – the degree of inequality more than doubled (from .115 in 1979 to .257 in 1991).[57]

Comparisons of the degree of inequality between different countries are difficult, because of differences in measurement methods and dates. However, a recent study[58] has shown that in the mid-1980s income inequality in Britain, as measured by the Gini coefficient, was greater than in most countries in northern Europe, though less than in some countries in southern Europe and in the US. It also shows that since then, while in most countries the degree of inequality was falling, or rising only slightly, in Britain it was rising rapidly, with the result that by 1991 Britain was more unequal by this measure than any of the other countries measured.

Another international comparison has been made by the United Nations Development Programme (UNDP), using the ratio of the richest 20 per cent of incomes to the poorest 20 per cent of incomes as the measure. On this basis, inequality in Britain has become greater than in any of the other 13 European countries measured, greater than in the US and Japan, and greater also than in half of the 47 countries measured in the developing world.[59]

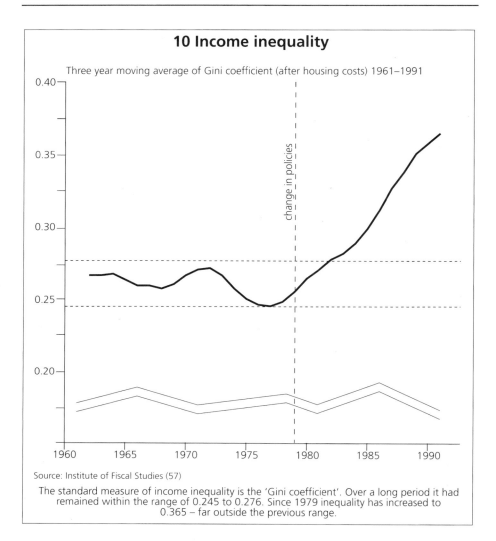

10 Income inequality

Three year moving average of Gini coefficient (after housing costs) 1961–1991

change in policies

Source: Institute of Fiscal Studies (57)

The standard measure of income inequality is the 'Gini coefficient'. Over a long period it had remained within the range of 0.245 to 0.276. Since 1979 inequality has increased to 0.365 – far outside the previous range.

Growing poverty

The most conspicuous consequence of the increase in income inequality has been a corresponding growth in the numbers in poverty. In wealthy countries it is not enough merely to ensure that all citizens have the bare minimum for physical survival so that they do not actually starve to death. Rather, it is necessary to prevent citizens falling into poverty in the sense that they are excluded by lack of money from the things in life regarded as normal and necessary by the rest of society. This concept of relative poverty

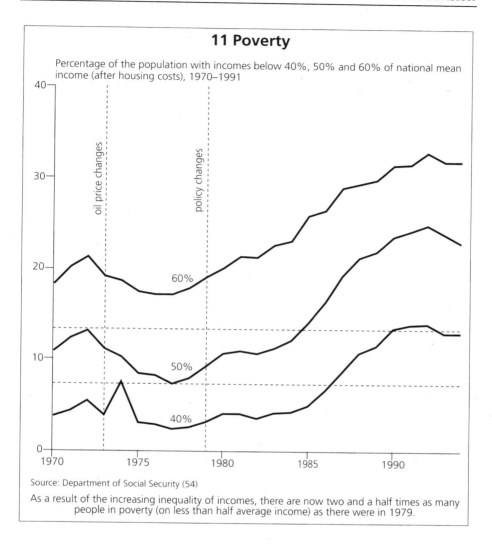

11 Poverty

Percentage of the population with incomes below 40%, 50% and 60% of national mean income (after housing costs), 1970–1991

oil price changes

policy changes

60%

50%

40%

Source: Department of Social Security (54)

As a result of the increasing inequality of incomes, there are now two and a half times as many people in poverty (on less than half average income) as there were in 1979.

is not new – Adam Smith supported it more than two centuries ago when he saw the need for the provision of 'not only commodities which are indispensibly necessary for the support of life but whatever the custom of the country renders it indecent for creditable people, even of the lowest order, to be without'.[60]

Relative poverty is inherently difficult to measure. One measure is the level of income represented by the means-tested benefits provided by the government. However, this is designed to meet only the barest basic needs, and it is reckoned that an income about 40 per cent greater than this is needed to prevent exclusion from much of what is taken for granted by the population in general.

The most widely used measure of poverty is 50 per cent below the national average income. This is the level the European Commission regards as necessary to keep people above in order to prevent social exclusion.

On both these measures, it is clear that since 1979, despite the general rise in national prosperity, there has been a substantial increase in the total number of people in poverty, and a particularly large increase in the number of children in poverty:

- the number of people dependent on income-related benefits increased by 50 per cent to 14 million (24 per cent of the total) in 1994/5;[54]
- the number of people with incomes below 50 per cent of national average income increased by 168 per cent to 13.4 million (24 per cent of the total) in 1994/5;[54]
- the number of children in families living on or below income support level increased to 29 per cent of the total in 1992;[61-2]
- the number of children in families with incomes below 50 per cent of national average income trebled to 4.2 million (32 per cent of the total) in 1994/5;[54] and
- in 1993 the proportion of families with below half the average income was the second highest in the EU, and the proportion of children in these families was the highest in the EU.[63]

On all these measures the incidence of poverty is higher than the national average in minority ethnic groups, in Scotland, Northern Ireland and the North, and in deprived inner city areas;[64] and is particularly high for children in one-parent families, 71 per cent of whom were in families with incomes below 50 per cent of the national average in 1993/4.[54]

All these measures tend to understate the true extent of poverty because the figures on which they are based exclude people who are homeless or living in institutions, and because they take no account of the various ways in which living can be more expensive and difficult for people with small incomes. For example, people without cars or freezers tend to have to shop in smaller quantities at more expensive small shops. Small consumers have to buy their gas on tariffs that can be twice as high as for large consumers, and people with small incomes often have to use prepayment meters, which are more expensive, and they are more vulnerable to disconnection. They cannot get mortgages to buy their homes and they cannot normally get bank cards or credit cards; most do not even have a bank account.

While people with small incomes are more likely than other people to need credit, they are much less well placed to get it. Friends and family are likely to be poor also, and borrowing on credit cards or bank or building society loans is usually unavailable. They are therefore likely to have to borrow, when they have to, from licensed moneylenders, whose interest rates are typically more than ten times as high, or from unlicensed ones whose rates are higher still.[65] Families with incomes below £100 a week are nine times as likely to fall into debt as families with incomes above £400 a week.[66]

People on low incomes have also been hit disproportionately by a number of cost increases in rents following deregulation, in water charges following privatisation, in public transport costs following cuts in subsidies, and in charges for school meals, books, journeys, home help, meals-on-wheels, day centres and other council services following reduced central government grants and capping of council budgets.

Health and social consequences

The growth of inequality and poverty has caused not only material hardship for large numbers of people, but also social exclusion and ill health. People on low incomes tend to be unable to go out for meals, to stand rounds of drinks in pubs, to entertain friends or exchange presents with them, to send their children on school trips, to go on holidays, to take part in sports and other leisure pursuits, to join in a whole host of activities that bring people together and make social life rich, varied and agreeable. In consequence, they tend to be forced into social isolation and to suffer disproportionately from stress, anxiety, depression, sickness and shortened life expectancy.[64]

Children are particularly affected – those in low-income homes tend to have poorer health, lower educational attainment and a higher probability of becoming involved in crime or having a teenage pregnancy.[67] A recent survey[68] of 179 local authorities and 36 health authorities found that children in deprived homes tend to be underweight and below average in height. It found pockets of rickets due to lack of vitamin D, widespread anaemia from lack of iron, and a rising incidence of tuberculosis. Perinatal and infant mortality rates are more than 50 per cent higher among children in social class V (the families of unskilled workers) than in social class I (the families of those with professional occupations), and children in social class V are four times as likely to suffer accidental death.[64]

Studies have shown higher rates of suicide, attempted suicide and acute mental illness in deprived areas[69] and higher rates of sickness in lower socio-economic groups and less prosperous regions.[70] Death rates from coronary heart disease, which used to be 50 per cent higher for the poorest socio-economic groups, have become three times as high.[71] Life expectancy at birth is seven years less for people in social class V than for those in social class I,[72] and death rates in the 15–64 age range are more than twice as high.[73] Death rates for people living in hostels are more than five times as great as for people living in normal homes, and for homeless people they are more than twenty times as great.[74]

The longitudinal study made by the government's Office of Population Censuses and Surveys[73] has shown that the gap between the social classes in mortality rates has been *widening*, and a King's Fund study headed by the government's former chief medical officer has found that, among the very poor, mortality rates have stopped going down and have begun to go *up*.[75] Life expectancy for men, which has been gradually rising over a long period, has started to *fall for social classes IV and V*.[76]

An important point is that in relatively rich countries, like Britain, better health and longer life expectancy seem to be associated less with higher absolute standards of living than with lower degrees of *inequality*. In developing countries, life expectancy tends to rise steadily as income per head increases. But in developed countries, this no longer happens – once basic material needs are met, further increases in income do not normally lead to further increases in life expectancy.[77] What *is* associated with higher life expectancy is greater equality of incomes – the greater the degree of equality, the higher the life expectancy.[78–9]

It appears that not only among the poorest groups, but elsewhere in the income range, sharp income differences restrict the scope for friendships and social activities and give rise to stress, tension and anxiety. These, in turn, are associated with worse health and shorter lives than in societies with similar average income levels but less inequality and greater social cohesion.[78] Thus, increasing inequality brings material hardship and social exclusion to the poor; but it also has far more widely pervasive effects, undermining social cohesion and worsening the quality of life throughout society to a degree that can be clearly measured in terms of worse health and shorter life expectancy.

Social division

The changes since 1979 have already been highly damaging. If they continue into the future, their consequences could be even more serious. In the early 1990s, the rapid rise in inequality of the 1980s slowed down and in the latest period for which figures are available, 1992/3 to 1994/5, there was even a slight reversal of the previous trend – due mainly, it seems, to the fall in unemployment, the ending of the poll tax and increases in other taxes. However, this has made only a small dent in the changes from the previous years, and it remains to be seen whether the further changes in taxes in subsequent years, and the further widening of the gap in earnings, will have brought a resumption of the trend towards increasing inequality. Meanwhile, it can be calculated that, if the trend for the period 1979 to 1994/5 as a whole continued to 2010, by then:

- average incomes would have doubled over three decades; the incomes of the richest 10 per cent would have nearly trebled, but incomes of the poorest 10 per cent would have *fallen* by 15 per cent;[54]
- the gap in incomes between the top 10 per cent and the bottom 10 per cent would have widened from 4¼ times as much in 1979 to more than 15 times as much in 2010;[54]
- income distribution in Britain would have become as unequal as in Brazil and more unequal than in most other developing countries;[80] and
- over half the population would be in poverty.[54]

Such a sharp increase in inequality in such a short period would be entirely unprecedented and gravely damaging. The high degree of social stability and cohesion that has been experienced in Britain has been made possible by the equalising effects of two world wars and their subsequent consolidation by full employment, the welfare state and a progressive system of taxation. The shift back to far greater inequality since 1979 has already done much to undermine this social cohesion; a continuation towards greater inequality still would risk its total breakdown.

If recent trends continued, there would be a substantial proportion of people in poverty, with little prospect of getting out of it, with no share in rising national prosperity and little stake or participation in society more generally. For many of them this would lead to despondency and alienation; for some it could lead to crime or extremist politics. The steep gradient of income distribution would put strong pressures on the somewhat better placed to try to join the groups doing very well at the top, combined with keen anxieties not to sink down to join those with no prospects at the bottom. Even those at the top would find the pleasures of affluence constrained by insecurity and tension.

Continuing increases in inequality will bring a society that is increasingly fragmented, with mounting divisions and tensions, with rising crime and violence, and with a growing threat of social breakdown and political upheaval. Such a prospect is neither appealing nor necessary.

Inequality is *not* a requirement for rapid economic growth. In Britain, economic growth has been *slower* in the period of rising inequality (see Chapter 5); and in other OECD (Organisation for Economic Cooperation and Development) countries faster economic growth has been associated with *less* inequality.[81] World Bank studies covering a wider range of countries[82] have led to the conclusion that 'if anything, inequality is associated with *slower* growth'.

The shift to greater inequality has *not* been universal and it is *not* inevitable. The only other OECD countries to match Britain in this respect are the US and New Zealand. And, in all three countries, the trend has been associated with specific developments. In Britain, these have been widening inequalities in earnings, changes in the social security system, changes in the tax system and rising unemployment.

All four of these developments are affected by, or are the direct consequence of, the public policies followed in Britain since 1979. It therefore follows that by changing these policies it will be possible to check, and in time reverse, the dangerous trend towards ever increasing inequality.

Widening inequalities in earnings

Ever since 1886 (when records were first kept) right through to 1979 the differential between higher and lower earnings changed remarkably little, with the top decile of earnings between two-and-a-quarter and two-and-a-half times the bottom decile. Since 1979, however, the gap has widened markedly until, by 1997, the top decile has become more than three times as high as the bottom. If this trend continued, by 2010 the top decile of earnings would be more than four times as high as the bottom decile – a gap nearly twice as great as in 1886.[83]

There have also been widening gaps between non-manual workers and manual workers, between skilled manual workers and unskilled manual workers, and between full-time workers and part-time and casual workers.[83-5]

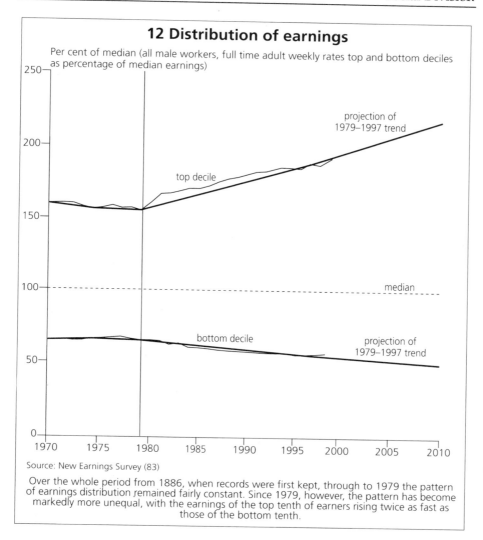

12 Distribution of earnings

Per cent of median (all male workers, full time adult weekly rates top and bottom deciles as percentage of median earnings)

projection of
1979–1997 trend

top decile

median

bottom decile

projection of
1979–1997 trend

Source: New Earnings Survey (83)

Over the whole period from 1886, when records were first kept, through to 1979 the pattern of earnings distribution remained fairly constant. Since 1979, however, the pattern has become markedly more unequal, with the earnings of the top tenth of earners rising twice as fast as those of the bottom tenth.

There are also substantial gaps (slowly diminishing) between men and women; and also gaps (not diminishing) between different industries, regions and ethnic groups.[83,85-6] There has also been a substantial increase in the number of people with earnings below the poverty line.[86]

This widening of inequality in earnings is not something that has been happening everywhere. On the contrary, the OECD, in its review of recent trends in earnings observes:[87] 'No clear tendency emerges of a generalised increase in earnings inequality. ... In fact, the UK and the US stand out

13 International trends in earnings inequalities

Ratio of the lower limit of the tenth decile of male earnings to the upper limit of the first decile of male earnings

United States

France
Britain
New Zealand

France
US
Germany

Japan
Italy
Finland

Japan
Britain
Italy
Finland
Sweden

Germany
Sweden

5X
4X
3X
2X

1980   1985   1990   1995

Source: OECD (87)

Between 1979 and 1995 in Britain the gap between top and bottom earnings widened by a third. There was a similar widening of the gap in the United States. In this they were out of line with most other countries where the pattern of earnings remained little changed.

as the only countries where there has been a continuation of a pronounced rise in earnings inequality.'

The OECD figures make clear that, since 1979, earnings inequalities have risen more steadily in Britain than in any of the other 17 countries measured except the US; earnings inequalities in Britain are now greater than in any of the other countries except the US (and also France where, however, they have been diminishing); and in Britain, the incidence of low pay (defined as less than two-thirds of median earnings) is higher than in any of the others except the US.[87] The trend in Britain has been away from the rest of Europe and towards the situation in the US, where over the past ten years real wages have been *falling* for 60 per cent of earners and where, in the 1980s, 70 per cent of the total increase in incomes went to the top 1 per cent.[88]

The exceptional changes in Britain and the US are not coincidental; they are largely the result of government policies to give freer play to market forces in general, and to establish a 'flexible' labour market in particular.

In Britain, part of the increase in wage inequality in the 1980s and 1990s appears to have been associated with changes in the pattern of labour demand.[89] Partly because of the introduction of new technology-based systems in industry and parts of the service sector, there has been increasing demand for people with skills, and falling demand for unskilled manual workers, leading to shortages and higher pay for the former, but disproportionate unemployment and declines in pay for the latter. The problem has been accentuated by weaknesses in vocational education and training, and by underlying weaknesses in basic education, which mean that many people are unable to benefit from training, even when it is available.

There are other changes resulting directly from government policies that have had important effects at the lower end of the earnings distribution. These include:

- the discontinuance of incomes policies (which tend to compress differentials);
- the rise in unemployment together with measures specifically intended to weaken the bargaining power of trade unions;
- the privatisation of local council services, which has resulted in the introduction of contractors using low-paid labour;
- the increased use of part-time and casual labour;
- the absence of minimum wage legislation; and
- the abolition of wages councils – a survey of job centre vacancies in sectors formerly covered by them found that half the jobs were offering pay below what the wages council rate would have been, and more than three-quarters were paying below what a family would receive on income support.[90]

Meanwhile, at the top end of the income distribution, remuneration has soared. According to Incomes Data Services,[91] the highest paid directors of the largest companies – those in the FT–SE 100 – had average pay increases of 12.6 per cent in 1996, 9.9 per cent in 1995, and 22.2 per cent in 1994 –

several times the rate of inflation and several times the average rate of increase for their employees. An analysis of 288 quoted companies[92] found that in 1982 the highest paid director's remuneration was equivalent to eight times that of the average male worker, but by 1992 it had risen to sixteen times as much.

These disproportionate increases in top earnings are not explained by any sudden improvement in performance. The British economy (and that of the US) has not been getting markedly more competitive relative to other countries, where there has been no comparable surge in top pay. An analysis of 288 companies found that over the period when directors' pay increased so greatly, there was only a very slight relationship between pay rises and company performance in the early years, and none at all in the later years.[92] An analysis of the privatised utilities reveals that directors' remuneration has risen sixfold since privatisation – largely going to *the same people as before,* without any evidence of commensurate improvements in their capabilities or performance.[93]

The recent extremes of high pay at the very top, so far from being necessary for competitiveness in the market, are in fact the result of an *imperfection* in the market, which actually *reduces* the efficiency of the economy.[94] It is simply that in Britain and the US the directors of large companies, particularly in monopoly utilities, have found themselves in an environment where there is little to stop them paying themselves as much as they please.[95]

The increasing inequality in earnings is by no means inevitable – it has not been experienced in other countries. In the long run, one of the most important ways of reducing earnings inequality will be to bring about major improvements in vocational education and training, and in the basic education that provides the foundation for them. This will increase the number of people with skills that are in demand and reduce the number of people whose lack of skills makes them vulnerable to low pay and poor employment prospects. The same market forces that have brought about the recent increases in inequality will then pull the other way to narrow the range of inequality. The present government's emphasis on education and on the additional training provided through the welfare-to-work scheme is thus highly relevant. However, it will be a long time before the full effects of these measures are felt.

The planned introduction of a national minimum wage will have a more immediate effect. It will take over the role of the disbanded wages councils in ensuring at least a basic floor for people in low-paid activities, many of whom are isolated and not unionised. At the same time, it will help reduce the gap between male and female earnings (the majority of beneficiaries are likely to be women). It will also bring in extra revenue from income tax and national insurance and reduce the cost of family credit, currently paid to top up the incomes of families on very low earnings – or, in effect, to subsidise employers who pay wages too low to live on.

It will not affect international competitiveness because very low pay is mostly in services like catering and cleaning, which are not internationally traded. And it should not adversely affect employment. A string of empirical studies[95–100] have shown, both in the US and Europe, that where the national minimum wage has been set at a fairly low level there has been no significant effect on costs and, if anything, a small increase in employment. Even if the minimum were set at a higher rate, such as half average male earnings, as urged by the Low Pay Unit, a survey by the Chartered Institute of Management Accountants found that most respondents did not believe this would 'cause them to reduce staff numbers or increase their prices'; and a survey for *Personnel Today* magazine showed that 86 per cent of personnel chiefs did not believe it would cost jobs in their organisation.[101]

Other recent measures which, even if they do not directly increase their earnings, at any rate may be expected to add to the security and wellbeing of people on low pay, are the strengthening of general employment rights, particularly for part-time and casual workers, and the adoption of the Social Chapter to give Britain's workers the same rights as those in other European countries. The most important contribution towards improving pay at the bottom – which has not yet been achieved – will be a return to full employment (see Chapter 4).

At the other end of the income scale, remuneration at the top is likely to be more difficult to affect directly. In Britain and the US, a market culture has focused on maximising returns to shareholders and top directors. What is needed is a shift towards the stakeholder culture more common in most European and Far Eastern countries. There, senior people in business tend to see themselves as having wider responsibilities, not just to themselves and their shareholders, but also to their workers, suppliers, distributors and customers, and to the environment and to society more generally. The right to make profits in a free economy is seen as balanced by the duty to behave as good citizens of the community that provides them with the means to prosper. This sense of civic responsibility at the top has been found to be helpful for social cohesion and conducive to long-run growth and business success in countries as varied as Germany, Japan and Malaysia.

If there is a case for a minimum wage at the bottom, there is also one for *maximum* remuneration at the top, as a percentage of the turnover of the organisation or as a multiple of the lowest paid employee; and a case for companies giving *all* their staff proportionately the same fringe benefits as their top directors. If concerns over inflation or commercial prudence are felt to limit the size of pay increases felt to be appropriate for the workforce, then social responsibility should imply a similar limit to the size of increases at the top, and the adoption of a code of good practice in relation to the wider community.

Some companies already behave responsibly. Others may be encouraged to do so through organisations such as Business in the Community and Business in the Environment. Informal measures to change the climate may be reinforced with requirements for fuller disclosure, with greater use of the powers of the regulators of monopoly public utilities, or, ultimately, with institutional changes, possibly on the lines used successfully over many years in Germany, where major companies have a second, higher, board charged with taking a wider perspective of the company's responsibilities.

However, changing a whole business culture takes time. Meanwhile, there is one fair, practical and speedy way to tackle astronomic pay at the top – taxation (see section after next).

Changes in social security

The second major factor in increasing inequality has been changes in the social security system. There used to be provision for most social security benefits to be up-rated each year in line with the rise in inflation or national average earnings – whichever was greater. This ensured that those depending on social security benefits for their income shared equally with the rest of the population in rising national prosperity. In 1980, however, the link with average earnings was ended and since then benefits have been up-rated only to take account of inflation. This has meant that their real value has been frozen, while other incomes have continued to rise, resulting in a steadily widening gap between those dependent on benefits and the rest of the community. For example, unemployment benefit fell from 36 per cent of average income in 1983 to only 28 per cent in 1995.[102]

A series of other changes have also worsened the position of people dependent on benefits. Some benefits have been cut, some have been subjected to more restrictive conditions and others have been abolished altogether. For example, child benefit has been increased by less than the rate of inflation, unemployment benefit has been curtailed, sickness benefit and invalidity benefit have been replaced, the maternity grant has been abolished and the lump sum cash grants that used to be available for meeting special crisis needs have been replaced by loans that have to be repaid. The effects of these policy changes have been compounded by other longer-term changes that have increased the numbers of people needing social benefits – the ageing population, the huge rise in unemployment, the increasing unevenness and uncertainty of earnings with more part-time and temporary work and self-employment, the increasing numbers of people on very low pay, and the rise in divorce resulting in a higher proportion of one-parent families.

Changes in the social security structure between 1979 and 1997 have followed a pattern: there has been a steady scaling down of the role played by benefits such as the basic pension, child benefit and unemployment benefit that are paid on a universal basis to all who come within defined categories of eligibility, and a steady building up of benefits such as income support, family credit and housing benefit which are subject to a means test. The idea has been to cut costs and prevent the development of a 'dependency culture' by targeting benefits on those who are shown by a means test to really need them. This may sound sensible enough in theory, but the results in practice have been quite different from those intended.

The procedures for claiming means-tested benefits tend to be cumbersome, time-consuming and tiresome for claimants and administrative staff alike. Partly because of this, many people entitled to benefits do not in fact claim and get them. Whereas take-up is almost 100 per cent for universal benefits such as child benefit and the basic pension, the Department of Social Security estimates that people who are entitled to benefits but do not claim them amount to 12–21 per cent of those eligible for income support, 10–29 per cent for council tax benefit, and about 29 per cent for family credit.[103] Altogether, it is estimated that a total of between £1.6 billion and £3.2 billion in means-tested benefits went unclaimed between 1993 and 1995,[103] with more than a million people not getting the benefits which they were eligible for,[103] and therefore having to subsist on incomes even lower than the benefit level.

The complexity of the procedures makes them confusing, with the result that errors are common. An analysis by the Audit Commission[104] revealed a 20 per cent error rate in income support payments in 1995/6, giving rise to wrong payments totalling £653 million in the course of the year. The procedures also give scope for fraudulent claims; housing benefit in particular has attracted the attention of organised crime, with bogus claims amounting to as much as £2 billion a year.[105]

The procedures can also involve rigidities and delays. It used to take six weeks to process a claim for family credit (to top up the low pay of a prospective new job) – after which it could not be changed for six months. In a world where new jobs are often low-paid, part-time, temporary and precarious, with earnings varying greatly from week to week and the possibility of renewed unemployment ever present, uncertainties about the size and likelihood of future entitlements often brought stress and hardship to unemployed people considering taking on a new job. These problems have been addressed by the introduction of a new fast-track system, but it is not yet clear whether the replacement of family credit by a new tax allowance will bring further problems of inflexibility and delay.

While the processes are slow and inaccurate, they are by no means cheap to administer. The cost of administering the basic retirement pension is equivalent to only 1 per cent of the value of the pensions paid out, and child benefit 2 per cent, but the means-tested income support costs 11 per cent and the cost of administering the loans from the Social Fund amounts to no less than 45 per cent of the value of loans.[106]

A further very important problem with means-tested benefits is their effect on work. When an unemployed person receiving means-tested benefits starts a job, or an employed person takes on a better job or works for longer hours, the extra earnings automatically trigger deductions in means-tested benefits, which can leave people very little better off as a result of working.

Change in Income after £1 Pay Rise

Gross pay rise	£1
Income tax	–20p
National insurance	–10p
Net pay rise	70p
Family credit reduction	-49p
Housing benefit reduction	–14p
Council tax rebate reduction	-4p
Net rise in income	*3p*

Source: Low Pay Unit.[107]

The extent of the deductions depends on family circumstances, hours worked and levels of earnings. Not many people face the effective marginal 'tax' rate of 97 per cent in the example above, but it is estimated that about 100,000 families face effective marginal 'tax' rates of 90 per cent or more, and 420,000 of 80 per cent or more.[97] It is often claimed that people with plenty of money will find marginal income tax rates of more than 40 per cent a disincentive to work; it can well be imagined how the incentives of people with very little money will be affected by marginal rates more than twice as high.

The 'poverty trap' built into the means-tested benefits system means that many people stand to lose in tax and withdrawal of benefits almost all they could gain in earnings, unless they can get a job that is very well paid, which is rarely available, or they can work for very long hours, which for many women is simply not possible. Thus, the present system, far from preventing the growth of a 'dependency culture', effectively locks many people into a dependency on benefits that is permanent, inescapable and disheartening.

The means-tested system of benefits suffers from an insoluble internal contradiction. As the increasing spread in earnings makes the lowest pay ever lower, benefit levels have to be depressed to make them less attractive than earnings. But they also have to be kept above absolute poverty levels, particularly for families with children. Since some earnings are already below poverty levels, there is an increasingly intractable policy dilemma: either benefit levels are depressed below the lowest wage levels, bringing increasing hardship and health risks for the families dependent on them; or else they are raised above minimum earnings levels, in which case the poverty trap becomes deeper and more people stand to get no financial benefit from working longer, or indeed at all. It is a system that combines increasing harshness for those struggling to live on benefits with a complete disregard for classical economics notions of 'incentives' for those expected to seek work without significant reward.

A further feature of the present system, which may undermine its longer-term durability, is that an increasing reliance on means-tested benefits made available only to those in greatest need will not only increase inequalities but will also tend to polarise society into two distinct groups. Instead of social security being a system which everybody contributes to and which everyone benefits from, as of right, it will come to be seen as a system for giving benefits to the poor by levying taxes on the better off. In time, those dependent on benefits may increasingly resent being locked into poverty and dependence, while the better off may increasingly resent the level of taxes needed to pay for a system which they derive no personal benefit from. There is thus a risk of a society increasingly split between rich and poor, increasingly perceived in terms of givers and receivers: 'successful' and 'undeserving', with increasing tension and conflict between them.

The present system of means-tested benefits is then: mean, slow, rigid, unfair, inefficient, prone to error and abuse, and costly to administer. It has built-in contradictions. It keeps people from working and it polarises society, accentuating inequalities and fomenting social divisions. The effect of its 'targeting' is to lock people into dependency. As a residual safety net for a tiny number of exceptional cases (the original intention), it may be useful; but as the main mechanism for providing social security in the twenty-first century, it is manifestly and utterly inadequate. The system does not need reviewing; it needs replacing.

The various hazards in life – such as becoming disabled or unemployed – are too many and serious for individuals or families to be able to protect themselves. If community means anything, it means caring about the misfortunes of others and ensuring that their needs are met. Commercial insurance is not available for most of the risks, and is never likely to be on any basis that covers everyone adequately. The only practical way of doing so is through a modern system of social insurance.

Trying to get by on the cheap with a means-test-based system of benefits is not working. It is costing a great deal without providing real security. It would be better to pay more for a system that really worked with higher contributions from everybody in a position to pay them in order to qualify for specified benefits in the event of specified situations. It can be fair and simple to administer, with no scope for abuse: if you meet the criteria, you get the money; if not, you do not. Such systems are already in place in other European countries and they work.

There is only one drawback, and it is a big one. Any system that automatically provides enough to live on for everyone who qualifies under the criteria will need substantially higher contributions than we have now. Part of this could be covered by removing the anomalous upper limit on employees' national insurance contributions. This alone would bring in an extra £4 billion from people with high earnings; but more would be needed from everyone else too.

This need not cause concern lest it place excessive burdens on the economy. Social insurance schemes are essentially systems of transfer payments, and contributions to them do not constitute a real 'burden' any more than premiums for house insurance or life insurance – they are simply a prudent way of making financial arrangements to cover risks. Moreover, the considerable amount of empirical research on the subject confirms that the level of social security expenditure has little if any effect on economic performance.[108]

There may be difficulties in moving to the higher contribution levels needed to cover adequate benefit levels on a universal basis. However, the full change does not have to be made overnight. The important thing is to decide on the direction to be taken – the changes can then, if necessary, be phased in over a period of years.

Meanwhile, there are immediate problems that will not wait. In the short run, the only way of alleviating hardship will be to raise benefit levels within the system as it stands and replace the Social Fund system of loans with grants. To ensure that at least things do not get worse, it will be necessary to provide now for future benefit levels to be up-rated in line with average earnings and not just inflation. The present government has made a useful start with a disproportionate increase in child benefit, but it is not yet clear how far it will be prepared to increase other benefits by more than inflation or whether it will restore the Social Fund to a grants basis.

Also urgently needed are a combination of changes to reduce the poverty trap. An important start has been made with the welfare-to-work initiative, which, in addition to counselling, training and a subsidised period of employment, relaxes some of the benefit disregards, provides tax relief for child-minding and gives the equivalent of an increase in family credit with a new tax allowance for low earners. However, effective marginal rates of 'tax' are still high and extend over a greater number of people. Dismantling the poverty trap will be a slow and expensive business, but it will provide a payoff in due course, not only in more employment and less inequality, but also in rising revenues from income tax and national insurance.

Changes in taxation

The third main factor in increasing inequality has been changes in the tax system. Traditionally, the tax system in Britain has been progressive – it has borne more heavily on the rich than on the poor and so has tended to reduce inequality. Between 1979 and 1997, however, the previous government brought in a succession of changes in taxes. These have greatly reduced the extent to which their overall effect is progressive and have therefore contributed importantly to the increase in inequality.

Since 1979, the highest rate of income tax on earnings has been reduced from 83 to 40 per cent, and the standard rate from 33 to 23 per cent –

changes that disproportionately favour the highest earners. The investment income surcharge has been abolished; the threshold for inheritance tax has been raised and the rates at which it is levied on large estates reduced; and tax relief has been given for the Business Expansion Scheme and Personal Equity Plans. These changes have been hugely favourable to the wealthiest taxpayers, but are of no benefit to the poorest 50 per cent of the population who have assets (other than homes and pensions) of less than £450.[26] Rates on property (which were proportionate to value) have been replaced first by the flat-rate poll tax and then by the council tax (in which the bands rise much less than proportionately to value), to the benefit of richer people with more valuable homes. At the same time, greater reliance has been placed on indirect taxes, which tend to be regressive, with higher rates of VAT and its extension to domestic fuel, which bears particularly heavily on the poorest families.

Over the period between 1978/9 and 1994/5, the share of income tax and national insurance in total government revenue fell by one-sixth, while the share of VAT more than doubled.[109] While by no means all the changes have been regressive, the balance of the total effects of tax changes has been overwhelmingly towards greater inequality. For example, between 1978/9 and 1993/4, reductions in income tax amounted to £32 billion, of which half (an average of £6000 a year) went to the top 10 per cent of taxpayers, and 30 per cent (an average of £35,800 a year) to the top 1 per cent, while the bottom half of taxpayers got an average of only £340 a year, and the poorest families, with too little income to pay income tax, gained nothing at all.[110] The revenue forgone would have been enough to increase total public spending on social security by 40 per cent. The issue was not that the country could no longer 'afford' the welfare state, but rather that the government's priority was to reduce taxes for the better off rather than improve welfare for the worse off.

It would not be feasible suddenly to reverse all the tax changes of the past two decades. But nor is it necessary to accept for ever the consequences of these changes – a tax system that is unfair and does not play its part in reducing inequalities. There are many ways in which the system can be made fairer and more effective.

The present top rate of income tax of 40 per cent in Britain is lower than in most other developed countries.[106] A higher top rate of 50 per cent on incomes above £100,000 would yield an additional £1 billion, or an extra £2.5 billion if levied on incomes above £50,000.[112] An even higher rate of 60 per cent or more on the very largest incomes would not yield large revenues,

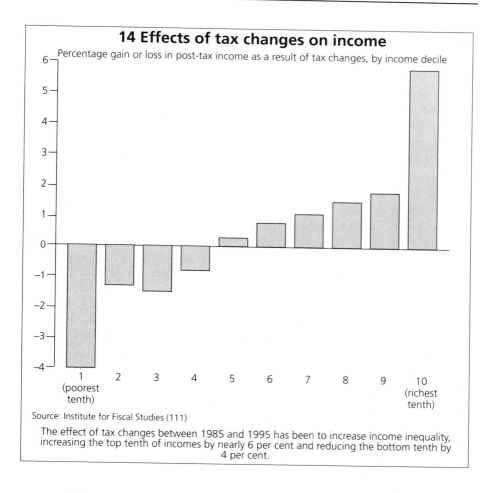

14 Effects of tax changes on income

Percentage gain or loss in post-tax income as a result of tax changes, by income decile

Source: Institute for Fiscal Studies (111)

The effect of tax changes between 1985 and 1995 has been to increase income inequality, increasing the top tenth of incomes by nearly 6 per cent and reducing the bottom tenth by 4 per cent.

but would help reduce the extremes of inequality arising from the very highest incomes.

In terms of likely yield, even more important than increasing the top rates of income tax will be taking steps to reduce the scope for the many kinds of avoidance and evasion, which result in some of the highest incomes attracting relatively little tax. The use and abuse of trusts, overseas tax havens and the wide range of special tax reliefs available, the favourable tax treatment given to share options and other top-income perks, and the failure due to under-staffing to prevent widespread under-payment and fraud give rise to tax revenue losses estimated at up to £9 billion, of which half goes to the top 10 per cent of incomes.[106]

The numerous tax reliefs provide a parallel welfare state for the better off. They are not usually considered in discussions of what the country can 'afford', but their cost in lost tax revenue is nonetheless real and substantial –£1.5 billion on profit-related pay, £3 billion on mortgage interest relief, £8 billion on pensions, £1 billion on private education, and more again on tax-free Personal Equity Plans and TESSAs, the ending of the investment income surcharge, the under-rating of the more expensive properties for council tax, and the £6800 tax free allowance for capital gains, in addition to the £4195 allowance everyone gets for income tax.

The various reliefs, incentives and loopholes in the present tax system cost between them at least £30 billion a year – equivalent to more than 60 per cent of the total receipts from national insurance contributions. It is perverse to have such large-scale generosity targeted on the *better off* sections of the community in times when funds are short for so many other social needs. Some rolling back of this top people's welfare state would do much to reverse the increase in inequality.

Shifting the tax burden onto those better placed to pay it is often opposed on two grounds: it would undermine work incentives and it would make Britain uncompetitive. Both are spurious.

The view that high marginal rates of tax destroy the incentive to work is widely held, but not supported by the evidence. Empirical research on the subject has been inconclusive, suggesting that there is little in it one way or the other.[110,112-14] This is because higher marginal tax rates have two effects. These are the substitution effect (if people can keep less of what they earn at the margin, they may be more likely to choose more leisure instead of work) and the income effect (if people can keep less of what they earn at the margin, they may work harder or longer in order to keep up a particular post-tax income and standard of living). The two effects influence different people in different ways, and many people have little control over how long they work anyway. The two effects tend to cancel each other out, making little overall difference to the time and effort put into work, at least not in the 40–60 per cent range of marginal income tax in prospect – although for people facing effective rates of 90 per cent or more in the poverty trap it may be a very different matter.

The argument that higher taxes would make Britain uncompetitive also does not stand up. At present, taxes in Britain are *lower* than in most of the countries with which we trade. Even an increase of a quarter would do no more than bring taxes in Britain up to the average of the EU.[31] Anyway, empirical evidence shows no clear link between the level of taxation and expenditure and the pace of economic growth.[97]

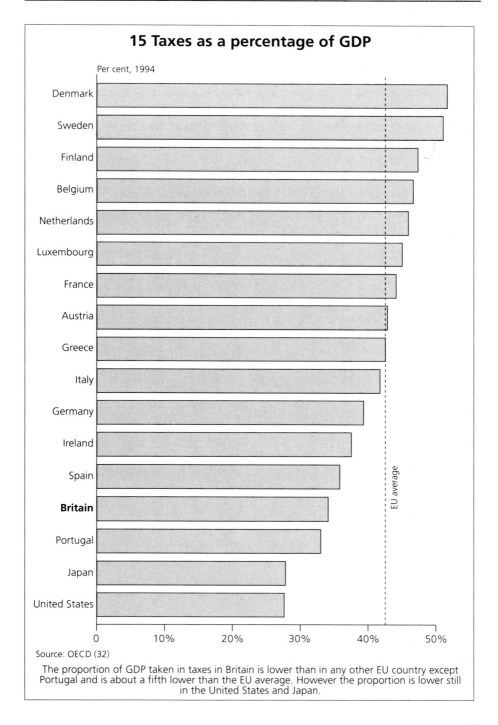

15 Taxes as a percentage of GDP

Per cent, 1994

Denmark	
Sweden	
Finland	
Belgium	
Netherlands	
Luxembourg	
France	
Austria	
Greece	
Italy	
Germany	
Ireland	
Spain	
Britain	
Portugal	
Japan	
United States	

EU average

0   10%   20%   30%   40%   50%

Source: OECD (32)

The proportion of GDP taken in taxes in Britain is lower than in any other EU country except Portugal and is about a fifth lower than the EU average. However the proportion is lower still in the United States and Japan.

However, for reducing inequality the need is not for higher taxes, but for fairer taxes. There are three main grounds for requiring better off people to pay more tax. First, responsibility – if people have the right to receive higher incomes, this should be balanced by the duty to pay higher taxes. Second, practicality – people who are better off are better placed to pay more. And third, least personal cost – according to the classic economic principle of diminishing marginal utility, the more pounds you have already, the less each extra pound is worth to you, and hence the less the pain to you if you have to pay higher rates of tax on higher earnings.

The first two budgets of the present government have been usefully redistributive. But there is still a very long way to go before the tax system is as fair as it needs to be.

Unemployment

The fourth main factor in increasing inequality in Britain has been the rise in unemployment. It worsens the situation in three ways.

First, it brings large numbers of people with varied income levels down to the level provided by social benefits at the bottom of the income distribution range. Second, this puts pressure on the social security budget by increasing costs and reducing contributions, making it more difficult to raise the level of benefits. Each extra 1 million unemployed costs £3.75 billion in social security benefits.[113] And third, it reduces trade union bargaining power and so tends to reduce wages, particularly for unskilled people at the bottom end of the income distribution.

Accordingly, reducing unemployment must be an important element in any package of policies to reduce the growth in inequality. It will also be important for many other reasons. It is considered more fully in Chapter 4.

Targeting poverty

There is now widespread recognition that inequality and poverty have been growing and that they are leading to social exclusion and division. The present government has declared the reduction of poverty to be one of its major objectives and it has taken many steps, including setting up a special Social Exclusion Unit, to help bring this about. However, many different policy areas have a bearing on the problem and there are many differing views on what needs to be done, how much needs to be done and how soon.

It would be helpful to take up Tony Atkinson's proposal[115] that we should set a national poverty target and provide mechanisms for monitoring progress towards it. We already have specific numerical targets for inflation, education, health care and many other areas. Why not also for poverty?

What is proposed is that we take the measure used by the European Commission – the percentage of people with incomes below half the national average – as the single basic indicator of social exclusion. The government should set a target for poverty, just as it does for inflation, of reducing the percentage to a particular level by a particular date. It should then arrange for the General Statistics Office to publish an annual report on progress on poverty reduction, just as the Bank of England does on inflation. The report should publish the various statistical indicators, which should be made available quickly, like the main economic indicators, not years later as they are now; and it should comment on progress towards the target and on the various factors, including policy measures, helping or impeding it.

Such a target and annual report would demonstrate the importance the government attached to poverty reduction, and setting numerical targets would provide a benchmark for success. It would help ensure that this objective was not crowded out by all the others with numerical targets already set for them. By focusing on outcomes, it would not prejudge the particular policy instruments best suited to achieving them. The provision of an informed measurement of progress would ensure that where results were good, success would be publicised and applauded; and where results were disappointing, there would be a stimulus to do more or to try different approaches to reach the target. Thus, it would bring poverty reduction into a more central position among national policy-making priorities.

4 Employment

Is mass unemployment here to stay?

Unemployment has risen from an average of 2 per cent in the first three decades after the war to an average of more than 9 per cent since 1979. The official government figure ranges between 2 and 3 million, but the real level is around 5 million. Current levels of unemployment carry a high personal and social cost and massive economic costs – lost output equivalent to more than 8 per cent of GDP *each year*, lost government revenue of more than £16 billion a year (the equivalent of more than one-fifth of the income tax yield), and additional government expenditure of more than £8 billion a year (the equivalent of nearly one-quarter of the NHS budget).

Permanent mass unemployment is neither unavoidable nor 'a price well worth paying'. It can be ended by changes in macroeconomic policy and in education, training and social security policies. It will be necessary to address skill shortages, capacity constraints, inflationary pressures and international payments problems. This will take time. The new government has made a useful start in some areas, but not in others.

The rise in unemployment

Between the wars, unemployment was very high, but after the Second World War it was believed that better macroeconomic policies would put an end to mass unemployment once and for all. Over the period from 1946 to 1973, unemployment in Britain averaged only 2.1 per cent,[116] and for much of that time the number of unfilled job vacancies exceeded the number of people unemployed.

In 1973, however, there was a global economic upheaval following the trebling of oil prices. In Britain, this brought balance of payments deficits and International Monetary Fund (IMF) pressure to introduce deflationary policies, which caused unemployment to rise to more than 6 per cent in 1977.

By May 1979, unemployment had fallen back to 4.1 per cent. However, a new government took power and introduced major changes in economic policy, causing a further steep rise in unemployment to a postwar record of 13.0 per cent in 1982. Since then, unemployment figures have remained

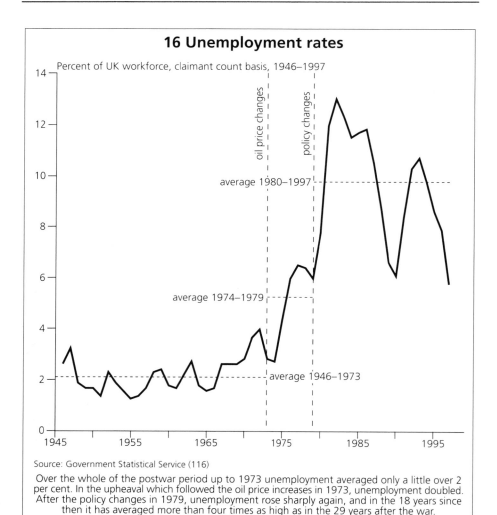

16 Unemployment rates

Percent of UK workforce, claimant count basis, 1946–1997

oil price changes

policy changes

average 1980–1997

average 1974–1979

average 1946–1973

1945   1955   1965   1975   1985   1995

Source: Government Statistical Service (116)

Over the whole of the postwar period up to 1973 unemployment averaged only a little over 2 per cent. In the upheaval which followed the oil price increases in 1973, unemployment doubled. After the policy changes in 1979, unemployment rose sharply again, and in the 18 years since then it has averaged more than four times as high as in the 29 years after the war.

permanently high, ranging between 1.7 million and 3.3 million at different points in the economic cycle.

Because people move in and out of unemployment, the total number of people affected by it is greater than the number recorded as unemployed at any one time. In every year from 1984 to 1995, about one person in five had experienced unemployment in the course of the previous five years.[117]

The incidence of unemployment has been particularly high in the North of England, Scotland, Wales and Northern Ireland. It has particularly affected the unskilled, the young, single parents and ethnic minorities – in the spring of 1994, 33 per cent of black men were unemployed, including 51 per cent of those aged 16 to 24.[118] It has also had a disproportionate impact on children. One household in five with children has nobody in a job – the highest proportion of any country in the EU.[119]

Moreover, high as they are, government figures used in the past to measure unemployment have greatly understated its true extent. Because they were based on the number of people claiming unemployment benefit or a jobseeker's allowance, the unit of measurement changed each time the government tightened up the benefit conditions. A study by the Royal Statistical Society[120] identified 30 changes in the basis of the figures since the method was introduced in 1982, almost all of which have had the effect of making the figures lower. It concluded that the figures provided an unsatisfactory measure of unemployment and should be replaced.

The new government has decided to use instead the figures from the Labour Force Survey, which are not susceptible to manipulation and are comparable with the basis used in other countries. However, even the new figures do not include the large number of people who have dropped out of the labour market altogether. Many older men have made use of special redundancy packages to take early retirement. The number of men aged 50 to 59 who were not economically active rose from 4 per cent in 1975 to 21 per cent in 1995, and the number aged 60 to 64 rose from 16 per cent to 50 per cent.[121] Large numbers of younger men have also dropped out. As a result, according to the Labour Force Survey,[122] there are more than 2 million people who are not in work but who would want a job if they could get one, who are not included in the government's count of claimants.

In addition, there are people in part-time work, some of whom say they would rather work full time if they could. The extra time they would like to work is equivalent to a further 500,000 full-time-equivalent jobs.[123-4]

Taking together those counted as unemployed on the official measure with those wanting work but not counted and those working part-time who would like to work full-time, gives a total shortage of jobs of more than 5 million[123] – more than double the officially recorded unemployment figure. Unfortunately, this figure, which represents the true scale of unemployment, has *not* been falling much in the recovery phase of the economic cycle. The prospect, then, is for the indefinite continuance of lack of employment for about 14 per cent of the population who would like to be in work.

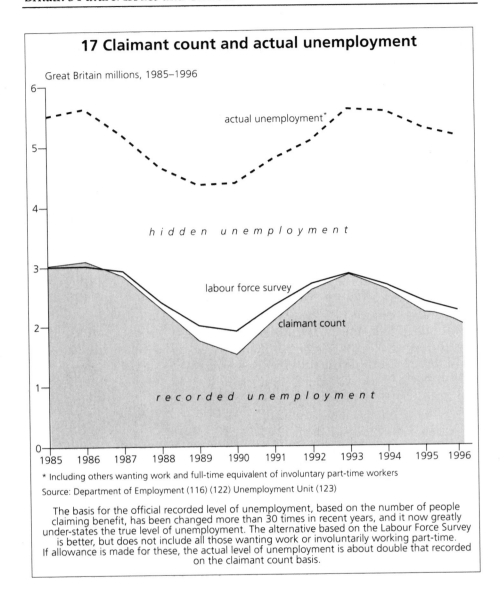

17 Claimant count and actual unemployment

Great Britain millions, 1985–1996

actual unemployment*

hidden unemployment

labour force survey

claimant count

recorded unemployment

* Including others wanting work and full-time equivalent of involuntary part-time workers

Source: Department of Employment (116) (122) Unemployment Unit (123)

The basis for the official recorded level of unemployment, based on the number of people claiming benefit, has been changed more than 30 times in recent years, and it now greatly under-states the true level of unemployment. The alternative based on the Labour Force Survey is better, but does not include all those wanting work or involuntarily working part-time. If allowance is made for these, the actual level of unemployment is about double that recorded on the claimant count basis.

The effects of unemployment

The most obvious effects of mass unemployment are the economic ones arising from the loss of output of the people who are not in work. With real unemployment at around 5 million, more than 14 per cent of the potential labour force is not being used, compared with about 2 per cent in the conditions of full employment in the 1950s and 1960s. If the wasted 12 per cent were all at work, total national output would clearly be greater, although probably not by as much as 12 per cent – for those who are unemployed tend to have fewer skills and qualifications than those in work, and it has been calculated that on average their productivity would be about one-third less.[125] Hence, a return to full employment should increase national output by more than 8 per cent.

The loss of more than 8 per cent of potential output, *year after year*, is waste on a substantial scale. The cumulative loss of output due to unemployment since 1979 is equivalent to more than the *entire* output of the economy over a whole year. The loss in 1997 was more than £63 billion. This would have allowed an increase of more than £24 billion in government expenditure (equivalent to an increase of more than 70 per cent in expenditure on the NHS), and an increase of more than £39 billion in net personal incomes (equivalent to more than £600 a head for every woman, man and child in the country). The economic cost of mass unemployment is not trivial.

In some ways, the personal and social cost is even more serious. Falling into unemployment can be a major trauma. Two in three entrants to unemployment lose their jobs at a week's notice or less;[126] only one in ten gets redundancy payments;[126] and unemployment benefit is equivalent to only 14 per cent of national average earnings,[127] which is the lowest proportion for any country in Europe except Greece.[128] It is available for only six months and subject to stringent conditions. Nine out of ten unemployed young people aged 16 and 17 receive no benefit at all.[129]

Even for those who qualify for means-tested income support and housing benefit, unemployment normally involves a drop in income of at least a half.[126] This is just about enough to cover basic essentials, but little extras like a chocolate bar, a drink at the local, or bus fares are not covered; shoes, clothes and toys for the children are a real struggle; holidays, household repairs and replacement of furniture, furnishings or appliances are normally out of the question – hence exceptional needs can often only be met by running into debt or cutting back on food or heating.[130-2] Unemployment has become one of the main causes of poverty. More than 70 per cent of children in households without an earner are in ones with incomes below half the national average.[133] Unemployment is also a major cause of mortgage repossessions and homelessness.[134]

One consequence of poverty through unemployment is being unable to join in social and recreational activities with other people – and worse, being unable to buy their children fashionable clothes or to pay for them to participate in special events, such as school trips.

The psychological effects are in some ways even worse than the financial hardship. In a society in which the work ethic is still strong, people without a job tend to feel themselves a failure, to lack confidence and self-esteem, and to suffer from stress and depression.[135] They often feel humiliated in their encounters with staff at jobcentres and benefit offices, and looked down on in pubs and clubs where people talk about 'unemployed lay-abouts' and 'benefits scroungers'.[126]

A survey has found that unemployed people need to see their doctor more often than those at work, are twice as likely to drink heavily and are more than two and a half times as likely to develop mental illness.[136] The incidence of parasuicide is much higher – 19 times as high among those unemployed for more than a year.[137] And unemployed people suffer worse general health and earlier death.[138–40]

Finally, the rise in unemployment has stimulated the growth of the 'black economy',[126] and the level of unemployment among young men has been closely associated with the level of burglaries.[141] A survey by chief probation officers found that almost 70 per cent of convicted offenders were unemployed.[142]

Thus, mass unemployment is very expensive both in economic terms and in human costs. It is eroding the fabric of society. To identify what policies will reduce it and, over a period, bring about a return to full employment, it is important to examine the real and perceived causes of unemployment.

The culture of dependency

It is sometimes argued that unemployment is largely the fault of the unemployed themselves, that they are work shy and unenterprising, corrupted into a culture of permanent dependency by the attractions of an easy indolent life on welfare benefits. What is needed, it is said, is to cut benefits to a minimum, make eligibility conditions more stringent, and tell anyone unemployed to 'get on yer bike'. This explanation of unemployment, while convenient for those who would like to reduce the level of taxes needed to pay for welfare benefits, is not supported by the evidence.

First, unemployment was relatively low before the First World War, very high between the two wars, very low for the first three decades after the Second World War and very high again in the past two decades. If indolence and lack of enterprise are the explanation, then why are these qualities in only limited evidence in the first period, strongly present in the second, absent in the third and strongly present again in the fourth? It is not credible that the supposed moral decay should have infected most other industrial countries at the same time and in similar degree; that it should have suddenly doubled in the two years after 1979, or that it should have subsequently varied substantially from year to year in line with the stage in the economic cycle. It is reasonable to suppose that there will always be a few lazy or unscrupulous people who will seek to take advantage of any social system; and it is possible that general attitudes to work will change – gradually over a period. It is completely implausible to suppose that basic attitudes and behaviour will change on such a scale, in both directions, and as abruptly as the figures for unemployment and in countries with very different cultural patterns and institutional arrangements.

Second, the activity rate figures. Male activity rates have been falling steadily, but female ones have been *rising*. It is hardly likely that the former indicate an increasing aversion to work on the part of males and the latter an increasing enthusiasm for work on the part of females; *both changes happening at the same time.*

And, third, the realities of life on the dole. Unemployment normally involves a sharp drop in income, serious financial hardship and dependence on a welfare system that is neither comfortable nor unconditional. And this is compounded by social isolation and personal stress. It is implausible to suppose that many people find this a preferable way of life. Moreover, the social pressures to find employment are compounded by internal ones. Studies of the unemployed have shown that their pressing desire is not for higher benefits but *to get back to work;*[126] and a study commissioned by the government specifically to gauge the extent to which the long-term unemployed were lapsing into a 'dependency culture' found no evidence of its existence. On the contrary, it found that the chances of people getting a job depended entirely on the job opportunities available and their suitability for them in the eyes of prospective employers.[143]

Flexible labour markets

It is often argued that a more flexible labour market would bring down unemployment. Too many employment regulations inhibit employers from taking on new staff and too high wages mean that workers 'price themselves out of a job'. Consequently, we need to dismantle employment protection legislation, reduce the power of the unions and have a more flexible (ie lower) pay structure, particularly for those with low skills who would otherwise face a declining demand for their services. Government policies in Britain since 1979 have already gone some way along this road and the US, which has gone much farther, is cited as an example to emulate.

The British labour market has become the most deregulated in Europe. However, it was during the period when deregulation and union weakening were proceeding most quickly that unemployment was rising most sharply. It is now much higher than it was when the labour market was less flexible.

In the rest of Europe, several of the countries with the best unemployment records over the period 1983–96 – Germany, Norway, Portugal, Sweden and Switzerland – had particularly *high* degrees of labour market regulation and unionisation. A survey[144] of employers in Britain and six other European countries found that, on balance, rules about such things as minimum notice, unfair dismissal, severance pay and statutory requirements to negotiate redundancies with unions, brought *higher* employment – their deterrent effect on recruitment was more than offset by their deterrent effect on dismissals.

The most evident consequences of labour market deregulation in Britain have been an increase in the desire of employers to limit their commitment to their employees by using short-term, temporary contracts, and a greater willingness to 'down-size' their workforces. It is no coincidence that this has led to a greatly increased feeling of job insecurity, bringing a sharp drop in employees' morale and commitment,[145] damaging productivity and giving rise to stress, ill-health and marital problems.

Whether pay flexibility, meaning flexibility downwards, particularly for the least skilled and lowest paid, brings any significant increase in jobs is questionable. Britain's record for creating new job in the 1980s and 1990s is rather unimpressive by comparison with other European countries. Moreover, the majority of the increase in jobs has been in low-skill, low-pay, part-time, insecure ones, offering poor prospects and an inadequate basis on which to support a family. The rising inequalities in pay have been a major factor in increasing inequality and poverty (see Chapter 3). The OECD warns:[146]

> OECD societies also confront some worrying inequalities which are straining the social fabric. In some countries, such as the United States and the United Kingdom, earnings have become considerably more unequal ... this can lead to more marginalisation, an increase in poverty, and exacerbation of budgetary pressure on existing social

safety nets ... the risk now facing a number of OECD countries is that labour market exclusion can easily turn into poverty and dependency.

The example of the US as the way ahead is not encouraging. While it is true that in recent years new job creation in the US has been greater than in Europe, this appears to owe more to rising population, low interest rates and budget deficits than to a flexible labour market.[147]

Unfortunately, the downside of a flexible labour market in the US has been even more marked than in Britain. Between 1990 and 1996, when real wages rose by 20 per cent in Europe, they *fell* by 1 per cent in the US.[148] In the same period, US GDP rose by 16 per cent, with the benefit going predominantly in higher profits, dividends and share values. Since 80 per cent of US households receive no dividends at all, and three-quarters of all dividends go to 2.5 per cent of households, the result has been a substantial redistribution from wage-earners to wealth-owners.[149]

Since 1979, even male university graduates have suffered falls in real earnings, while men with fewer than 12 years of schooling have experienced a 27 per cent drop in real hourly earnings.[150] Many of the new low-skill, low-pay jobs do not even cover basic subsistence needs – 60 per cent of US households in poverty have someone *in work*, but earning too little to support a family.[146]

Low pay and poor prospects for young, less-educated men have been associated with a sharp rise in crime.[151] The prison population has been rising at nearly 9 per cent a year, and in 1993 was equivalent to 1.9 per cent of the workforce, with a further 1.5 per cent guarding them at an average cost of more than $30,000 per head a year.[151] One-third of all black American men between the ages of 18 and 30 are in prison, awaiting trial, or on bail.[149]

Even if further labour market deregulation and even lower pay for the worst paid resulted in some increase in employment, the social costs of the poor quality of the jobs, the increase in poverty, inequality and insecurity, and the probable rise in crime would be likely to outweigh any economic benefits. This is therefore not a promising way to deal with unemployment. On the contrary, it is high-skill, high-productivity, high-pay jobs that are needed, not only on social grounds, but to improve the country's economic performance.

New technology and skills

Another frequently cited explanation for the rise in unemployment is the increasing adoption of new technology. If a new robot or computer can do the tasks formerly done by several people, is it not plausible to suppose it will result in several people being out of a job?

This can and does happen. However, the direct loss of jobs is less than is commonly supposed and tends to be offset by an indirect *gain* in jobs elsewhere. For example, when new technology is introduced in the production of a product or service, it normally results in higher labour productivity. The initial effect of this may be labour shedding; but the secondary effects may be expected to be job *creating*. The gain from higher labour productivity may be used to reduce prices, leading to higher sales and more jobs elsewhere in the plant, or to savings for consumers enabling them to spend more on other things. It may be used to pay higher wages, leading to higher incomes and spending by the workers, or to pay higher dividends, leading to higher spending by investors. It may be ploughed back into new investment, leading to higher spending on capital goods. Or it may be used for some combination of these. But, whichever way the fruits of higher productivity are used, they may be expected to give rise to increased spending elsewhere, leading to greater activity and more jobs to offset the initial loss of jobs.

This is why replacing horses and carriages with motorcars, or handwritten manuscripts with printed books and handmade goods with factory-made products did *not* lead to a general reduction in employment after the Industrial Revolution. It is also why successive decades of rising labour productivity from other causes such as mechanisation, better management methods or improved training have not been associated with rising unemployment. It also explains why countries such as Japan and Korea, which make particularly extensive use of robots and other kinds of automation, do not have higher than average levels of unemployment.

Moreover, this assessment of the effects of new technology on employment is supported by comprehensive empirical evidence. The Policy Studies Institute undertook four major surveys,[152-5] which mapped the diffusion of new technology across British manufacturing industry and found that the adoption of new technology did indeed often lead to some direct loss of jobs, with a tendency for the loss to be greater with more extensive use and with more advanced kinds of application. However, they also found that in some plants it brought no change in jobs and in some a *gain* in jobs. Also, the average net loss was fairly small compared with losses from other causes – a total loss of 36,000 jobs a year in the whole of manufacturing industry between 1981 and 1987, equivalent to an average of less than two jobs per factory per year.

Further analysis[156] of the data in terms of the *total* change in jobs from all causes, including the *indirect* effects of new technology, showed that while the plants using new technology had some loss also in their total employment, the plants that did *not* use it experienced a decline in their total employment three times as great. Whereas more extensive use and more advanced applications were associated with more direct job losses, in terms of *total* employment they were associated with *fewer* job losses – indeed, use of robots was associated with an actual *increase* in total employment. Thus, the evidence suggests that if allowance is made for the indirect as well as the direct effects, the overall impact of new technology on employment is probably not negative at all.[157]

Results consistent with these findings have also emerged from the few empirical studies that have been done in other countries: for example, the surveys undertaken in parallel with the PSI one in 1983 in France[158] and Germany[159] and other studies undertaken in Spain, Ireland, Denmark, Italy, Austria, Japan and New Zealand.[160–1]

Thus, new technology has not turned out to be the mass job killer it was sometimes forecast to be. On the whole, its use has been welcomed, not merely on the grounds of its contribution to competitiveness and longer-term job protection, but also on account of the opportunity offered for higher pay and better working conditions. A major PSI survey on industrial relations[135] found that shopfloor attitudes to new technology were overwhelmingly favourable. It was associated with more skill, responsibility, interest and diversity of tasks. A PSI survey of robot users[162] in fact found that expected shopfloor opposition failed to materialise and that improved work conditions and better labour relations were among the more important benefits experienced.

While fears about the general impact of new technology have been exaggerated, there is one aspect that does give grounds for concern. PSI surveys[155] found that where there were direct job losses resulting from the use of new technology, the decrease in shopfloor jobs was substantially greater than the decrease in non-shopfloor jobs, and the decrease in *unskilled* shopfloor jobs was more than ten times as great as the decrease in skilled shopfloor jobs. This decrease in unskilled jobs was accompanied by persistent scarcities of people with the highest skills, such as microelectronics engineers. Indeed, the shortages of people with key skills was cited as much the most important obstacle to the adoption of new technology – and this applied across all industries, regions, sizes of plant and degrees of use, and also in all the other countries in which similar surveys were undertaken.[161]

Whereas, in principle, direct job losses through the introduction of new technology should be broadly offset by corresponding gains in new jobs generated elsewhere, there is a problem. The new jobs may be in different plants, industries, towns or even countries, and may not become available immediately. Also, they will generally require substantially higher levels of skill than the old ones they displace. Hence, new technology offers the possibility of replacing poor old jobs with better new ones – but only if adequate skill levels are acquired for taking them up.

While the introduction of new technology throws things into particularly sharp focus, similar considerations apply more broadly. Throughout the economy, demand is falling for many kinds of old unskilled jobs, particularly in declining industries, while demand is increasing for professional, managerial and technical jobs requiring a high level of skills. It is therefore imperative, not only for fuller employment, but also for international competitiveness and economic development, to ensure that national skill levels are high enough to pick up the job opportunities of the future.

In this area Britain has been falling behind other countries. British managers tend to be less qualified than those in other European countries and, more strikingly, a succession of international comparative studies have shown the *general* level of skills and educational qualifications in Britain to be lower than in competitor countries.[163–5] For example, the proportion of the workforce educated to craft level is twice as high in France and the Netherlands and three times as high in Germany. In 1993, 27 per cent of the working age population in Britain had no qualification at all.[166]

These low figures are partly the result of market forces failing to produce enough industrial training in Britain. While the best firms have had excellent training schemes, others have seen no point in making an investment in training when the investment may later be lost if the newly-trained employee subsequently decides to change jobs. Instead, they have hoped to get by with poaching people who have already been trained elsewhere. However, specific industrial training is only feasible where people have sufficient general education to be able to benefit from it, and the unsatisfactory level of skills today is partly a reflection of underlying weaknesses in education over a period of many years.

Fortunately, in recent years there have been important improvements. For example, between 1979/80 and 1994/5 the percentage of young people entering higher education more than doubled[166] and, although the proportion is still lower than in most other European countries, this is largely compensated for by high staying-on rates and by more mature students coming later into full-time higher education, or becoming part-time students, for example at the Open University.[167] There have also been increases in the proportion of students staying on at school after the minimum leaving age and in the proportion gaining qualifications before leaving.[168]

However, the proportion of 16–18 year olds in full-time education or training is still one of the lowest in Europe,[168] as is the proportion of secondary students in vocational training.[192] Spending on education as a percentage of GDP is lower than it was two decades ago, and lower than in most other European countries.[168]

There is a clear need to expand and improve training in industry; but beyond that there is a need to improve general education standards to ensure that no one leaves school without basic literacy, numeracy and IT skills.

The National Commission on Education[169] has suggested that the key to this will be to strengthen the foundations of education by reducing class sizes in primary schools, particularly in the first two years, and by extending nursery education to all three–five-year-olds. The new government has declared that education is its number one priority, and has set targets for improvements in attainment – but it will need to supply major additional funding over a number of years for them to be met.

The welfare-to-work scheme includes provision for a major expansion of training opportunities for young and long-term unemployed people, which will help make more employable some of the people who have hitherto found particular difficulty in finding jobs. While there can be nothing but benefit from making labour markets more 'flexible' in the sense that people are better trained and more skilled and adaptable, and in consequence more employable, it should not be supposed that this alone will be enough to put an end to unemployment. Edward Heath's government set up the Manpower Services Commission, which generated a massive increase in training – but not in employment because there was no comparable increase in jobs for the newly-trained people. Germany has long had one of the most highly trained workforces in Europe – but this has not prevented a serious increase in the level of unemployment.

The social security system

A further argument is that at least a part of unemployment can be attributed to the operation of the social security system: on the one hand social security contributions make labour more expensive to employers, on the other the basis on which social benefits are paid discourages people from taking jobs.

It is undeniable that employers' social security contributions make labour more expensive than it would be if wages were the only costs involved. However, this can hardly be a specially adverse factor in Britain, since employers' contributions in Britain are less than half as high as in every other EU country except Denmark, partly because benefit levels are higher in other countries and partly because a higher proportion of their costs are financed from employers' contributions.

The way social security benefit entitlements are calculated means that when someone who has been unemployed starts a new job, the new earnings are partly or wholly offset by corresponding deductions in benefits, which can lead to an effective 'tax' rate of more than 90 per cent (see Chapter 3). A new job therefore needs to be quite highly paid for it to bring a worthwhile improvement in income. The jobs accessible to people who have been unemployed are often low-pay, part-time and precarious, and cuts in hours and earnings, or a return to unemployment, can mean a delay in getting benefits restored. This 'poverty trap' means that many unemployed people who would like to take a job are effectively discouraged from doing so.

For lone parents, the majority of whom would rather be in a job than on benefit, there is the further problem that the need for additional expenditure on child-minding makes most job possibilities unremunerative.

The new government is seeking to mitigate both these problems by introducing working families tax credit at a higher rate than the family credit it is replacing. This will improve the return from low-paid jobs. It is also providing a six-month wage subsidy to employers taking on young and long-term unemployed people, providing help for lone parents in the form of a new child-care tax credit to cover 70 per cent of the cost of child care, and providing more facilities for supervised activities for schoolchildren after school hours and during school holidays.

These should all be helpful. However, marginal rates of withdrawal for most recipients of the new working families tax credit will still be from 68 to 79 per cent. Of those previously unemployed who take subsidised jobs under the welfare-to-work scheme, it remains to be seen what proportion would have got jobs anyway even without the subsidy, and what proportion merely displace people employed already. OECD studies suggest that these two categories applied to 90 per cent of the jobs in job-subsidy schemes in Australia, Belgium and the Netherlands. Even more crucial, it remains to be seen what proportion remain employed after the subsidised period is over. A recent study of new jobs taken by the unemployed found that only 13 per cent of them lasted more than nine months.[170]

The working families tax credit is not due to come into effect until October 1999, and the child-care tax credit until April 2000. Even so, the combination of measures should prove of value in due course.

Work sharing

Another approach is work sharing. If the total amount of work is limited, is it wise to have some people working longer hours than they wish, while others have no work at all? Would it not make more sense to share out the work available, with those in a job working shorter hours in order to make jobs available for those at present unemployed?

In the past, the fruits of higher productivity were taken partly in higher pay and partly in shorter working hours. In the course of the past century, in Europe the average number of hours worked each year fell from 3000 to 1700,[171] and in Britain the number of hours worked per week fell by one-third between 1861 and 1980.[172]

However, in the 1980s, while average weekly hours tended to continue to fall in other European countries, in Britain they have been rising and are now the highest in Europe.[119] It has been estimated that if hours in Britain had continued to fall in the 1980s and early 1990s it would have created an extra million jobs.[172] If, in the future, hours in Britain were cut to meet the average for the rest of the EU (by three and a half hours a week), it would imply an 8 per cent increase in the total number of jobs.

Accordingly, there would at least seem sense in welcoming the EU directive giving employees the right to refuse to work more than a maximum of 48 hours a week. Beyond that, various proposals have been put forward for bringing about shorter hours and, in France and Italy, there are government proposals for a maximum working week of 35 hours in the years 2000 and 2001 respectively. Both proposals are encountering opposition from employers, and in Britain too there would be problems.

The majority of those working particularly long hours in Britain are people on low rates of pay, who reckon they need the long hours to get a reasonable income. People who are self-employed or in senior professional and managerial positions, see long hours of work as a route to advancement (in contrast with continental European countries where working excessive hours tends to be viewed as an indicator, not of enthusiasm, but of inadequacy). Where a shorter basic working week is agreed, employers tend to provide for it by increasing overtime, cutting out marginal tasks or installing labour-saving equipment, and not necessarily by taking on extra

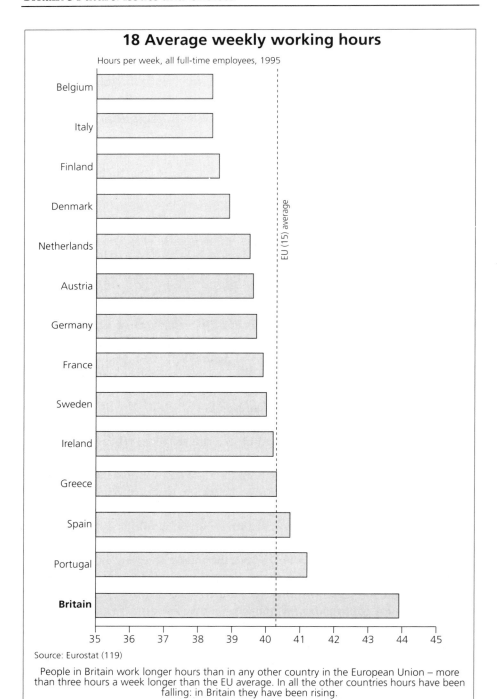

18 Average weekly working hours

Hours per week, all full-time employees, 1995

Source: Eurostat (119)

People in Britain work longer hours than in any other country in the European Union – more than three hours a week longer than the EU average. In all the other countries hours have been falling: in Britain they have been rising.

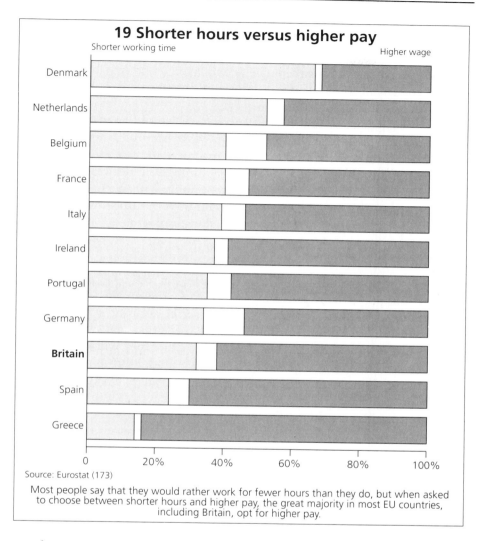

19 Shorter hours versus higher pay

Shorter working time — Higher wage

Denmark	
Netherlands	
Belgium	
France	
Italy	
Ireland	
Portugal	
Germany	
Britain	
Spain	
Greece	

0 20% 40% 60% 80% 100%

Source: Eurostat (173)

Most people say that they would rather work for fewer hours than they do, but when asked to choose between shorter hours and higher pay, the great majority in most EU countries, including Britain, opt for higher pay.

people to replace the missing hours. Where they wish to take on extra staff, they sometimes have difficulty rearranging work patterns or finding people with appropriate skills from among the unemployed.

Probably the most important difficulty lies in the attitudes of employees and employers. A Europe-wide survey found that most people would prefer to work shorter hours than they do but, if given a choice between shorter hours and higher pay, in every country except Denmark and the Netherlands (where pay is much higher than in Britain) the majority expressed a

preference for higher pay.[173] So, shorter hours with correspondingly less pay tends to be unacceptable to employees; while shorter hours with the same weekly pay tends to be unacceptable to employers – and may be expected to put up costs, add to inflation and impair competitiveness. Public subsidies to help bridge the gap could be expensive.

The alternative of encouraging earlier retirement would be easier to achieve, but would go against the need to move towards *later* retirement because of the pension problems arising from an ageing population (see Chapter 2).

Thus, sharing existing work more widely through shorter weekly hours or earlier retirement would be better than continuing with the present level of unemployment; but, bringing it about would involve difficulties and would not provide a full solution to the problem of unemployment.

Direct job generation

Spreading existing work over more people can only be a second-best solution compared with providing *more* work. Improving education and training and removing anomalies in the social security system will be valuable in removing some of the obstacles that prevent people taking up the jobs that are available; but it is doubtful whether they will actually make *more* jobs available, at any rate on the scale required. It is therefore likely to be necessary also to make use of macroeconomic policies to expand effective demand and generate extra jobs directly.

In Britain, unemployment increased from an average of 2.1 per cent between 1946 and 1973 to an average of 9.7 per cent between 1980 and 1995. The increase was triggered initially by increases in oil and world commodity prices in the early 1970s; but the high levels of unemployment, which have continued subsequently, have been associated primarily with the abandonment of the Keynesian macroeconomic policies that kept demand high and unemployment low during the earlier period in favour of monetarist macroeconomic policies, which have involved bouts of severe deflation. These were supposed, in theory, to eliminate inflation and, after a while unemployment also; but, in practice, they have had only limited success against inflation and they have kept unemployment at very high levels compared with those suffered in the interwar period.[174]

In most other EU countries, unemployment has also become high for similar reasons – the reversion to more traditional macroeconomic policies, giving more priority to containing inflation and public borrowing than to achieving full employment, and economic growth. This has been reinforced in recent years by a concern to meet the convergence targets set for economic and monetary union (EMU) at the expense, if necessary, of higher unemployment.

These traditional economic policies, and the arguments advanced in their support, bear a striking resemblance to the economic policies and arguments of the interwar years. The reasons for the shift from prewar orthodox policies (which failed) to postwar Keynesian policies (which succeeded) and back to traditional policies (which failed again) appear to owe less to appraisal of the evidence than to shifts in fashion among the élite opinion leaders who form the conventional wisdom of the day – to 'the herd-like behaviour of policy intellectuals and policy-makers, who too often fall in thrall to a conventional view that commands such universal approval that nobody dares question it'.[175]

The experience has been very different in Japan and the newly industrialised countries of east Asia where, until very recently, rapid economic growth has kept unemployment very low. The experience has also been very different in the Scandinavian countries and Austria. They too were exposed to higher oil and commodity prices in the early 1970s, but they continued to give priority to full employment; and achieved it by maintaining a higher general level of demand and generating an increase in jobs in the public sector. This gave them a continuing high level of employment and good social services, albeit at the expense of high taxation.[128,176] Only in the 1990s have these countries experienced high unemployment as a result of succumbing to the same change in economic fashion, together with the need to meet the EMU monetary targets.

The basic Keynesian insight – that full employment and fast economic growth can be achieved by government measures to raise effective demand and thereby draw into use the economic resources that remain unused when demand is too low – remains valid, and can be used again. Indeed, it will *have to* be used again if we are to secure a return to full employment. For other measures, useful and necessary as they will be, will not be enough unless they are undertaken in the context of a rising level of demand to create the needed extra jobs.

An increase in demand can take several forms. One is to increase demand for general consumer expenditure by increasing personal incomes, for example by reducing the level of personal taxes. However, this has the disadvantage that much of the extra expenditure will go on imported consumer goods, thereby creating more jobs in other countries, but not in Britain.

Another way is to reduce company taxation with a view to increasing private sector investment, thereby creating extra jobs in the investment goods industries and at the same time strengthening the competitiveness of British industry. However, unless the tax cuts are carefully targeted, there is the risk that the savings will be used to pay higher dividends, thereby increasing personal consumption instead of investment.

Probably the most reliable way of ensuring that the increase in demand has a direct impact on jobs is by increasing government expenditure in ways that involve creating more jobs. It is anomalous that people who could be usefully at work are unemployed at a time when we need more people to work in our schools, hospitals and care services and to improve our environment, infrastructure and housing stock, but we cannot 'afford' to employ them because of a self-imposed commitment to traditional concepts of 'sound finance'. The lesson of Keynesian economics is that, in so far as additional activities in these socially desirable areas involve the use of resources that would otherwise be left idle, there is no 'real' cost in undertaking them, even if it involves a bookkeeping deficit in the public accounts.

Even in terms of traditional economics, the net cost of direct job generation is much less than is commonly supposed. This is illustrated by the modelling of a scheme[177] for the creation of a million new jobs ('real' ones, full-time, at normal rates of pay): 150,000 each in housing, education and health, 100,000 each in care in the community, environmental projects and energy conservation, and 250,000 further jobs as the indirect consequence of the other ones.

It is estimated that the creation of these jobs would cost the government £16.9 billion. However, the new jobs would bring savings in welfare expenditure of £2.9 billion, and gains from additional receipts from national insurance of £2.9 billion, from income tax of £2.7 billion and from indirect taxes of £1.4 billion – a total of £9.9 billion in all. Hence, the *net* cost to the government would be only £7 billion. This is a sizeable sum, but it would be 'a price well worth paying' for bringing about a significant reduction in unemployment and a valuable improvement in public provisions in health, education and other areas at the same time.

Constraints on action

The demand management policies that maintained full employment in Britain in the 1950s and 1960s, and in the EFTA (European Free Trade Association) countries through the 1970s and 1980s also, can still in principle bring full employment and faster growth in the years ahead in Britain. However, Britain's situation today is in some ways very different from that in the 1950s and 1960s, and there are four constraints that may impede the adoption of more expansionist economic policies – capacity, skills, inflation and international interdependence.

Capacity limits

Increases in demand will only bring increases in output so long as there is spare capacity available to bring into production. At present, there is some spare unused capacity.[178] Two decades of on-off deflation have brought low levels of investment resulting in a weak stock of productive capital, particularly in manufacturing, and any sustained increase in demand is likely to run up against capacity limits, beyond which further increases in demand will result not in higher output but merely in higher inflation. Indeed, recent analysis suggests that a decline in the capital stock has become a major factor in unemployment.[179] It will therefore be necessary to rebuild the capital stock to match the proposed increase in employment (see Chapter 5).

Skills shortages

Similarly, any sustained increase in demand may in time run up against increasingly serious skill shortages as a result of past inadequacies in education and training. Hence, the importance of the new policies to give much higher priority to education and training.

Inflation

The third potential constraint is inflation. On the face of it, there is little reason for supposing that demand management policies to maintain full employment are inherently inflationary. In the 1946–70 period, when unemployment was most of the time kept below 2 per cent, inflation averaged only 3.6 per cent a year;[174] but since 1979, when demand management policies were abandoned and unemployment has been very much higher, inflation has most of the time been higher too.

However, it is argued that the economy now behaves in a way that is different from the 1950s and 1960s in that an expansion of demand is believed now to bring overheating and inflation at much higher levels of unemployment than hitherto.[176] For example, it has been estimated that in the four largest economies of the EU in the 1973–9 period, when unemployment fell below about 4 per cent, there tended to be inflationary wage increases; by 1994 this tended to happen when unemployment fell below about 9 per cent.[180] With NAIRU (nonaccelerating inflation rate of unemployment) having apparently become so high, it is argued that high unemployment has to be accepted, because the alternative is high inflation, which would be worse. There are three points of relevance to this.

First, inflation is *not* necessarily worse. Runaway inflation is disastrous, but moderate rates of inflation – say 4–6 per cent a year – though not desirable, are nothing like as damaging as high unemployment and economic depression. Rising prices can be allowed for, and social benefits can be indexed to compensate for higher prices, but there is no way of compensating for lost jobs or lost output. *Some* inflation can actually be helpful in making the labour market more flexible. With a little inflation, adjustments in pay relativities can easily be made by some having larger money increases and others having smaller ones. With zero inflation, adjustments can only be made by some having increases and others having to accept actual *cuts* in pay – which is much more difficult to achieve. A little inflation can also be helpful in encouraging borrowing for investment by enabling debts to be repaid in slightly depreciated currency, thereby lowering the effective rate of interest.

Second, the real rate of inflation may in fact be lower than is commonly supposed. Inflation, as currently measured, is based on GDP, the standard measure of output. However, although convenient and universally used, GDP has a number of important deficiencies – among them, it is claimed, a tendency systematically to understate increases by not making adequate allowance for improvements in quality and variety. For example, modern cars, cameras and personal computers incorporate so many improvements that they are markedly superior to their predecessors of a few years ago, but these improvements in value to the consumer do not show as increases in 'output' in the statistics. Similarly, the increasing variety of choice available – in colour, size, television programmes, holiday destinations or whatever – although potentially of value, also do not show in the statistics. Accordingly, it is argued, GDP systematically understates real rises is value, so the official inflation figures based on it regularly overstate the real extent of inflation. It has been estimated that in the US over the past two decades, inflation has been overstated by an average of 2–3 per cent a year.[181] If this is true of Britain, it follows that the official inflation target of 2.5 per cent inflation is, in reality, the much more ambitious target of no inflation at all.

And third, the NAIRU theory, on closer examination, is not a very helpful basis for economic policy. It is never certain what the NAIRU rate *is* – estimates vary greatly at different dates and with different experts at the same date, and tend, after a time lag, to go up with the actual level of unemployment. The figures offered do not anyway fit the theory of higher rates for NAIRU being associated with greater rigidities in the labour market. Average estimates of the NAIRU level were low (at 2.9 per cent unemployment) between 1969 and 1973, when supply side weaknesses were reckoned to be ubiquitous, but much higher (at 6.7 per cent unemployment) in 1995/6, after 16 years of measures supposed to have brought a fundamental correction of supply side weaknesses and, in particular, the break-up of rigidities in the labour market.[182]

A recent analysis of the relationship between unemployment and inflation[182] demonstrates that there is an asymmetry present, which has important policy implications. In the periods of deflation between 1981 and 1983, and again between 1991 and 1993, a rise of 2 per cent in unemployment brought a 4 per cent reduction in wage increases; while after 1986 each *fall* of 2 per cent in unemployment was associated with only a 1 per cent increase in wage inflation. Since 1993, the fall in unemployment, which NAIRU theory predicted would bring renewed inflation, has in fact brought about no increase in wage inflation at all.

The lesson from this is that the external shocks of the 1970s brought special inflation problems. The *over rapid* expansion of demand in the boom of the late 1980s also generated inflationary pressures, but the more moderate and steady expansion of demand in recent years has *not* brought higher inflation. It follows that previous demand restraints based on the NAIRU theory have been unnecessarily restrictive, and further expansion of demand to reduce unemployment should be feasible without risk of undue inflationary pressures.

That said, there may be times in the future when falling unemployment could produce a tight labour market giving rise to inflationary pressures. To guard against this, it would be prudent to work out a basis for a national compact on incomes. In recent years, incomes policy has been anathema to employers, unions and government alike. This is because, in Britain in the past, incomes policies were introduced at times of crisis, in a hurry, without careful preparation, often in a rigid form and, sometimes, initially not allowing for any increases at all. Sooner or later, they all broke down.

However, incomes policies have been more successful in other European countries, where it is customary for employers, unions and government to seek a partnership in pursuit of their mutual interest in avoiding inflationary settlements – employers to get expanding markets, unions to get full employment and government to get industrial harmony. There are many obvious difficulties, but the chances of success will be greater if the arrangements are put in place during a period of economic stability, rather than waiting to be overtaken by a crisis.

One approach that clearly will *not* work is the policy of imposing tight pay curbs on the public sector, while merely exhorting restraint on the private sector. This merely causes public sector pay to fall further behind, thus accentuating problems in recruitment and declines in morale, while the private sector simply takes no notice. While there is a *general* interest in reducing inflation, there is a *specific* interest for each individual to get as big an increase as possible. The only way to bring the two together is through an openly acknowledged and freely agreed national incomes policy.

International interdependence

The fourth constraint on the adoption of more expansionary policies is international. With economies becoming more and more interdependent, it is becoming increasingly difficult to overcome unemployment in one country on its own. General measures to expand demand can lead to a surge in imports and unmanageable overseas payments deficits – as happened to France when it attempted to go it alone with expansion in the early 1980s. The best prospect of sustained expansion and a return to full employment is therefore through joint action in concert with other European countries – as was proposed by the European Commission with the Delors plan a few years ago, and more recently by the Jospin government in France; and is likely to be taken up by other countries in the EU now that all but two of them have left-of-centre governments. This is part of a wider question on how to prosper in an increasingly global market system – which is considered in the next chapter.

5 The Economy

What are the prospects for faster economic growth in an increasingly global market system?

A global market system is developing in which economies are becoming increasingly interdependent, with international trade growing much faster than output, international investment growing even faster than trade, and international financial movements growing very much faster still.

This is tending to bring wider choice and lower prices for consumers; but it is also generating market forces that are turning national sovereignty into a hollow concept. In the short run, national governments are unable to stand up against speculative pressures in the financial markets – on the day Britain was forced out of the ERM, turnover on the London market was ten times as great as the total value of the foreign exchange reserves. In the longer term, the need of governments to compete for inward investment tends to apply downward pressure on wages, taxes, labour conditions, environmental protection and public spending on social welfare – and Britain is more than twice as dependent on inward investment as any other country in Europe.

The British economy, once the strongest in the world, has been performing less well than others over a very long period. In 1950, Britain had the highest income per head of any country in Europe except Switzerland. By 1992, it had been overtaken by Germany, Denmark, France, Norway, Belgium, Austria, Sweden, the Netherlands and Italy, and it soon could be overtaken by Ireland, Spain and Portugal as well. There is a pressing need for new policies to improve economic performance – but in the context of the constraints placed on independent government action by the forces of the global market. Fortunately, many of the policies needed can be adopted without running up against market forces. Other objectives can be achieved by joining with other governments to coordinate policies at an international level.

Forces driving globalisation

There are a number of forces, which, in combination, are causing the leading world economies to work increasingly as a single market system. Some have been evident for several decades, others are more recent, but all are likely to continue, with important effects, in the decades ahead.

Trade liberalisation

Seven successive rounds of cuts under the auspices of the General Agreement on Tariffs and Trade (GATT) led to drastic reduction in average tariff levels from about 40 per cent in the late 1940s to about 5 per cent in 1993.[183] In December 1993, after seven years of negotiations, the GATT Uruguay Round was finally concluded, with provision for:

- industrial tariffs to be cut by a further third;
- phasing out of the MFA (Multi-Fibre Arrangement), which restricted imports of textiles and garments by the industrialised countries;
- reduction of agricultural support; and
- extension of fair trade principles to international trade in services.

Largely as a result of the removal of these barriers, world trade has been rising rapidly. Over the period 1985–96, total world merchandise trade rose by about 5 per cent a year – more than twice as fast as output;[184] and the GATT Uruguay agreement is expected to bring increases of a further 1 per cent a year or more.[185]

For manufactures, the rise has been even greater. Over the whole period 1950–94, total world exports of manufactures have risen no less than 27-fold – more than three times the rise in world production of manufactures.[186] International trade in services has been rising more rapidly still, and is now equivalent to more than one-quarter of world exports of goods.[187]

Developments in transport

Since the 1960s, there has been a revolution in transport, which has brought more reliability, shorter journey times and much lower costs. This has been brought about by a tenfold increase between 1960 and 1990 in typical oil tanker sizes and the introduction of bulk carriers for ores, grains and heavy chemicals; containerisation of shipments of manufactured goods, with special trains and lorries, roll-on/roll-off ferries and giant ocean carriers; the construction of motorway networks; and the use of larger lorries, electric and diesel railway locomotives, and larger, faster and more economical jet aircraft.

The process is continuing, with further improvements in vehicles and aircraft, the development of new high-speed rail networks, and the opening of the Channel Tunnel and other major new tunnels and bridges.

Revolution in telecommunications

The use of fibreoptic cable, satellite links and digital transmission and switchgear has made telephone links cheaper, more reliable and more convenient, and made possible the introduction and widespread adoption of new services such as telex, fax, e-mail and mobile phones. These are making it more feasible than before to integrate financing, sourcing, marketing and production operations on an international scale and to manage them efficiently from a distance.

Changes in finance

The widespread abolition of foreign exchange controls and restrictions on movements of capital, together with the revolution in telecommunications, have made it easier, safer, quicker and cheaper to move money from one country to another.

In many industrial countries, savings have become increasingly concentrated in banks, insurance companies, pension funds and other financial institutions. In Britain, for example, between 1957 and 1995 the proportion of shares held by individuals has fallen from 65 per cent to 18 per cent, and the proportion held by pensions and insurance companies has risen from 12 per cent to 51 per cent. Financial deregulation has led to mergers and trans-national link-ups, bringing a further increase in the proportion of business handled by large organisations. These financial institutions are far better placed than individuals for making effective use of the new opportunities for international financial transfers.

These developments have resulted in a spectacular increase in the scale of international financial transactions with dealings on world foreign exchange markets amounting to an estimated $150 billion a day in the mid-1980s[188] and about $1300 billion a day in 1995[189] – ten times the value of total world output.[190]

Growth of multinationals

The removal of barriers to trade and financial movements, and improvements in transport and telecommunications, have been of particular value to large multinational companies and have helped them expand greatly their international operations. In Britain, it is estimated that more than half the sales of the top 100 companies are overseas, and 14 of the top 200 companies have more than 90 per cent of their earnings from overseas.[191] Worldwide, it is estimated by the UN that multinationals now probably account for a third of total production and half of total exports of non-agricultural products.[192]

Technology transfer

New technologies, in manufacturing production, in design and in the product itself, have become a major factor in industrial success, particularly in some of the fastest growing new industries. With the accelerating pace of technological change, shortening product life cycles and increasing research and development (R&D) costs, the rewards of using new technologies early and effectively have increased, and so also have the penalties for falling behind. Accordingly, companies that are strong in technology have been seeking to get a wider international payoff by transferring new technology to other companies in the same group, by licensing arrangements with other companies, by joint research projects, and by mergers and takeovers.

Cultural convergence

International news media, particularly television, have made people much more aware of what people in other countries are doing, wearing, eating, drinking, seeing and listening to. More and more people are getting first-hand experience of other countries through their work, education or holidays. This has been leading to much greater familiarity with, and acceptance of, foreign products and services, and a tendency towards international convergence in tastes and fashions. With increasing similarity of consumer demands in different countries, it has become feasible and profitable for producers to achieve economies of scale by supplying similar products and services to markets in a number of different countries.

Common markets and free trade areas

In addition to the broader global developments, there have been a number of regional developments towards the establishment of free trade areas, common markets and other kinds of regional integration.

In Europe, the original common market of six countries set up in 1958 has been deepened into a fuller single market and widened to include 15 countries, with free trade or common market agreements with a number of other countries, several of which are likely to become members later. Elsewhere, many other new groupings have been set up, including NAFTA (North

American Free Trade Association), MERCOSUR, the Andean Community, ACS (Association of Caribbean States), FTAA (Free Trade Agreement for the Americas), APEC (Asia-Pacific Economic Cooperation Conference), ASEAN (Association of South East Asian Nations), SADC (Southern African Development Community) and CIS (Confederation of Independent States), the latter consisting of most of the republics that became independent after the break-up of the Soviet Union.

It is possible that some of these regional groupings will develop into protectionist economic blocs. So far, however, their main effect has been to stimulate the growth of international trade within the regions and, on balance, probably to help, rather than hinder, the development of a wider global market system.

Former Soviet bloc

The collapse of communism in the former Soviet bloc has been followed by attempts by Russia and the newly independent republics and former satellite countries to move to a market economy. This will bring into the world market system an industrialised area with a population of nearly 400 million people – more than in either the EU or NAFTA.

Russia and the republics of the former Soviet Union have been attempting to make this fundamental change without the benefit of suitable institutions, infrastructure, managers, entrepreneurs, clear plans, or outside help on any significant scale. Not surprisingly, all of them have run into difficulties, with output falling to levels far below those achieved previously. It will be some years before their economies are strong enough to make an impact on the world market system.

The former satellite countries of eastern Europe have also run into difficulties, but ten of them have applied for membership of the EU. Although it will be several years before even the first ones become full members, all have Europe agreements to help prepare them for membership and some have already attracted substantial western investment. It is thus likely that they will be integrated into the world market system more quickly than the countries of the former Soviet Union.

China

For more than a decade, China has been moving towards an increasingly market-based internal system and, in recent years, has begun to open its economy to the rest of the world. Economic growth, though unevenly distributed, has been extremely rapid, averaging 12 per cent a year in the five years 1992 to 1996.[193] Inward investment averaged $32 billion a year between 1953 and 1995 – nearly double the amount coming to Britain.[194] Merchandise exports nearly trebled between 1990 and 1995 – to more than half the size of Britain's.

With a population of 1.2 billion, China is potentially both a very large exporter and an enormous market. Hitherto, the very large number of people has been offset by their very low incomes and average productivity. However, it can be calculated that if productivity per head of the Chinese in the whole of China were to match that of the Chinese in Hong Kong, the Chinese economy would be nearly as large as those of the US, the EU and Japan combined.[1] Given the extremely rapid rate of growth of the Chinese economy in recent years, this possibility seems less remote than it once did. While there must be doubt about how long such high economic growth rates can be sustained, particularly in the absence of political change, it seems likely that in the coming decades China will constitute a very important addition to the world market system.

Implications of globalisation

This combination of developments is enormously enlarging the area covered by the world market system and greatly expanding the volume of inter-national trade, international investment and international financial move-ments. This is making national economies more closely interdependent, with events determined far more than hitherto by impersonal market forces, and far less than hitherto by national government policies. It is bringing useful benefits, but also serious problems.

Consumption

In a free trading system, countries tend to specialise in areas in which they have the greatest relative advantage. This helps achieve more efficient use of resources, with the resulting improvements in productivity bringing higher output and lower costs. Accordingly, consumers should be able to benefit from wider choice and lower prices, and thereby enjoy higher levels of con-sumption.

It is difficult to quantify how far consumers have in fact benefited from the theoretical gains of the widening market system. In Europe, it is claimed, with some plausibility, that the rapid economic growth of the six member countries of the Common Market in the 1960s was largely due to the economic and psychological gains resulting from its establishment. However, it can also be noted that in the 1960s the European countries with the fastest growth rates of all were Spain and Greece, which were members of neither the Common Market nor EFTA.[195]

A major study undertaken for the European Commission[196] estimated that the establishment of the Single European Market in 1992 should bring a 4.5 per cent gain in GDP by 2002. In the event, growth in most EU countries since 1992 has so far been modest, but it can be argued that this is due to other factors, such as attempts to meet the Maastricht convergence criteria, and that without the benefit of the Single European Market the performance would have been worse.

In 1993, the GATT Secretariat attempted to quantify the benefits of trade liberalization on a global scale.[185] It estimated that the Uruguay Round should bring a net gain of $230 billion a year by 2005 – roughly equivalent to an extra three-quarters of 1 per cent of world GDP. Much of the benefit is expected to come from reduced agricultural protection, which it is estimated has been costing consumers in the EU an average of $450 a head each year, in the US $360 and in Japan $600.[197]

Production

Globalisation is involving not only huge increases in trade, but also changes in the production process itself. While much of the production of goods, and even more so of services, is still undertaken at a local or national level, a growing proportion is being handled on an international, even global, level. Capital is raised on international markets; staff are recruited internationally; machinery, spare parts, materials, technologies and specialist services are imported; marketing is planned and sales made on a world market; and profits are declared, dividends are paid and taxes become due in a number of different countries.

As a result, the concepts of where something is 'made' or where a company is 'based' are becoming increasingly blurred. So also, sometimes, are reckonings of national loyalties, social benefits and tax liabilities.

Competition, ever wider, keener and more effective, is the main instrument through which the benefits of higher overall productivity are to be obtained. But competition is inevitably double-edged, bringing both gainers and losers. British producers will have access to much more of the world for finance, recruitment, R&D, equipment, systems, business services, materials and components; but so too will their competitors in other countries. They will have expanding opportunities to sell in world markets; but they will also have stronger competition in their home market. Those that are more successful in competition will expand and prosper; those that are less successful will run into difficulties or fail altogether.

This already happens within a country, but within a country there is often scope for government measures to cushion the shock for firms, industries or regions in difficulty, and to help them build new capacities to compete more effectively in new areas. The difference with competition in a global economy is that there is normally very little prospect of external help for firms or countries that fall behind. Consequently, competitiveness, constant and continuing, becomes not a desirable goal but a life-and-death imperative.

Investment

Globalisation is bringing a steady increase in international direct investment, which doubled between 1984–89 and 1990–95.[198] Inward investment to Britain quadrupled between 1981–85 and 1991–95,[199] and in 1995 amounted to nearly $30 billion[194] – far more than in any other European country.

There is no area in which international competition will be keener than in investment, for it is the key to future productivity, competitiveness and growth. Multinational companies, faced with increasingly wide choices of location for their new investments, will tend to prefer those that look likely to be the most profitable for the company. Governments increasingly see the need to compete with one another for inward investment and modify their policies to make location in their country as attractive as possible. There is a danger that, as competition for inward investment gets keener, governments will come under increasing pressure to try to attract investment in ways that may be detrimental to other objectives. For example:

- Pressure to keep marginal rates of income and corporation taxes as low as possible may force governments to adopt regressive tax structures or become unduly dependent on indirect taxes.
- Pressure to keep taxes in general low may restrict the scope for needed public services and other activities requiring government expenditure.
- Pressure to keep labour costs low may discourage the provision of a fair labour market or safe and healthy working conditions.
- Pressure to minimise government interference may make it more difficult to impose regulations for company law, consumer protection and environmental issues.

There is thus a danger that pressures to attract vital investments could bring about a steady erosion of standards that are necessary to maintain for a good quality of life.

Trade

The increase in trade has made national economies more interdependent and this has reduced government control over them. In the first two decades after the war, governments in most industrialised countries used macro-economic policies fairly successfully to ensure full employment and economic growth. In more recent times, fewer governments have used macroeconomic policies in this way. Where they have tried (as in France in the early 1980s and in Britain a few years later), the attempt to achieve economic expansion in one country has been frustrated by balance of payments difficulties and exchange rate pressures. This is because, with the expansion in trade, imports are becoming an increasingly large part of the economy, and an even larger part of any expansion in the economy. Government attempts to accelerate growth or reduce unemployment through general expansionary fiscal or monetary policies tend to suck in greater volumes of imports, thereby diluting the expansionary impact on the home economy and at the same time weakening the balance of overseas payments.

As trade continues to grow faster than output, economies will become more closely interlocked and governments will be left with diminishing scope for independence in macroeconomic policy – particularly in Britain where trade volumes are already high. By 2010, imports are forecast to be equivalent to two-thirds of total consumer expenditure.[1]

Financial movements

In some ways, national control of the economy is more seriously under-mined by financial movements than by trade movements. The removal of currency controls, changes in the structure of financial institutions and improvements in technology have combined to produce currency move-ments that are much larger, and act much more quickly, than movements in physical trade. Current annual turnover in the world's foreign exchange markets is ten times the world's annual GDP.[190]

Part of this is needed to cover the increase in international trade in goods and services. Companies need other currencies for their purchases and sales, and sometimes feel a need to buy ahead as a hedge against future exchange rate fluctuations. Part is needed for the increase in foreign direct investment and part for the parallel growth in international portfolio investment. For example, in 1991 UK mutual funds were estimated to have 39 per cent of their assets invested abroad, and UK pension funds 20 per cent.[200] Total foreign investments of the mutual and pension funds of the five leading countries amounted to more than $6000 billion[200] – the equivalent of more than 13 times their total foreign exchange reserves.[187]

It is estimated[190] that the world's 'basic' needs for international trade and investment account for only about 2 per cent of total foreign exchange transactions. Arbitrage, hedging and other 'legitimate' activities account for rather more. The overwhelming majority of transactions, however, are accounted for by speculation – buying or selling with a view to making a profit from price changes. London is the world's leading foreign exchange market and turnover on it has risen from an estimated $90 billion a day in 1986, to $460 billion a day in 1995.[200] It is estimated that about 79 per cent of it is in the hands of foreign institutions[201] and between 90 and 95 per cent of it represents purely speculative transactions.[202]

The high proportion of speculative transactions makes the market very volatile and the sheer scale of business makes it difficult for any government to control. On 'Black Wednesday', 16 September 1992, the day when the pound was forced out of the ERM, it is believed that turnover on the London market rose to about 50 per cent above the average level that year to somewhere in the region of $450 billion.[200-1] In a single day, turnover was greater than the value of total imports and exports over the whole *year*, and more than ten times as great as the total value of the foreign exchange reserves.[203]

In the face of this pressure, sterling was forced down, despite government efforts to save it with tough talk, support from other central banks, raising the base rate to 15 per cent and short-term rates to 100 per cent, and selling $15 billion or more from foreign exchange reserves.[201]

In this particular instance, there is a valid argument that the government entered the ERM at too high a rate, that at the time of the crash sterling was manifestly over valued, and that the government had unwisely rebuffed earlier offers of a managed realignment of exchange rates. The devaluation was thus desirable and at some stage inevitable. The action of the markets overturned inappropriate policies of politicians and represented a healthy and beneficial dose of reality.

The same could not be said of the attack on the French franc a year later. It was *not* over valued, inflation in France was *lower* than in Germany, and there was no objective rationale for devaluation. Yet, despite determined opposition from the central banks in France and Germany, market pressures were strong enough to disrupt the whole ERM system. What was involved was not the wisdom of the market being imposed on irresponsible politicians, but irresponsible speculators speculating on the speculations of other speculators, on such a massive scale as to overturn the central policies of the elected governments of two of the strongest countries in Europe.

Again in 1997, the economies of several east Asian countries, previously regarded as exceptionally dynamic and competitive, were suddenly destabilised by massive speculative financial movements.

With their overwhelming power and capacity to be irrational, capricious and damaging, the operations of the financial markets are one aspect of the emerging global market that has no apparent benefits, but obvious potential dangers.

Fatalism versus neo-Luddism?

Thus, globalisation brings benefits through international specialisation according to the greatest relative advantage. It also has more unwelcome implications – fiercer competition (with difficulties for the less successful); the need to attract international investment (risking downward pressures on labour standards, social services and care of the environment); and increasing economic interdependence and massive financial movements (bringing loss of national control over the economy and rendering ineffective the measures that had been used in the past to secure full employment and faster economic expansion).

Some people view these latter aspects as advantageous. They see no point in cushioning the blow for those who do not fare well in competition; they welcome the dismantling of the welfare state; and they trust the judgement of the market for economic management more than they do that of politicians. Others accept that globalisation may have a serious downside, but believe it will be more than offset by the gains from free trade. And still others are more doubtful about the overall net benefits, but believe that globalisation has to be accepted anyway because it is irresistible and uncontrollable.

However, there are others who are beginning to question whether globalisation is really worthwhile. Will the gains from more global efficiency be as great as is claimed? Will they be distributed in a way that will allow more than a few to benefit from them? If, to compete, we have to accept *lower* wages, *curtailed* social services and a *deteriorating* physical environment, will we really be better off? If the markets are predisposed to restrictive economic attitudes, will they not impose permanent deflation and unemployment, with erratic volatility as well? In short, will the benefits outweigh the problems? Would it be better to opt out of globalisation and reclaim control of our economic destiny?

As the drawbacks of globalisation become more apparent, a case can be made for a kind of neo-Luddism – forgoing the potential efficiency gains of the new global system in favour of keeping a more humane and caring society behind a comfortable wall of protectionism. However, the cost of outright rejection, both in disrupting existing arrangements and forgoing future opportunities, would be heavy.

Fortunately, there is no need to make a straight choice between fatalistic acceptance and neo-Luddite rejection. In relation to the needs of the British economy, there are some areas where globalisation poses no problems, some where a British government is not as powerless as it might at first appear, and some where it should be possible, by working together with other governments, to *regulate* the global market system to make it better serve our common needs. What *are* the needs of the British economy? And how will it be possible to meet them within the constraints of the global market system?

Britain's economic performance

England was the first country to go through the Industrial Revolution and, though the process was painful, it brought us the highest standard of living in the world. Although other countries subsequently industrialised too, in 1950 Britain still had the highest GDP per head of the 15 countries that now form the EU.[204]

However, by 1973, Britain had been overtaken by Sweden, Denmark, West Germany, France and the Netherlands.[204] By 1993, Britain had been overtaken also by Belgium, Luxembourg, Austria and Italy.[204] Early in the next century, it seems likely that Britain will be overtaken also by Finland, Ireland, Spain and Portugal – leaving Greece as the only country in the EU still with a GDP per head lower than Britain.

The economies of other industrial countries grew faster than Britain's while they were catching us up – and have gone on growing faster since leaving us behind. Over the 43 years between 1953 and 1995, Britain's economy grew by an average of 2.2 per cent a year.[205] Over the same period, the US's grew by 2.8 per cent a year, France's and Italy's by 3.8 per cent, Germany's by 4 per cent, Japan's by 6.7 per cent, and the OECD countries' as a whole by 4 per cent – nearly twice as fast as Britain's.[206]

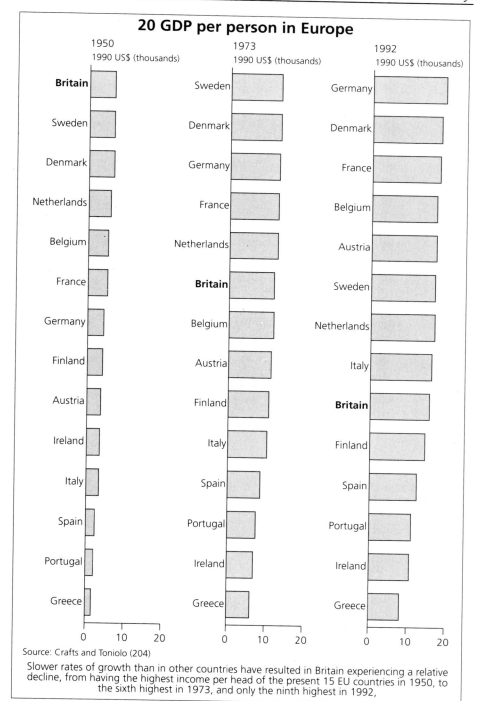

20 GDP per person in Europe

1950
1990 US$ (thousands)

Britain	
Sweden	
Denmark	
Netherlands	
Belgium	
France	
Germany	
Finland	
Austria	
Ireland	
Italy	
Spain	
Portugal	
Greece	

0   10   20

1973
1990 US$ (thousands)

Sweden	
Denmark	
Germany	
France	
Netherlands	
Britain	
Belgium	
Austria	
Finland	
Italy	
Spain	
Portugal	
Ireland	
Greece	

0   10   20

1992
1990 US$ (thousands)

Germany	
Denmark	
France	
Belgium	
Austria	
Sweden	
Netherlands	
Italy	
Britain	
Finland	
Spain	
Portugal	
Ireland	
Greece	

0   10   20

Source: Crafts and Toniolo (204)

Slower rates of growth than in other countries have resulted in Britain experiencing a relative decline, from having the highest income per head of the present 15 EU countries in 1950, to the sixth highest in 1973, and only the ninth highest in 1992,

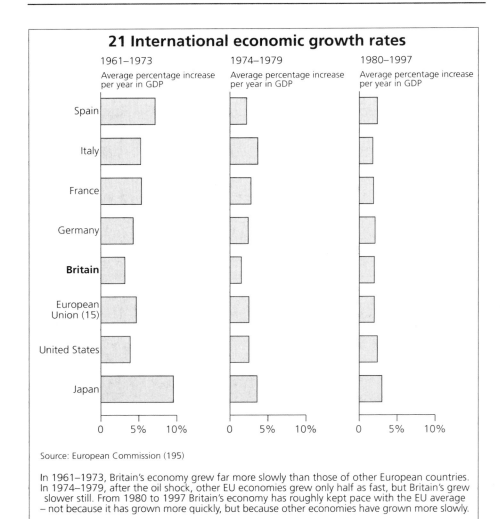

21 International economic growth rates

1961–1973
Average percentage increase per year in GDP

1974–1979
Average percentage increase per year in GDP

1980–1997
Average percentage increase per year in GDP

Spain · Italy · France · Germany · **Britain** · European Union (15) · United States · Japan

0 5% 10%

Source: European Commission (195)

In 1961–1973, Britain's economy grew far more slowly than those of other European countries. In 1974–1979, after the oil shock, other EU economies grew only half as fast, but Britain's grew slower still. From 1980 to 1997 Britain's economy has roughly kept pace with the EU average – not because it has grown more quickly, but because other economies have grown more slowly.

It is sometimes claimed that Britain's economic performance was poor in the 1950s and 1960s because of various weaknesses, but that after the change of government in 1979, new policies corrected the earlier weaknesses, bringing a stronger economy and better performance. If so, it does not show in the figures. Average growth over the period 1950–1973 was 3 per cent a year; 1974–1979 (the period upset by the oil shock) 1.5 per cent; and 1980–1997, 1.9 per cent – more than a third *less* than in the period before the 'weaknesses' were removed.[205]

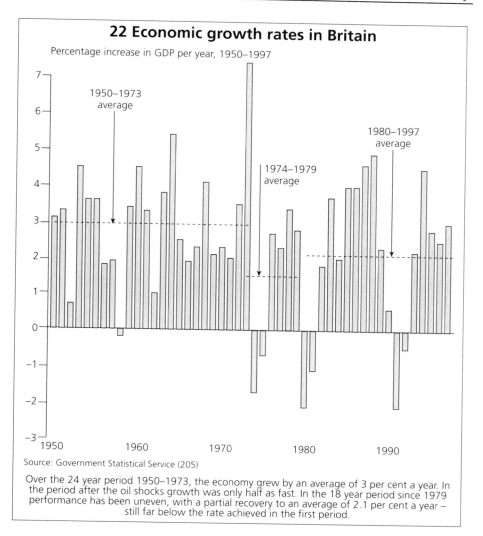

22 Economic growth rates in Britain

Percentage increase in GDP per year, 1950–1997

1950–1973 average

1974–1979 average

1980–1997 average

1950   1960   1970   1980   1990

Source: Government Statistical Service (205)

Over the 24 year period 1950–1973, the economy grew by an average of 3 per cent a year. In the period after the oil shocks growth was only half as fast. In the 18 year period since 1979 performance has been uneven, with a partial recovery to an average of 2.1 per cent a year – still far below the rate achieved in the first period.

This relatively poor rate of economic growth has been reflected in an increasingly uncompetitive performance in overseas trade. Over the period 1970–1996, the volume of imports of manufactures rose more than twice as fast the volume of exports of manufactures, and the volume of imports of *finished* manufactures rose more than three times as fast.[205] During the 1970s and 1980s, in most of the main manufacturing sectors, imports accounted for a growing share of home market consumption and exports accounted for a falling share of manufacturers' sales.[205]

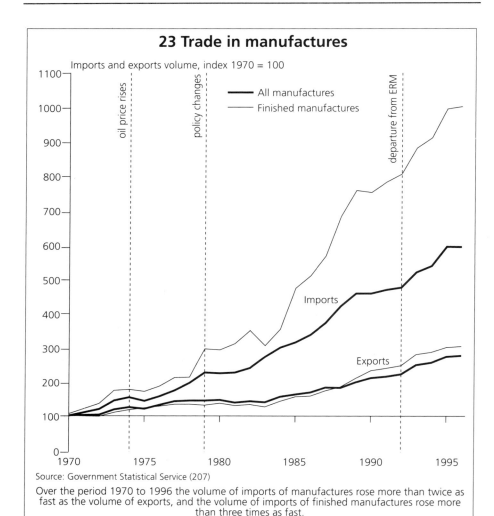

23 Trade in manufactures

Imports and exports volume, index 1970 = 100

— All manufactures

— Finished manufactures

oil price rises

policy changes

departure from ERM

Imports

Exports

Source: Government Statistical Service (207)

Over the period 1970 to 1996 the volume of imports of manufactures rose more than twice as fast as the volume of exports, and the volume of imports of finished manufactures rose more than three times as fast.

In the early 1950s, there was a large surplus of exports of manufactures over imports. Since then, the surplus has declined steadily, turning into an increasing deficit after 1983. For most of the 1950s and 1960s, this was largely offset by falling world prices for food, energy and raw materials. In the early 1980s, it was more than offset by a sharp rise in invisible earnings and the coming on stream of North Sea oil, which transformed an oil deficit of £4 billion in 1976 into an oil surplus of more than £7 billion in 1985.[207]

24 Balance of payments

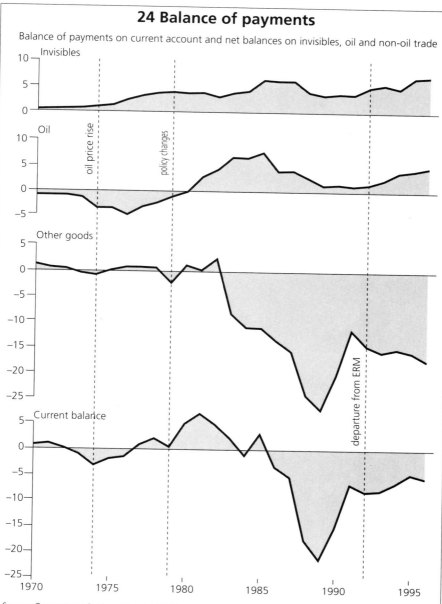

Balance of payments on current account and net balances on invisibles, oil and non-oil trade

Source: Government Statistical Service (207)

In the early 1980s rising earnings from oil and invisibles brought balance of payments surpluses despite a deteriorating balance in manufactured goods. Reduced earnings from oil and invisibles and a further worsening in manufactures brought record deficits in the late 1980s. The enforced devaluation in 1972 improved the balances of both invisibles and manufactures, but the recent rise in sterling is likely to bring further large deficits.

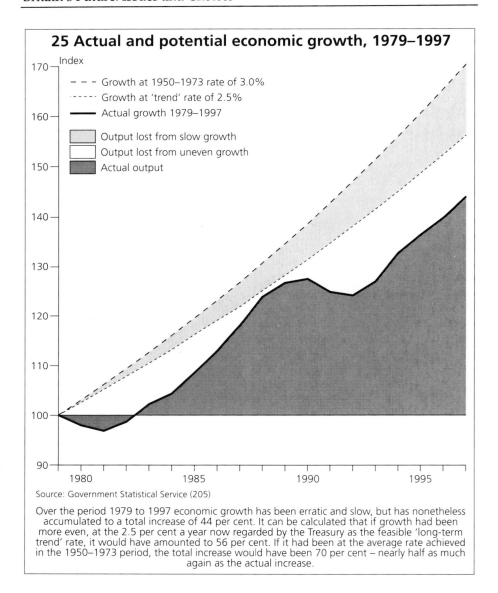

25 Actual and potential economic growth, 1979–1997

Index

- - - Growth at 1950–1973 rate of 3.0%
······ Growth at 'trend' rate of 2.5%
—— Actual growth 1979–1997

▨ Output lost from slow growth
▢ Output lost from uneven growth
▨ Actual output

Source: Government Statistical Service (205)

Over the period 1979 to 1997 economic growth has been erratic and slow, but has nonetheless accumulated to a total increase of 44 per cent. It can be calculated that if growth had been more even, at the 2.5 per cent a year now regarded by the Treasury as the feasible 'long-term trend' rate, it would have amounted to 56 per cent. If it had been at the average rate achieved in the 1950–1973 period, the total increase would have been 70 per cent – nearly half as much again as the actual increase.

However, in the late 1980s, when invisible earnings declined and oil prices fell, there was nothing to offset the decline in manufacturing earnings, and the deficit in the overseas balance of payments rose to more than £20 billion.[207] Since then, there has been some recovery in earnings from oil and invisibles, but the large deficit in manufactures has continued.

Thus, over a long period Britain's economy has been growing more slowly than those of other similar countries. In the past two decades, it has been growing more slowly than before and has been becoming less competitive internationally.

This weak performance has been expensive. Between 1979 and 1997 Britain's GDP increased by a total of 41 per cent.[205] It can be calculated that if growth in this period had been at the same rate as between 1950 and 1973, the total increase would have amounted to 70 per cent – three-quarters more.[205] GDP would now be one-fifth greater, with scope for correspondingly higher levels of personal consumption and improved standards of public services.

To achieve better economic performance in the future, it is important to identify the causes of poor economic performance in the past.

Causes of poor performance

Many explanations have been advanced for Britain's relatively poor economic performance. Some focus on the government's economic policies. These include political opportunism and incompetence, with erratic stop–go changes; obsessive concern with inflation, with deflationary measures bringing unnecessary recession; overvaluation of sterling, damaging industry by making imports cheap and exports uncompetitive; keeping interest rates higher than in other countries, making investment expensive; favouring consumption over investment and city interests over manufacturing interests; and failing to ensure adequate investment in science and technology, in education and training, and in the economic infrastructure.

Other explanations are of a more general kind. These include a national nostalgia to remain a world power, reluctance to give up empire and continuing insistence on much higher defence spending than other comparable countries; a cultural tradition that favours arts over sciences and the professions over industry and trade; a political system that makes it difficult to confront hard choices or to pursue longer-term goals; a class structure that encourages adversarial attitudes in politics and industry and makes national cooperation difficult; an education system that reaches high standards for a few, but leaves many with no qualifications at all; industrial training that fails to equip enough people with modern skills; industrial management that is strong on finance but weak on science and engineering and industrial relations; trade unions with outdated structures and attitudes and prone to disputes; a capital market that is 'efficient' in forcing industry to yield continuous high dividends at the expense of investment for longer-term growth; a civil service that is secretive and remote from science and industry; and a political system that tends to think in the short term and to defer difficult decisions.

There is some validity in most of these explanations. The causes of a poor past economic performance are numerous, complex and interacting, and some of them are deep-seated and difficult to change, even over a long period. Nevertheless, if two elements of Britain's past economic policy were changed – the excessively high priority given to the containment of inflation, and the excessively high parity sought for the exchange rate for sterling – we could expect to see better results in the future.

Deflation

In the 1950s and 1960s, the main objectives of economic policy were economic growth and full employment, and the main means of achieving them were Keynesian measures to maintain a generally high level of demand. With the change of government in 1979, the objectives of economic growth and full employment were made secondary to an overriding preoccupation with checking inflation. Severe deflation was used as a deliberate policy for 'squeezing inflation out of the system'.

The new policies brought two recessions, during which the economy actually *shrank*. Many firms collapsed and unemployment rose sharply (see Chapter 4). Over the whole period from 1979 to 1997, the economy grew at only two-thirds of the average rate achieved in the 1950s and 1960s and unemployment remained very high.

Moreover, the deflationary policies that prevailed over most of the past two decades depressed not only current output and employment, but also the investment needed for a better performance in the future. Investment in manufacturing industry, vital for international competitiveness, fell in 1982 to 31 per cent below the 1979 level, and over the 17 years from 1980 to 1996 it averaged 10 per cent *below* the 1979 level, and, as a percentage of GDP, *fell* by one-third.[205,208]

Investment has been low because high interest rates have made it more expensive, and low levels of consumer spending have reduced confidence in future prospects. Instead of being encouraged to undertake investment to profit from supplying an expanding home market, industrialists have been wary. They fear that continuing deflation might leave them with a depressed home market and expensive excess capacity. At the same time, high unemployment has encouraged firms to look for cheap labour instead

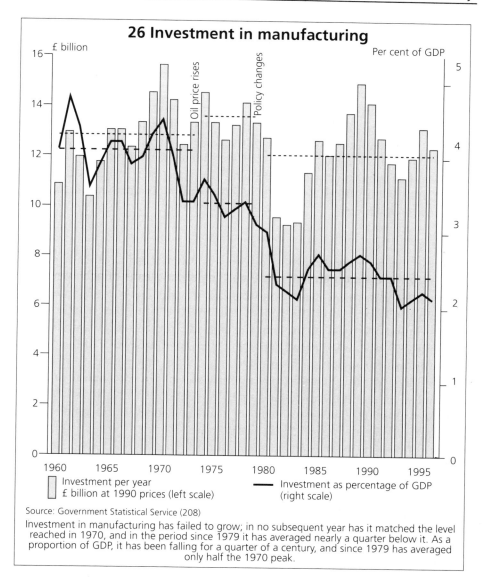

26 Investment in manufacturing

Source: Government Statistical Service (208)

Investment in manufacturing has failed to grow; in no subsequent year has it matched the level reached in 1970, and in the period since 1979 it has averaged nearly a quarter below it. As a proportion of GDP, it has been falling for a quarter of a century, and since 1979 has averaged only half the 1970 peak.

of improving training or investing in new plant to raise productivity in the future. The prevailing deflationary policies have left industry, not leaner and fitter, but merely smaller and weaker.

This has meant that, even when the deflationary policies were for a while abandoned in the runaway boom of the late 1980s, after many years of low investment, British industry lacked the capacity to meet the sudden increase in demand. As a result, the bulk of the surge in consumer spending went on imports, to the benefit of foreign suppliers and at the expense of a record deficit in Britain's balance of overseas payments .

Despite all their costs, deflationary policies have not even been particularly effective at containing inflation. Since 1979, inflation in Britain has been around the average for the OECD countries, and higher than in Germany, France, Switzerland, Austria, the US and Japan, in all of which unemployment has been lower than in Britain.[206] Inflation in Britain has also been higher than in the 1950s and 1960s, when unemployment was much lower and growth was faster.

Sterling

The other key factor in Britain's poor past economic performance has been the determination to maintain a high exchange rate for sterling, even when economic circumstances made it unsustainable, or a lower rate would have been more advantageous. The policy has resulted in a damagingly overvalued pound for most of the postwar period,[209] enforced devaluations in 1949 and 1967, and an enforced departure from the European ERM in 1992.

The reasons for seeking a high exchange rate for the pound were partly sentimental – a strong pound was seen as a sort of virility symbol, an indicator of Britain's strength and standing in the world – and partly political – a high parity had the short-run effect of making imported consumer goods and foreign holidays cheap, which was popular.

However, seriously overvaluing the pound has had highly damaging economic effects. It has made exports of manufactures very expensive, leading to reduced profitability and lower sales in overseas markets. It has made imports of manufactured goods very cheap, providing strong competition in the home market, and this too has led to reduced profitability and lower sales. Manufacturing firms that could have been competitive and prosperous if they had been allowed to trade at a realistic exchange rate, have had a struggle to survive at all, or have gone under altogether. Many products that Britain used to manufacture are now no longer made in Britain at all – although they are still produced profitably in other European countries.

The direct impact of too high an exchange rate has been reinforced by the impact of the measures taken to try to keep the pound artificially high – high interest rates and deflationary fiscal policies – leading to lower investment and reduced competitiveness.

An indication of the cost of an overvalued pound can be ascertained by looking at what happened when its value was reduced. In 1931, when Britain left the gold standard and the exchange rate of the pound fell by 24 per cent, GDP rose by 20 per cent over the next five years, manufacturing output rose by 58 per cent, exports rose sharply, imports fell sharply, wages rose, prices fell and unemployment fell by 1.5 million.[206] In 1949, when the pound was devalued by 30 per cent against the dollar, output and exports rose sharply. When, as a result of the collapse of oil prices, the pound depreciated by 12 per cent in the 18 months up to the end of 1986, exports of manufactures rose by 17 per cent over the next three years and manufacturing output by 18 per cent. In 1992, when the pound was forced out of the ERM and depreciated by 15 per cent, there was a surge in exports and Britain recovered from the recession.

While Britain has long suffered from an overvalued currency, other countries have benefited from the opposite. After the war, to help recovery of the devastated economy, Germany's exchange rate was set at a very low level, which was made even more competitive by a devaluation of 21 per cent in 1949. This gave recovery a powerful boost and ushered in a long period of high exports, high investment and rapid growth. Similarly, after the war, Japan was given an initially competitive exchange rate, which helped bring high exports and many years of rapid economic growth. For France, two devaluations in the 1950s helped set the country on course for a period of rapid growth. The 'tiger' economies of east Asia all started their rapid economic development on the basis of highly competitive exchange rates.

More recently, as a result of many years of economic success, the German and Japanese currencies have become *too* strong with the result that even these countries have now been impeded by high export prices and have been experiencing markedly slower growth rates. Policy makers in Britain mistakenly supposed that the strong currencies of Germany and Japan were the *cause* of their economic success, when in fact they were the *result* of it. Attempts to maintain the pound at artificially high levels, far from strengthening the economy, have been a key factor in *weakening* it.

Policies for faster growth

Throughout the industrialised world, fast economic growth has been strongly and clearly associated with high investment, particularly productive investment in manufacturing and investment incorporating new technologies. Between 1960–73 and 1973–92, when economic growth slowed down in most industrial countries, the rate of growth in their capital stock fell by about a half.[210] In the 1973–92 period, the rate of growth in capital stock was lower in Britain than in other European countries, barely one-third of the rate in the US and only one-fifth of the rate in Japan.[210] Fixed investment per year in manufacturing in Britain in 1992–4 was *lower* than in 1961–73, more than two decades before.[205]

Productive investment can be seen as the main *cause* of economic growth. Investment in new equipment, new buildings, better trained people and an improved infrastructure makes possible not only increased total output, but also improved productivity and hence an economy that is more competitive internationally. A high rate of investment brings not only a larger aggregate capital stock, but also one embodying a higher proportion of new, more efficient equipment. This leads to better quality, lower costs, stronger competitiveness, more sales, higher profitability – and, in turn, further investment and still better productivity.

However, the causality may also be seen the other way round, namely that *economic growth* causes investment. A recent analysis of investment and growth in a number of countries, to identify leads and lags and possible causality, found a strong tendency for investment to follow growth but not for growth to follow investment, the implication being that 'it seems that investment responds to better growth opportunities rather than creating them'.[211]

The explanation for this is that an expanding market is the most important requirement for high investment. Investment will only be profitable if there is a market in which the products of the investment can be sold. If an economy is growing slowly, unevenly or not at all, there is little incentive for investment because there may be no market for the output from it. Instead of a flow of profits, the investment would merely yield costly excess capacity. But if there is rapid growth, there will be an expanding market to offer the prospect of the rising sales needed to make investment profitable – thus providing the finance for further investment to supply further expansion in the market. In a fast growing economy, high investment is likely to come about more or less automatically.

Thus, there is a circularity in the process. Investment is the basis for growth, but growth is also the basis for investment. Higher investment tends to go with faster growth, which goes with still higher investment, which goes with still faster growth. Lower investment tends to go with slower growth, still lower investment and still slower growth. The key requirement of successful economic policy is to get out of the low investment/slow growth cycle and onto the high investment/fast growth cycle.

A number of things can be done to encourage higher investment. One is to keep interest rates low. High rates of interest discourage investment by making it more expensive, particularly for longer-term projects so that only projects with the quickest, safest and highest payback are able to go ahead.

A second is to introduce measures to redress the short-term bias of the stock market and the tax system. The stock market has many features that are prejudicial to investment.[212] One is that companies that pay out most of their profits in immediate dividends are likely to see their market values appreciate, while those that put more aside for investment to produce more growth later are likely to see their values marked down and their future threatened by takeovers. This short-term bias has in the past been reinforced by the corporate tax system. This gave tax credits on dividends to pension funds and insurance companies, thereby encouraging them to pay out their profits in dividends. Since these institutions now own more than half of all shares,[213] the discouragement to investment was substantial – sufficient, it has been estimated, to depress company investment by about 5 per cent.[214]

An attempt to correct this short-term bias has already been made in the new government's first budget, which removed the favourable tax treatment of dividends paid to pension funds. A further step would be to revert to earlier arrangements that provided a more general preference in tax treatment for profits ploughed back into investment rather than distributed as dividends. Another would be to increase the rate of stamp duty. The higher transaction costs would discourage people from switching funds to make short-term gains. Perhaps the most important step, though, would be to tighten conditions for takeovers so that companies investing for future growth would not risk being taken over if in the meanwhile their dividends were lower.

A third area in which there is scope for action is in the provision of specific incentives for investment in new technologies. In Britain, there used to be government schemes for giving grants for investment to develop applications in microelectronics and robotics, and these were effective in encouraging investment in these areas.[215–16] In other countries, such as Australia, Canada, France, Japan, the Netherlands and the US, there are special tax incentives for expenditure on research and development. They seem to be a relatively efficient way of encouraging firms to spend more on R&D.[217]

Valuable as particular measures to promote investment may be, they will not, *on their own,* be enough. However good the incentives, companies will still not invest unless they are confident there will be a market for the product of their investment. For the incentives to work, the key requirement is to provide a context of *growth* – or at least the expectation of it.

Thus, it will be necessary to complement the specific measures aimed at increasing investment with more general macroeconomic policies aimed at stimulating growth and with a competitive exchange rate. These will provide the prospect of an expanding home market together with higher sales in export markets and will discourage excessive import penetration of the expanding home market. These policies will not only foster investment by British companies, they will also encourage inward investment from overseas.

Unfortunately, the new government has not chosen to adopt this approach. So far, it has continued with the previous government's preoccupation with trying to combat inflation by using relatively deflationary policies to avoid the risk of 'overheating'. It has made the Bank of England independent and made it responsible for monetary policy, with the sole objective of keeping inflation below 2.5 per cent. In the US, the Federal Reserve Bank is responsible for keeping inflation down, but is also required to take account of growth and employment. Given the very narrow objective it has been set, the Bank of England, taking a very cautious view of possible inflation risks two years ahead, has imposed a succession of increases in interest rates, which have become much higher than those in other European countries – in itself a major deterrent to investment.

Worse, the relatively high interest rates in Britain have attracted international speculative funds to London, which have pushed the value of sterling up to even more unrealistically high levels than before. As a result, imports have become extremely cheap and are flooding into the home market, while British exports have become impossibly expensive and very difficult to sell. Faced with this double threat to their markets, many British companies, which managed to survive the two recessions of the previous government, now face a final knock-out blow from the new one. The declared aim of the policy is to eschew short-term expedients and provide long-term stability for future growth. However, without a viable short-term prospect, the prospects of long-term stability are poor. The first requirement for a better future is to survive the present.

One reason why the new government has continued with the broad thrust of the macroeconomic policies of its predecessors – indeed reinforced them by making the Bank of England independent and thereby giving up control of interest rates – is that it is what the markets want. The government appears to believe that it is desirable, even inevitable, to go along with the markets. In this age of globalisation, have circumstances changed so much that governments no longer have an effective choice? Is it true that globalisation precludes adopting the policies needed for faster growth in Britain?

The constraints of globalisation

In some ways, globalisation is nothing new. In the period before the First World War there were few restrictions on international trade or investment, or on movements of people. In Britain and other leading industrialised countries, international trade and international investment were, if anything, higher then than they are now.[218] The movement of labour between countries was less restricted than now, and currencies were locked into fixed parities by the gold standard.

In some ways, the globalising processes of the past few decades have merely been getting us closer to the free market situation that had already been reached nearly a century ago. However, there are some important ways in which the new global market system is different from the old.

First, the size of the leading multinationals and the complexity of their operations have become enormously greater, giving them more bargaining power over where to locate their operations.

Second, the size and speed of financial movements have grown many times faster still, bringing to the market system a new element that is both very powerful and potentially destabilising.

And third, the interdependence of the leading economies, and the consequent limits to control over their economies by national governments, which may have seemed quite acceptable in 1913, are a matter of much greater concern in an era when governments are expected to deliver economic growth, full employment, a welfare state, a sustainable environment and much else besides.

The multinationals

With their greatly increased scope over where to locate their investment, multinational companies put pressure on governments to cut wages, taxes, social security charges, environmental requirements and whatever to make their countries attractive for investment. However, it does not follow that the only feasible response for governments is to give in to these pressures, quickly and completely, hoping that by a 'flag of convenience' policy of lowering their standards farther and faster than other countries they will steal a competitive advantage. On the contrary, even now national governments still have considerable leverage with multinationals,[219] if they choose to use it, and can have far more if they act effectively together.

It needs to be remembered that, despite the wide ramifications of their activities, most multinationals still retain strong national roots. For example,

British multinationals in manufacturing have two-thirds of their sales in Britain and Europe, and nearly two-thirds of their assets, while British multinationals in services have three-quarters of their sales in Britain and Europe, and two-thirds of their assets.[220] They depend on Britain for many support services and for much of their senior management, and most of them exhibit a clear national identity. There are economic and cultural reasons for the concentration of key activities in Britain, and it would be costly and impracticable for them to move out of Britain altogether. *New* investment is potentially more footloose, but even here the extent to which multinationals are prepared to go outside their base areas can be exaggerated. For example, the $100 billion invested in newly industrialising countries in 1993 represented only 3 per cent of total investment in Europe, the US and Japan in that year.[221]

Foreign-based multinationals also usually have solid commercial reasons for their operations in Britain. They will see the situation in the round, with perceived disadvantages arising from any unwelcome government policies weighed against perceived advantages of Britain as a location. These include the use of the English language; a stable and democratic system of government; a competent and uncorrupt civil service; a fair and workable system of contract law and financial regulation; a strong base in science and technology; an educated labour force; a functioning infrastructure; a peaceful society; the availability of a range of incentives for inward investment; access to the British market; and, often the key point, access through the Single European Market, to the very much larger market of the EU as a whole.

The European dimension is a key factor. A British government on its own has some leverage because, although economic growth has been slow, the market is still large enough to interest companies. Also, there is potential bargaining power in the fact that, while inward investment to Britain has been larger than to any other EU country, outward investment *from* Britain has in most years been substantially larger still.[222]

On its own, any medium-sized country would be too small in the global market to be seen as indispensable to a large multinational. However, the EU as a whole constitutes such a major part of the total global market that even the largest multinational would be reluctant to be excluded from it. That gives the EU far more clout than the government of any one member country – but only, of course, to the extent that it negotiates as a single unit. There have already been initiatives to try to harmonise tax incentives for inward investment in an attempt to prevent EU member countries bidding against each other to their mutual disadvantage. There should be scope to reach agreement on EU standards in other areas, using Europe's collective bargaining power to achieve for all the member countries the protection of common standards, which individual countries would not be strong enough to maintain on their own.

Financial movements

A second worrying feature of globalisation in its present form is the massive scale of financial movements. These far exceed both the requirements of international trade and investment and the reserves available to governments for containing them. Because they are driven predominantly by speculation, they produce changes that are not only huge, but also erratic, unpredictable and often irrational. They give the market a volatility that is destabilising and damaging. The present market system, rather than smoothing necessary changes, accentuates and dramatises them, and magnifies the disruption and difficulties that ensue from them. Because the forces are far too great for any single country to withstand, they make a mockery of national sovereignty – national macroeconomic policy has to be distorted to fit the pressures of the market.

For Britain, as it happens, this poses no threat at present. In the past, its aim was to maintain the pound at an unrealistically high level. To do so it tried to offset the lack of market confidence in sterling by offering high interest rates and deflationary fiscal measures – both damaging to growth. If the aim of policy now were not to keep the currency *up* at unsustainable levels but to bring it *down* to more realistic ones, then the thrust of policy would be working with the market, not struggling against it. It would not matter if the measures needed to encourage investment and growth – lower interest rates and a more expansionist fiscal stance – led to a decline in confidence and a more competitive value for the pound. In fact, it would be desirable. If Britain aimed for a *lower* value for the pound, it would have little to fear from the markets. Nevertheless, the financial markets generally constitute a force that is so massive and potentially destabilising that it hinders, rather than helps, world economic development. Even George Soros, the speculator who made $2 billion from the collapse of sterling in 1992, has called for their effective regulation.[223] How should it be done?

Ultimately, it will be necessary to create a new global international system to provide, as the postwar Bretton Woods agreement was intended to, an ordered structure for international economic relations. It would need to be designed to keep a balance between different national economies on the basis of general expansion. It would probably need to be based on fixed exchange rates, but with a provision for periodic agreed adjustments. Because of the recent shocks to the world economic system, the need for this is now much more widely accepted than it was a few years ago: but even so, it is likely to take several years to get wide international agreement on a complete new system.

Meanwhile, a proposal offering scope for much earlier adoption has been advanced by James Tobin.[224] It is for an international levy on foreign exchange transactions. Profits on foreign exchange dealings are based on tiny margins on huge volumes turned over in very short periods, usually using borrowed money. Even a very small percentage levy would be large enough to make small-margin speculative dealing unattractive, while at the same time it would be small enough to provide little impediment to legitimate merchandise trade and industrial investment, where margins are much higher and time-scales much longer.

A levy would 'put sand in the wheels' sufficiently to dampen volatility, without detrimental consequences, but with the useful advantage of potentially generating considerable revenue. It has been estimated that a levy of 1 per cent on all transactions, with world foreign exchange market turnover of more than $1000 billion a day, even allowing for 20 per cent exemptions, 20 per cent evasion and a 50 per cent drop in turnover on the remainder, total revenue would amount to more than $700 billion a year.[188] If half went to the UN, the World Bank and the IMF it could make a useful contribution to world economic development. If the other half went to the governments in whose countries the transactions originated, it would be a useful increase in tax revenues from a source that would cost few votes.

Information for the levy would be relatively straightforward to collect. Most foreign exchange transactions are made through a limited number of major banks. The same computerised systems that are used to make the transactions and record them for purposes of internal control could easily be modified to give a full central record of transactions for the levy. The resulting database could be analysed to provide comprehensive and up-to-date information on financial movements. This would be of great value to international traders and investors, to governments and to the foreign exchange market itself.[190] It would also be a powerful new weapon through which to expose international money laundering and fraud, both of which are at present difficult to detect because of the huge volume of transactions.

One possible difficulty with such a levy is that if it were introduced at a high rate it might give rise to large-scale attempts at evasion – through use, for example, of non-participating tax havens or internal transfers within multinational groups. It has been estimated that if the levy were brought in at a very low rate – say 0.01 per cent – it would not be worth trying to evade. The information benefits would outweigh the costs and it still might yield as much as $30 billion a year in revenue.[190] While a levy at such a low rate might be successful in overcoming opposition because it would make so little difference, by the same token it would probably not be successful in materially reducing the scale of foreign exchange business and its potential for destabilisation. Accordingly, it would probably be necessary to start the levy at a very low rate, but with a provision for raising it to levels that were sufficient to reduce purely speculative transactions and with arrangements for sharper temporary increases to damp down exceptional movements in times of financial crisis.

To be successful, such a system would need the support of at least the Group of Eight (G8) main economic powers. A few years ago such a possibility looked fanciful and remote. However, the succession of currency crises in the 1990s, particularly the 1997 débâcle in the east Asian economies, the 1998 crisis in Russia, and the knock-on effects on the west, have made many finance ministers and central bankers more sympathetic to ideas of this kind. (When there are speculative crises, some speculators may win but central bankers and politicians always lose.) Support has even come from the *Economist.*[225] If put strongly on the G8 agenda by a British government, it could now prove more acceptable in the charged international financial climate.

Meanwhile, more immediately and definitely on offer, is membership of the EMU (economic and monetary union). Joining together in a common currency will automatically end the possibility of currency speculation within the group of participating countries. The euro, a new, strong and widely used currency with pooled reserves many times greater than those of any one participant, would be much better placed to see off speculation relative to other currencies. Joining the euro offers Britain other advantages – lower transaction costs, a more effective Single European Market, attractiveness to inward investment, and probably lower interest rates and a general boost to business confidence. Unfortunately, there are two problems with joining right away. First, Britain's stage in the economic cycle is out of step with the other 11 countries and, second, as a result of recent speculative movements, the pound is at present greatly overvalued relative to other European currencies. Joining the ERM at too high a parity did great damage to Britain's economy until the pound was forced out; with EMU the pound would be locked in permanently at a very uncompetitive rate and the economy would face the prospect of a prolonged depression. There are also a number of more general problems with EMU, which are considered in the next section.

Economic interdependence and EMU

The third problem presented by globalisation is the growing interdependence of national economies. As imports and exports account for an increasingly large part of economic activity, economic developments in Britain are increasingly tied in with developments in other countries, which diminishes the government's control over the economy. This is particularly important if the government wishes to reduce unemployment by expanding the general level of demand. Imports already account for more than one-third of GDP and are rising twice as fast as output.[205] If the general level of demand were raised in Britain, the impact on output and employment in Britain would be dissipated. This is because much of the increase in demand goes on imported goods or foreign holidays, boosting the foreign earnings of other countries, but bringing a mounting balance of payments problem to Britain.

Thus, the problem would be eased if Britain sought a competitive exchange rate for the pound instead of an overvalued one. This would (after a time) tend to increase exports, and so reduce overseas payments problems. At the same time, it would increase output and employment to supply mounting export demand, and thereby reduce the extent of general reflation needed. It should be possible to expand demand in ways designed to have the maximum effect on employment and the minimum effect on the balance of payments (see Chapter 4).

Even so, a general problem remains. Increasing economic interdependence restricts the ability of a national government (acting on its own) to secure full employment by raising the general level of demand. But, this constraint does not apply to Europe as a whole.

The EU countries are coming closer together and are devising new structures. They hope to achieve greater prosperity through pooling their fortunes in a common economic destiny. About 60 per cent of Britain's trade is now with its European partners and the proportion is growing, as it is in other EU countries. While for Britain alone to reflate its economy in an attempt to get back to full employment would bring problems, for the whole of the EU to reflate at the same time would be a much more practical proposition.

There could still be problems with the remaining trade with the rest of the world. The EU is nearly self-sufficient economically – imports from outside the area normally account for less than 10 per cent of total GDP.[195] Even if general reflation led to an increase in imports from the rest of the world, it would not make much impact on employment and growth within Europe. Nor would it be likely to cause balance of payments problems – in most years the EU has a favourable balance with the rest of the world.[226] Altogether, the EU accounts for about 28 per cent of the world economy and about 39 per cent of world trade.[263] Europe is large and important enough to be a major and constructive participant in the global economy; it is also strong and independent enough to go-it-alone if necessary. Britain alone cannot hope to stand out against the pressures of the global economy. A united Europe can.

But will it? Unfortunately, the moves towards closer union came at a time when the governments in most EU countries were following conservative economic policies and the Maastricht Treaty reflected this in three ways: in the unsuitable arrangements for convergence in preparation for EMU, in the lack of adequate arrangements for continued convergence after it, and in the arrangements for the new European Central Bank. The first has already given rise to difficulties and the other two are likely to in the future.

The Maastricht Treaty convergence criteria for EMU included, reasonably, the requirement for a period of exchange rate stability. Unfortunately, during the run-up period Germany was having problems absorbing former East Germany, and these resulted in a temporary adoption of abnormally high interest rates. Other countries, to keep their currencies aligned with the strong deutschmark, were forced to raise their interest rates as well. As they were already in recession, this unnecessarily prolonged the recession and kept up high levels of unemployment.

Another convergence requirement was that public sector deficits must not exceed 3 per cent of GDP. At a time of rapid expansion this would have presented no problem, but as many of the economies were in recession, the attempt to meet this criterion further accentuated the recession.

In the end, almost all the countries wishing to join have managed to meet the criteria, more or less; but all of them, even Germany, have had considerable difficulty in doing so. This suggests that the criteria had less to do with ensuring convergence than with enforcing conformity with certain ideas of economic management, which were arbitrary and inappropriate to the circumstances of the time. They merely prolonged the recession and unemployment and made the whole project more unpopular.

The second difficulty arising from the Maastricht Treaty is in maintaining convergence in the future. It will be necessary to achieve convergence of the different economies, not only at the time EMU starts, but permanently.

After monetary union, it will no longer be possible for a national economy that gets out of line with the others to adjust by changing its exchange rate. Similar problems already arise within a country when a particular region gets into difficulty, for example because a traditional industry is run down. In such circumstances, the same national currency is used throughout the country and there is no possibility of a local devaluation to help a particular region. However, within a country there are other mechanisms to help correct imbalances between regions. If a region is in difficulty, people may accept lower wages to keep their prices competitive; some people may move to other regions where prospects are better;[227-8] there may be government grants, tax incentives or infrastructure investment to help the region; and there will be many automatic fiscal transfers, with weaker regions paying less in tax and receiving more in social security benefits and government services.[229]

Within a country, these adjustment mechanisms are mostly automatic and unnoticed, but their combined effect can be considerable.[2] In a monetary union between otherwise *separate* countries, these mechanisms are not available. Wage differentials are not easily changed. People do not easily move to other countries because of differences in language, culture, customs, schools and social security. Fiscal transfers do not take place between countries when national budgets are still made separately for each country.

If particular countries run into difficulties in the future, alternative mechanisms will be needed to make the necessary adjustments. The main weight of this is likely to fall on the supranational EU central budget. It is likely to require a much bigger budget, a more progressive way of raising revenue, a drastic reduction in the share taken by agriculture, and a major expansion of expenditure on the structural, cohesion and other funds to help countries with problems. Such changes will probably need to be substantial and will certainly prove to be controversial.[2] They will involve large transfers. Whereas the internal transfers that at present take place *within* countries are largely unintended, unmeasured, unnoticed and uncontroversial, future transfers *between* countries will be deliberate, quantified and transparent.

The problems of trying to combine a single European currency with separate national economies have not yet been adequately addressed. Until they are, countries that for one reason or another fall behind will risk finding themselves locked into a permanent depression.

The third difficulty arising from the Maastricht Treaty lies in the arrangements for giving effect to EMU. The Treaty provides for the system to be under the exclusive control of a new European Central Bank. This will operate with the 'primary objective' of ensuring price stability. It will be entirely independent both of national governments and of the European

Commission and European Parliament. Price stability is, of course, an important objective, but it is not the only one. There are also other objectives of public policy to be considered, such as economic growth, competitiveness, full employment, social cohesion and environmental protection. Normally, reconciling different, often conflicting objectives is a matter of economic and political debate and complex assessment of where the best balance of advantage may lie. A system that takes two key policy areas – interest rates and exchange rates – removes them from democratic political control, and hands them to a group of bankers charged with giving overriding priority to the single objective of curbing inflation is a formula for abdicating political responsibility and institutionalising federally the economic dogmas that caused so much damage when practised by national governments separately. It implies that a central system, which could be used to bring joint reflation and expansion, is likely instead to be used to impose rigorously the lopsided policies that have brought slow growth and mass unemployment. If EMU is to bring prosperity rather than depression, it will be essential to widen the remit to include other objectives such as full employment and growth, and to establish a degree of political control over the Central Bank's policies.

A few years ago, such an aspiration would have seemed hopelessly unrealistic. When the provisions of the Maastricht Treaty were being negotiated, Germany pushed for the preoccupation with inflation (born of its own searing historic experience of it) and insisted on complete independence for the Central Bank. The majority of governments at the time were broadly in tune with this approach to economic policy.

Now the situation is different. The economic dogmas in fashion at the time of Maastricht are increasingly being called into question; and the majority of countries in the EU – including Britain, Germany, France and Italy – now have left-of-centre governments. The Jospin government in France, in particular, is keen for EMU to be run with full employment as a major objective, and has pressed for some overall political control of the Central Bank. The current global economic crisis has alarmed even conservative bankers and finance ministers into seeing recession as a greater threat than inflation and calling for concerted cuts in interest rates and other measures to boost demand. There is thus a real possibility that a British government seeking to broaden the terms of reference of the Central Bank and establish some political control over it will receive a positive response. And a reformed EMU, working to a more actively expansionist agenda, should allow economic interdependence to be used as a means of securing positive economic and social benefits.

6 The Environment

Will it be possible to secure a sustainable environment?

Wealth generation on its own is not enough. There is little to gain from achieving a faster rate of economic growth unless it is *sustainable*. Unfortunately, even the modest economic growth that has been achieved in the past few decades has taken forms that are manifestly *not* sustainable in the longer term. The increasing pressures on the physical environment are showing in many different ways – for example, traffic congestion in towns, erosion of the countryside, threats to wildlife, problems with water contamination and waste disposal, increasing air pollution, the growing hole in the protective ozone layer, and the threat of serious climate change.

In this chapter, two problems of particular importance are considered, along with the policies needed to deal with them – traffic growth and climate change. The more general pressures that world economic expansion and population increase are putting on global natural resources – oil, gas, metals, land, food supplies and water – are considered in Chapter 7.

Traffic growth

The motorcar is one of the most popular products ever invented. It offers the possibility of going almost anywhere, any time, by any route, quickly, door-to-door, in weatherproof comfort, together, if desired, with radio, music, telephone, office equipment, luggage and passengers. It can be used for commuting, shopping, school runs, social visits, trips to the country and holidays, taking the whole family if required. And all at a cost that is generally affordable, even if it is the third biggest item in family budgets after housing and food. Many people regard it as a great liberator, making possible trips that would otherwise have been slower, costlier, more awkward or altogether impracticable. In addition, some see it as a status symbol indicating the owner's power, success and position. It is little wonder, then, that a major aim of large numbers of people has been to acquire a car, or a second one, or a newer, bigger or better one.

Accordingly, the proportion of households with a car has risen from 15 per cent in 1951 to 70 per cent in 1995, with 25 per cent of households having

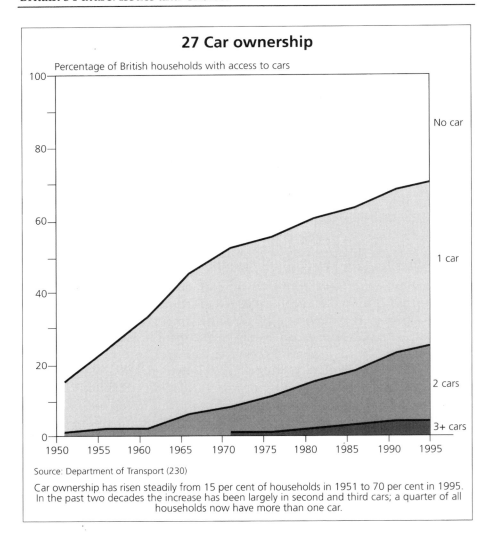

27 Car ownership

Percentage of British households with access to cars

Source: Department of Transport (230)

Car ownership has risen steadily from 15 per cent of households in 1951 to 70 per cent in 1995. In the past two decades the increase has been largely in second and third cars; a quarter of all households now have more than one car.

more than one.[230] Moreover, the somewhat higher figures in France, Germany and Italy, and the much higher figure in the US, suggest that there may still be some way to go before saturation levels are reached.[231]

Car traffic has gone up even faster than car ownership. It doubled between 1960 and 1970, and doubled again between 1970 and 1990. The Department of Transport estimates that it will increase by a further 34–51 per cent between 1990 and 2010, and by 62–91 per cent between 1990 and 2025.[231] The lower figure in each pair is based on a fairly modest rate of economic

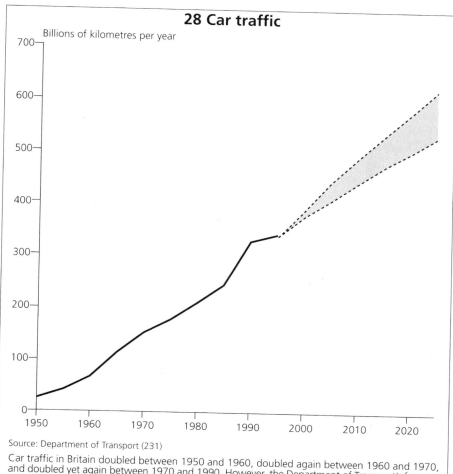

28 Car traffic

Billions of kilometres per year

Source: Department of Transport (231)

Car traffic in Britain doubled between 1950 and 1960, doubled again between 1960 and 1970, and doubled yet again between 1970 and 1990. However, the Department of Transport's forecast of a further increase of 62–90 per cent by 2025, although somewhat lower than earlier forecasts, seems likely to be constrained by environmental concerns.

growth (which should be attainable), the higher one on a rise in traffic faster than the average rate of economic growth (which is what has happened in the past). Both pairs are lower than the forecasts made a few years ago. They are therefore not far-fetched or fanciful. Even so, there are a number of reasons why further increases of this size will prove to be undesirable and, very likely, impossible.

The rise in car traffic is looking increasingly unsustainable in view of mounting problems with noise, accidents, air pollution, greenhouse gas emissions and, most obviously, congestion. The rise in car use (and also in lorry traffic) has led to peak-hour jams in many towns getting worse and spreading over longer periods and wider areas. Congestion is now also afflicting smaller towns and country and seaside areas, especially over weekends and during holidays. Even motorways are now prone to hold-ups, and are forecast to experience long periods of congestion in the future. The problems are particularly great in central London, where average traffic speeds have fallen to 10 miles an hour[231] – only one mile an hour faster than in 1912 and two miles an hour faster than a horse and carriage in 1890.[232]

In the past, transport policy focused on accommodating rising car numbers by building more roads and introducing traffic management schemes to use existing roads more intensively. However, roadbuilding has not only become more expensive, it is also attracting increasing opposition. New roads intended to relieve traffic congestion tend to generate extra traffic, thus creating renewed congestion. A particularly striking example of this is the M25 London orbital motorway. It was built to alleviate congestion, but within three years of opening in 1986 was carrying more traffic than the upper limit forecast for 2001, and has itself become a notorious blackspot for traffic jams. There are limits to how far traffic management schemes can coax more capacity out of the existing road network; they too, where they are successful, tend to end up generating more traffic and renewed congestion.

It seems then that the emphasis of public policy will need to shift from trying to *provide* for the insatiable growth in car traffic, to seeking to *check*, or even *reverse* it. To this end, it will be necessary to abandon past policies, which actually promoted more traffic, and bring in new attractive alternatives. This fundamental shift in policy objectives is reflected in the new government's recent white paper on the future of transport.[233]

Town and country planning

Part of the increase in car use comes from the inherent appeal of the car as a convenient means of getting about. But part, however, is the result of a number of social and economic developments that have generated additional *needs* for car journeys.

Over several decades there has been a tendency for people to move out of the big conurbations and go and live in country areas, either for their retirement, or to commute each day to jobs in the towns. This has given rise to great increases in long-distance commuting and in local traffic in country areas.

Traffic on country roads has also been growing as a result of people coming out of towns to the countryside, not to live, but just for the day or the weekend. With increasing prosperity and leisure, there has been a great increase in the numbers of people coming to the country to walk, cycle, ride, fish and play golf, and also a surge in other activities such as mountain-biking, motorbiking, hang-gliding, sailing, water skiing and power-boating. New facilities have been built to meet these demands. For example, new golf courses are being built at the rate of one-and-a-half a week, and planning permission has already been given for over 600 more.[234]

Since access to most of these recreational activities is, in practice, only feasible by car, they have generated a great increase in rural car traffic at weekends. They have brought traffic congestion to many seaside areas and places of outstanding natural beauty, and marked changes to the distinctive sights, sounds and smells of the countryside.

Other people continue to live in towns, but to drive out of them each day to jobs that have moved out. For several decades, industry has been moving out of inner cities, with their old buildings, constricted sites, difficult access, high rents and high labour costs, to new buildings with good services and lower rents on modern industrial estates in the suburbs, or to out-of-town sites near motorways. Warehousing and distribution centres have also been moving to out-of-town sites with good motorway access. And, more recently, offices have been moving to new business parks to benefit from lower rents, newer buildings and easier access for staff living in the suburbs.

Most of these jobs are at places not served by public transport and hence have to be reached by car – generating further daily traffic, particularly at peak hours.

More importantly, there have been major developments in retailing in the form of new shopping centres on suburban and out-of-town sites, all designed for access mainly by car. Some are very large. One, near Birming-ham, will be the biggest in Europe;[235] and one near Bristol has more shop-ping floor space than the centres of Bristol, Bath and all the other towns in the county of Avon combined.[236] The share of retail trade taken by out-of-town shopping centres rose from 8 per cent of the total in 1983 to 27 per cent in 1994;[237] and in 1996 three-quarters of all new retail space opened was in out-of-town locations.[238]

Over a period, these new developments have a devastating effect on nearby towns. They draw a large part of the business away from existing town centre shopping areas, cutting into their profits and making it difficult for them to invest in modernisation and expansion or, eventually, to stay in business at all. This makes the town centre drab, run-down and unattractive, leading to the departure also of offices, entertainments and other amenities. The new out-of-town centre acts as a leech, gradually draining the lifeblood out of the existing town centre, eventually leaving behind only an empty shell of decay.

These developments are not just hypothetical – they have already happened in many US cities where shopping in city centres has fallen, typically, to less than one-quarter of earlier levels. Offices have also moved out, with only about one-quarter of them still in the city centre in 'new' cities such as Houston, Dallas and Atlanta, as have other city centre amenities, leaving dead holes at the centre of cities, and a sprawl of scattered development and traffic congestion elsewhere.

Most western European countries, by contrast, have followed a very different approach. Major new out-of-town shopping developments have been strongly discouraged and the emphasis has been put instead on modernising and revitalising existing city centres. This has been done by creating attractive pedestrian precincts; building new shopping and leisure complexes on city centre sites; upgrading existing shopping streets by covering them over to make weatherproof arcades; improving access with better public transport into the centre and travelators or quiet and fumeless buses within the centre; and restricting traffic and parking for private cars. This has been attractive for citizens and profitable for business, for retail sales *increase* when streets are pedestrianised. Turnover has been exceptionally *high* in Munich, which has a largely pedestrianised city centre, exceptionally low car parking provision and an excellent public transport system.[288]

In Britain, planning controls were relaxed in the 1980s, leading to a surge in out-of-town developments. In 1993, the policy was reversed, with planning permission refused for further major new out-of-town developments – but without resources being put into redeveloping existing city centres or improving public transport services.

Locating new shops, offices and entertainment facilities near where people live, or at central locations easily served by public transport, would make our towns more convenient and attractive, and would give us more unspoiled and beautiful countryside. It would also reduce the *need* for much of the increase in car journeys generated by out-of-town developments.

If the three million or so extra homes expected to be needed for single people were mostly built not on rural land in the green belts around our towns but on the wasteland available for redevelopment in inner areas, people would be living nearer their jobs and leisure activities. They would probably be able to get to work on foot, or by bike or bus, so would have less need to use their cars.

The use of town and country planning controls to ensure that development goes where it is most useful to the community, rather than where it is most profitable to the developer, will be valuable in reducing the amount of unnecessary traffic that is generated by a *laissez-faire* system. But, it is only one side of a range of policies to reduce traffic. The other is to promote a shift in the ways people and goods move around. This is the objective of the government's new transport strategy.[233]

Walking

Walking still accounts for about 30 per cent of all journeys,[231] but could account for more – to the benefit of public health and the environment – if more were done to create a pedestrian-friendly environment. The overwhelming priority given to motor traffic in planning policy has meant that many places are difficult to reach on foot, or involve crossing roads with fast, heavy traffic. This can be hazardous, particularly for old people and children, many of whom do not have the option of going by car. Every year about 1000 pedestrians are killed on the roads[231] and walking is 17 times as dangerous as going by car for every mile travelled.[231]

We need wider pavements, safer crossings and lower speed limits in residential areas.[240] Department of Transport surveys show that more than 70 per cent of cars exceed the limit on 30 mph roads.[231] According to a report by the Parliamentary Advisory Council for Transport Safety,[241] about 160 children a year are killed in speed-related accidents, and the Transport Research Laboratory has estimated that the introduction of 20 mph speed limits could cut the number of deaths by two-thirds. It has also proposed modifications to the design of the front of cars. This would greatly reduce the severity of the injuries pedestrians suffer in accidents – at an extra cost estimated at only £11 a car.

It would be relatively cheap and easy to reclaim residential roads for local inhabitants by designating 'tranquil zones' with restricted access, very low speed limits, and priority for pedestrians and cyclists.

It would take much longer, and be much more expensive, to reclaim the city centres so that people could use them without the noise, fumes and danger of heavy traffic. The experience of many continental cities has been that if city centres are made more pedestrian-friendly, they become more attractive and more people use them, and they do so on foot – not because they are being penalised, but because with a traffic-free environment and shorter distances it is more *pleasant* than struggling through heavy traffic.

Cycling

In Britain, there are more bicycles than cars,[242] but most of them are rarely used. Cycling accounts for less than 2 per cent of all journeys in Britain, compared with 11 per cent in Germany, 18 per cent in Denmark and 27 per cent in the Netherlands[243] – all countries with high car ownership and higher standards of living than Britain's.

Since 1975, the average number of car trips per year in Britain has gone up by half, but the average number of bicycle trips has *fallen* by half. The main reason for the low and falling use of bicycles in Britain is that transport policy has given absolute priority to motor traffic, and cycling has become increasingly unpleasant and dangerous. In Britain, cyclists are 12 times as likely to be killed per mile travelled on the road as motorists,[231] and ten times as likely as cyclists in Denmark.[242]

Cycling is much cheaper and healthier than motor transport and there is little doubt that, given better facilities, far more people would use bicycles, particularly for getting to work each day. In London, only 4 per cent of people use a bicycle to get to work, compared with 30 per cent in Copenhagen, 43 per cent in Münster and 57 per cent in Groningen.[244]

The reason more people use bicycles in other countries is that provision has been made for them, with safe cycle lanes, cycle parking racks and sometimes other special measures, such as the scheme in Copenhagen for free loan of bicycles and the introduction of a legal requirement for Danish local authorities to ensure that it is safe for children to cycle to school – 60 per cent now do so.[242]

Suitable schemes will work in Britain too – already 18 per cent of commuters use bicycles in York.[244] A start has been made with plans to construct a 6500-mile national cross-country network of cycleways. What is now needed is higher priority for cyclists in towns, with generous cycle lanes in roads and separated tracks where feasible. Up to now, provision for cycling has taken less than 1 per cent of the total transport budget. New cycle routes are cheap to build – less than one-thousandth of the cost per mile of a motorway – and lines painted on roads are cheaper still. No other investment yields a larger or quicker return in terms of reduced congestion, pollution and accidents, and improved health.

Buses and trains

Car use has grown steadily, rail use has barely held level and bus use has fallen by 29 per cent since deregulation in 1985.[245] In other countries too, use of cars has risen relative to other forms of transport but not to the same extent as in Britain, where use of public transport is now the lowest in the EU.[231] These trends will only be reversed if public transport is made more attractive relative to cars.

Privatisation and deregulation have fragmented transport services, including timetabling and ticketing, and this has made them more difficult to use. The use of buses, for example, has on average fallen by 25 per cent since deregulation – except in London, where central regulation has been retained.[233] It is important to coordinate the various operators in a passenger-friendly way (with better information, through ticketing and improved interchanges), but the two main considerations are likely to be cost and quality of service.

Relative costs have moved in favour of the car. Between 1974 and 1994 the real price of petrol has fallen slightly, but the real cost of bus fares has been allowed to go up by more than 50 per cent, and of train fares by more than 90 per cent. Public transport fares in London are the highest of any capital in Europe, nearly double those in Paris and Copenhagen, and more than five times those in Rome and Madrid,[246] while intercity rail fares in Britain are among the highest in the world – far higher than in Germany, France, Italy or the US.

In most other European countries, it has long been recognised that the social and environmental benefits of high standard public transport systems make it worthwhile to subsidise their operation. In Britain, the policy has been to reduce drastically the level of subsidies – leading to higher fares, higher costs relative to cars, higher car use and more congestion. For this vicious circle to be reversed, it will be necessary to accept the need (and indeed the economic justification) for substantial public subsidy.

Park-and-ride schemes, whereby people park their cars on the outskirts of town and use a quick, cheap, frequent bus service to travel to the centre, is one way of encouraging people out of their cars and onto buses. Several towns are going ahead with them. In Oxford, where such a scheme exists, there has been a 40 per cent rise in the use of buses over the past ten years and car use has remained stable, compared with a 60 per cent increase in the rest of the country.[245]

The key to improving the attractiveness of bus services is speed. At present, buses are delayed (and made less efficient and more costly to run)

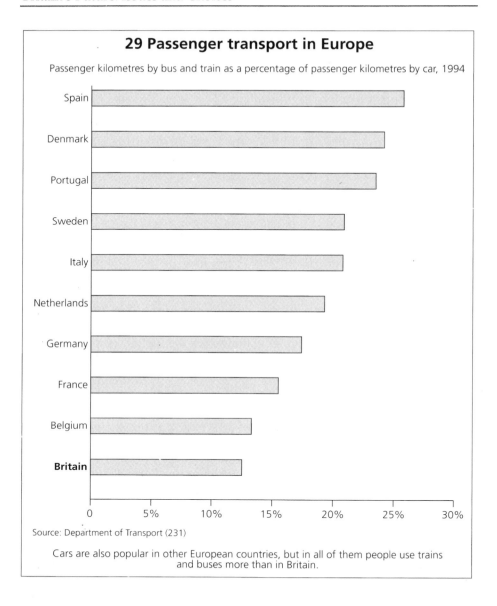

29 Passenger transport in Europe

Passenger kilometres by bus and train as a percentage of passenger kilometres by car, 1994

Spain

Denmark

Portugal

Sweden

Italy

Netherlands

Germany

France

Belgium

Britain

0   5%   10%   15%   20%   25%   30%

Source: Department of Transport (231)

Cars are also popular in other European countries, but in all of them people use trains and buses more than in Britain.

by the same traffic congestion as cars. They are made slower still when operators introduce one-man buses in busy areas, trying to reduce their own costs regardless of the extra congestion caused for everyone else. To make them attractive, buses in busy areas need to be *faster* and more reliable than cars. This can only be achieved by giving them priority use of the available

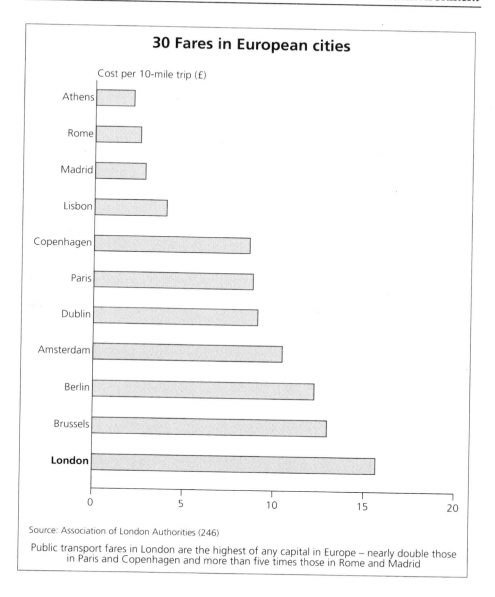

30 Fares in European cities

Cost per 10-mile trip (£)

Athens	
Rome	
Madrid	
Lisbon	
Copenhagen	
Paris	
Dublin	
Amsterdam	
Berlin	
Brussels	
London	

Source: Association of London Authorities (246)

Public transport fares in London are the highest of any capital in Europe – nearly double those in Paris and Copenhagen and more than five times those in Rome and Madrid

road space, with more rigorously segregated special bus lanes on key routes, and priority at road junctions, so that they can speed past the congestion resulting from higher car use.

Will the reduced capacity left for other traffic cause the road system to seize up? Surprisingly, no. Just as the extra capacity provided by new roads

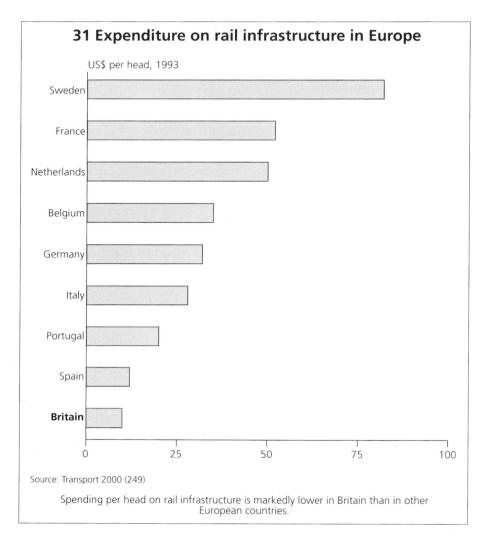

31 Expenditure on rail infrastructure in Europe

US$ per head, 1993

Source: Transport 2000 (249)

Spending per head on rail infrastructure is markedly lower in Britain than in other European countries.

tends to generate *extra* traffic, so conversely a reduction in available capacity tends to bring about a *fall* in the volume of traffic as people modify their times, routes, means of transport and destinations to take account of the reduced capacity. This phenomenon was demonstrated when the City of London was cordoned off, when Hammersmith bridge was closed, and when Birmingham's inner ring road was reduced from three lanes to two. The result, unexpectedly, was not seize-up, but a fall in the volume of traffic. Also, between 1980 and 1995, the volume of car traffic in outer London (where road capacity was less tight) increased by 40 per cent, in inner London (where capacity was tighter) it increased by only about 9 per cent, and in central London (where capacity was saturated) it did not increase at all – despite the increase of more than 60 per cent in national car traffic over the period.[231]

New track, signalling, rolling stock and amenities are needed to improve the standard of service on the railways and underground trains. This would require substantial investment sustained over a long period. Unfortunately, while year after year many billions of pounds have been spent on new roads, there has been no comparable level of investment in public transport. Investment in railways has been at only a quarter of the level in France and Germany. The growing backlog of investment is beginning to show in the deterioration in the quality of the service and in interminable delays in improvements. For example, the high-speed rail link to the Channel Tunnel is now expected to be completed all of 13 years late, while plans to construct high-speed links to other parts of the country have been put off to a date too remote to specify. There needs to be a major shift in investment from roads to public transport, and this is likely to require a much tougher use of the powers of the regulators and, if necessary, a return of the railways to public ownership and control.

Cars and lorries

While the main emphasis of policy should be on making alternatives more attractive, the reality has to be faced that on its own this is unlikely to be enough. It will need to be balanced by measures to make the car *less* attractive. The rationale for this is not based on punitive prejudice, bringing a damaging 'distortion' of the market, but rather on the need to introduce measures to correct the heavy bias in favour of the car, which is built into present arrangements.

The Royal Commission on Environmental Pollution estimates[247] that road users cost the country between £4.6 billion and £12.9 billion a year in air pollution, climate change, noise and vibration. A study undertaken at University College, London[248] estimates that if the full costs to society arising from private road users are taken into account (wear on roads, congestion, air and noise pollution, accidents and so on), total costs amount to between £22.9 billion and £25.7 billion a year. This compares with a total of about £14.7 billion a year they pay in taxes – equivalent to a subsidy of about £500 a year per car. Another study[249] puts the gap between environmental costs and tax receipts at twice as much – equivalent to a subsidy of about £1000 a year per car. It is therefore reasonable to contemplate introducing a range of measures to reduce this bias in favour of the car by making motorists pay more towards the costs they generate.

An obvious first step would be to scale down greatly the new road building programme. Another would be to use the existing road space more advantageously with more bus lanes, cycleways and pedestrian areas. And a third would be to start making charges for the capacity remaining. It is anomalous that the users of railways, ports and airports have to pay for the facilities they use, while users of roads have them provided free – even expensive new motorways, which in most other countries are subject to tolls.

The reason hitherto has been practical. There was no way of levying charges without causing delays and disrupting traffic. However, new electronic systems are now becoming available that can charge for use of roads without delaying traffic, charge at different rates at different times or places or for different categories of user, and automatically secure payment from users. Limited systems are already in use in Oslo, Singapore and other cities, and more sophisticated ones are being developed. One scheme devised for central London is estimated to be capable of cutting traffic by 17 per cent, pollution by up to 20 per cent and accidents by 5 per cent, while generating £400 million a year, which could then be invested in public transport.[250]

Such schemes unfortunately require major investment, take time to implement and are prone to mishaps while the technology is being perfected. Simpler schemes with flat-rate charges for permits to enter central areas of cities, or tolls for motorways, are easier to introduce and are already widely used in other countries. Easier still is a series of increases in petrol duty – such as the 6 per cent annual escalation already introduced in Britain – which increases the cost of using cars roughly in proportion to the distance travelled.

Other proposed measures include higher annual licence fees, higher charges for parking, levies on free parking space provided by offices in city centres and shops in out-of-town centres and, long overdue, withdrawal of the tax concessions for company cars. Company cars account for half of all new car registrations and, it is claimed, for three-quarters of the cars coming into central London. They have larger than average engine sizes and do greater than average mileages, particularly if they have free fuel.[233]

Would measures to reduce car use be too unpopular for populist politicians to contemplate? The motor industry is a powerful lobby with many jobs involved, and the devotion of motorists to their cars is well known and understandable. In recent years, however, public awareness of the problems

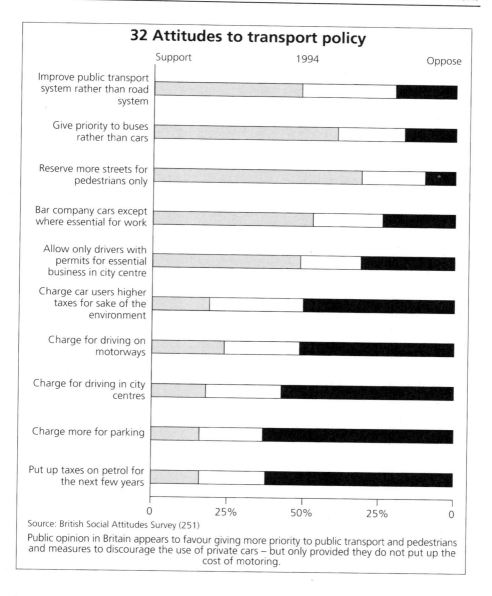

32 Attitudes to transport policy

Support   1994   Oppose

Improve public transport system rather than road system

Give priority to buses rather than cars

Reserve more streets for pedestrians only

Bar company cars except where essential for work

Allow only drivers with permits for essential business in city centre

Charge car users higher taxes for sake of the environment

Charge for driving on motorways

Charge for driving in city centres

Charge more for parking

Put up taxes on petrol for the next few years

0   25%   50%   25%   0

Source: British Social Attitudes Survey (251)

Public opinion in Britain appears to favour giving more priority to public transport and pedestrians and measures to discourage the use of private cars – but only provided they do not put up the cost of motoring.

arising from unlimited car use has been increasing. The 1994/5 British Social Attitudes Survey[251] found substantial majorities in favour of reserving more streets for pedestrians, giving buses priority over cars, improving the public transport system rather than the road system, banning company cars except where essential for work, and restricting access of cars to city centres. The

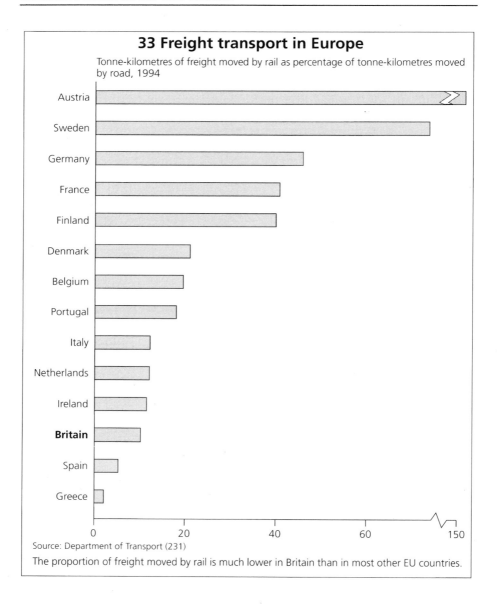

33 Freight transport in Europe

Tonne-kilometres of freight moved by rail as percentage of tonne-kilometres moved by road, 1994

Austria	
Sweden	
Germany	
France	
Finland	
Denmark	
Belgium	
Portugal	
Italy	
Netherlands	
Ireland	
Britain	
Spain	
Greece	

0   20   40   60   150

Source: Department of Transport (231)

The proportion of freight moved by rail is much lower in Britain than in most other EU countries.

same survey also found strong opposition to higher taxes on car users or petrol, to higher parking charges, and to charges for driving in city centres or on motorways. It seems likely that any measures that visibly increase the *costs* of motoring are unlikely to gain wide approval unless they are linked with public expenditure showing clear *benefits*, for example in the form of better public transport, preferably with the benefits being in evidence before the extra costs have to be paid.

Lorries are also a major factor in congestion, and lorry traffic has been rising even faster than that of cars. This is partly due to the shift from rail to road. As a result, the volume of goods going by rail, relative to the volume by road, is lower in Britain than in most other countries in Europe.[231] Motorway tolls, dearer fuel and higher charges for licences to reflect the disproportionate wear and tear and congestion caused by heavy goods vehicles, together with improved rail facilities and more effective use of the through-rail opportunities presented by the Channel Tunnel, could all help shift traffic back to the railways and thereby reduce the congestion caused by heavy lorries.

Air pollution

There are two main sources of air pollution. One is sulphur dioxide, which comes mainly from power stations and industry. In 1990, emissions per head in Britain were the fourth highest in the world,[252] but in recent years they have been falling.[253] The other is emissions from vehicle exhausts – nitrogen oxides, particulates, carbon monoxide, ozone, black smoke and aromatic compounds. In 1990, Britain's emissions per head of nitrogen oxides were also the fourth highest in the world,[252] exceeded only by the US, Greece and Denmark. Over a long period, emissions in Britain, as in other countries, had been rising, largely because of the increase in road traffic.

The various measures to reduce traffic congestion may also be expected to reduce air pollution, particularly in towns, and likewise the measures taken for emissions of greenhouse gases. There are a number of things that can be done specifically to reduce the air pollution from vehicles.

Between 1990 and 1995, there was a 21 per cent drop in emissions of nitrogen oxides.[253] This was the result of cleaner power stations and the adoption by the European Commission in 1989 of new regulations requiring all new cars sold after July 1992 to be fitted with catalytic converters. These sharply reduce emissions of nitrogen oxides and several other pollutants, so that as old cars are scrapped in favour of new ones fitted with converters the level of emissions goes down. However, they have the disadvantage of raising costs, reducing performance and increasing petrol consumption and, hence, emissions of carbon dioxide. Also, the benefits from fitting catalytic converters to new cars have been partly offset by the continuing increase in the total volume of traffic.

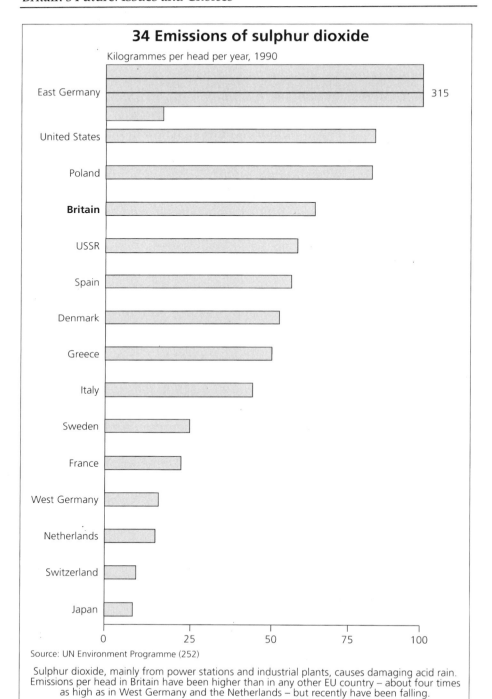

34 Emissions of sulphur dioxide

Kilogrammes per head per year, 1990

East Germany — 315

United States

Poland

Britain

USSR

Spain

Denmark

Greece

Italy

Sweden

France

West Germany

Netherlands

Switzerland

Japan

0   25   50   75   100

Source: UN Environment Programme (252)

Sulphur dioxide, mainly from power stations and industrial plants, causes damaging acid rain. Emissions per head in Britain have been higher than in any other EU country – about four times as high as in West Germany and the Netherlands – but recently have been falling.

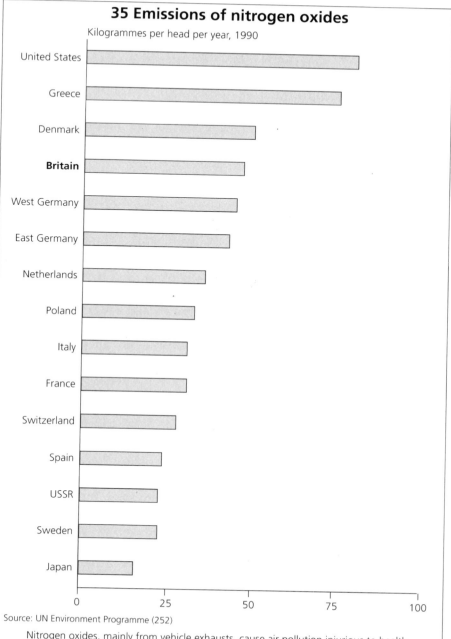

35 Emissions of nitrogen oxides

Kilogrammes per head per year, 1990

United States	
Greece	
Denmark	
Britain	
West Germany	
East Germany	
Netherlands	
Poland	
Italy	
France	
Switzerland	
Spain	
USSR	
Sweden	
Japan	

0   25   50   75   100

Source: UN Environment Programme (252)

Nitrogen oxides, mainly from vehicle exhausts, cause air pollution injurious to health. Emissions per head in Britain are higher than in most other EU countries, and there has been little progress in meeting targets for reductions – lower power station emissions have been offset by increased road traffic.

Another way of reducing air pollution from traffic is to modify the characteristics of fuels. Lead from car exhausts was an increasing problem; but a reduction in the permitted level of lead in petrol, combined with a tax differential in favour of lead-free petrol, has cut lead emissions in Britain by four-fifths in ten years.[253]

The European Commission has plans to require use of cleaner reformulated petrol and diesel fuel throughout the EU. It is already widely used in Italy, where it was made mandatory at the beginning of 1998, and in France where it will be mandatory from 2000.[254] It is also mandatory in California, where it has reduced the number of 'stage 1 smog alert' days in Los Angeles by half.[254]

Another way of reducing air pollution is to redesign cars to burn less fuel. The Royal Commission on Environmental Pollution has estimated[247] that improved engine efficiency, better transmission, reduced drag and reduced weight or size could between them reduce total fuel consumption by 10–30 per cent over five years, using current technology, and by 15–50 per cent within ten years using improved technologies. Several major manufacturers have already produced prototypes with dramatically better fuel consumption, but they have not yet put them into volume production.

Another approach is to move to a new type of fuel altogether, such as compressed natural gas, liquid petroleum gas, ethanol or methanol, all of which give off less pollution. Liquid petroleum gas and compressed natural gas are already used in more than a million vehicles in Italy. However, they involve high conversion costs for existing vehicles and require heavy pressurised fuel tanks. Also, a nationwide network of specially equipped filling stations would need to be installed before their use could become widespread.

Ultimately, the aim, particularly for traffic in towns, is to move to vehicles, not with reduced pollution, but with *zero* pollution. One recent development offering zero emissions is an engine that works on compressed air. It is planned to build 40,000 vehicles a year using the new engine, mainly taxis and delivery vehicles for use in Mexico City, where pollution is particularly bad.[255] It remains to be seen how successful they will be.

Hitherto, the main focus of attention has been on electric motors that produce no air pollution at all (except elsewhere in the generation of the electricity used), and are also quiet. Most of the major manufacturers have invested in the development of electric cars, but conventional batteries are very heavy in relation to the power delivered, which seriously restricts speed, acceleration and range; and the batteries need time to recharge. Few private motorists have yet been willing to accept these limitations.

All this will change with the development of higher performance batteries. Considerable investment has gone into this also – but the vital breakthrough has been 'just a few years away' for several decades, and there can be no certainty about when it will eventually come. Ultimately, the solution may come with fuel cells powered by hydrogen. This also has attracted substantial research, and great advances have been made, but it likely to be several years before the technology is developed to a stage at which it can be used economically on a commercial scale.[256]

Meanwhile, it seems likely that there may be a viable compromise in the form of hybrid vehicles. These have quiet, zero-emission electric motors for use in towns; but also clean, high efficiency petrol engines for use elsewhere to give greater range, easy refuelling, and recharging of batteries on the move. The petrol engine is used at its most efficient speed and so can be quite small and economical, with extra power for hills, acceleration or high speeds provided by using the electric motor at the same time. Electronic systems provide automatically the most efficient combination of drives, and a flywheel system enables energy from braking to be used to recharge the batteries.

Most major manufacturers have developed prototype hybrid cars and a few have put them into commercial production. Performance is claimed to be good, but the somewhat higher purchase costs have limited sales so far.

One thing that is abundantly clear about traffic-generated air pollution in towns is that it will not diminish of its own accord. The market provides an incentive for oil companies to sell more petrol, not cleaner petrol; and for vehicle makers to make bigger and faster vehicles, and more of them, not cleaner and more economical vehicles, and fewer of them.

The heavy investment that has gone into developing cleaner fuels and vehicles has only come about because the market has been 'distorted' by government interventions – in particular by the European Commission prescribing more stringent emission standards and by the state of California setting a requirement for 2 per cent of zero-emission vehicles by 1998 (which has recently had to be relaxed) and 10 per cent by 2003 (which has not so far been relaxed). Tax concessions have also played a part – in France and Sweden for electric vehicles, in Japan for a petrol-electric hybrid car, and in Britain for the use of lead-free petrol.

Global climate change

Probably the most important environmental issue of all, and also the most difficult to deal with, is global warming, the process by which the emission of greenhouse gases is making the world's climate steadily hotter, and also more violent and unpredictable. It is a process which, left unchecked, could ultimately make the planet uninhabitable.

In the past two decades, there have been disturbing changes in world climate patterns. Average global temperatures have been rising at an unprecedented rate. Nine out of ten of the planet's hottest years have been since 1983, and 1997 was the hottest year since records began. Average global sea levels have been rising.[257] The ice cover has been receding in both the Arctic and Antarctic. There has also been an increase in the frequency and severity of storms, floods, droughts and other extreme weather. In the first half of the 1990s, the incidence of 'weather related' disasters was six times as great as in the 1980s, involving a total cost estimated at more than $160 billion.[258]

These changes have been attributed to increased accumulations of certain gases in the upper atmosphere. These allow short-wave solar radiation to reach the earth, while preventing longer-wave infrared heat from escaping into space. They thereby produce a 'greenhouse effect', which has brought rising temperatures and disturbance of established weather patterns.

Four-fifths of the increase is attributed to carbon dioxide, which is produced by burning fossil fuels (coal, oil and natural gas) in power stations, industrial plants, heating and vehicles; most of the remainder to methane, which is given off mainly in the course of agriculture, waste disposal and mining; and some also from other gases, such as nitrous oxides, mainly from vehicles and aircraft.

Because the evidence for the greenhouse phenomenon was initially inconclusive, it aroused much controversy. To resolve it, 35 countries met in Geneva in 1988 under the auspices of the United Nations Environment Programme and the World Meteorological Programme to set up the Intergovernmental Panel on Climate Change (IPCC). Its purpose was to provide an authoritative assessment for governments of the state of knowledge on climate change. The project was the largest of its kind ever undertaken, and involved the participation of more than 200 scientists, nominated by their governments and drawn from all the leading organisations in the field.

The IPCC's first report[259] was published in 1990. It concluded that human activities were substantially increasing the atmospheric concentrations of greenhouse gases, and that this was bringing a long-term increase in global mean temperature of about $0.3^{\circ}C$ per decade, greater than seen over the past 10,000 years, and also an average rate of global mean sea level rise of about six centimetres per decade.

The report thus confirmed that global warming was in fact happening, and that if man-made emissions of greenhouse gases continued to increase, as they would on a 'business as usual' basis, temperatures would go on rising indefinitely, causing increasingly unacceptable damage. It estimated that a 60 per cent reduction in greenhouse gas emissions would be needed to prevent this happening. These conclusions were agreed *unanimously* by all the scientists taking part.

In 1995, the IPCC published a second report,[257] which made use of the additional evidence of the subsequent five years and of improvements in their climate models. The second report, agreed unanimously by leading experts from 96 countries, confirmed that global warming was happening, and modelled it more closely. It also scaled down the predicted rate of change by about one-third. It is now predicted that, if we continue with 'business as usual', average temperatures would rise by about 2^{0}C in the course of the next century, and that average sea levels would rise by about 50 centimetres.

Although the figures are lower than in the first report, the changes predicted over the next century are still very large. A change of 2^{0}C may not sound much, but it is in fact half the difference between the present average temperature and the average in the last ice age.[257]

Moreover, the *rate* of change is faster than in any period of recorded history – too fast for most trees and many plants and animals to adapt. It may be expected to cause deforestation, desertification and loss of biodiversity and, in some areas where food supplies are already a problem, it could be difficult to maintain agricultural production. Higher temperatures and reduced rainfall could exacerbate water shortages in dryer regions. Higher sea levels may be expected to threaten the homes and livelihoods of more than 40 million people and, eventually, submerge entire countries in some of the low-lying islands of the Pacific and Indian oceans.

It is too early to make reliable predictions for particular regions, let alone for individual countries. However, if average global predictions are applied to Britain then, over the next 50 years, London's climate would become like that of Bordeaux[260] – a not wholly unattractive thought. But it would not stop at that – over time it would become more like Rome, then Algiers, then Timbuktu. Meanwhile, the citizens of Timbuktu would be experiencing the drawbacks very much sooner. In the coming decades there will be net gainers as well as net losers from global warming, but in the long run all will be losers as the planet gets hotter and hotter, until eventually it becomes uninhabitable.

Long before then, it will not only get warmer, but weather patterns will become more erratic and extreme. The increasing frequency and severity of floods, droughts and storms in recent years falls well outside the normal range of fluctuations. The violence and unpredictability of short-term weather patterns may prove even more serious than longer-term gradual warming. There has already been enough increase in disaster claims for a group of 60 insurance companies to start campaigning actively for measures to check global climate change.[261]

Feedbacks have potentially more alarming implications. Climate systems are highly complex, and include a number of feedbacks that are not yet well understood. These may be negative. For example, warmer temperatures may cause plants or ocean plankton to adapt or multiply so that they absorb more carbon dioxide, thereby offsetting part of the increase in man-made emissions and *dampening* the process of global warming. Unfortunately, IPCC studies have identified more possibilities of *positive* feedbacks liable to *accelerate* the process. For example, plants and plankton may react to warmer temperatures in ways that reduce their capacity to absorb carbon dioxide;[262] deforestation due to warmer climate may reduce the amount of carbon dioxide absorbed by forests;[263] the thawing of previously frozen arctic tundra may release increased quantities of methane;[264] and, potentially most worrying of all, melting arctic pack ice may destabilize ocean currents.[263]

Ocean currents play an important but imperfectly understood part in the world's weather system. An important one starts under the pack ice in the North Atlantic at the Odden Feature east of Greenland. It is predicted that, as a result of global warming, the year-round polar ice cap will disappear entirely in the course of the next century. Already the ice east of Greenland has been receding and, as a result of this, the Odden Feature has failed for three years in succession.[265] This has never happened before, and the consequences are unknown.

Recent research drilling in the Greenland ice sheet has revealed new information on past climate patterns. The relatively steady climate of the past 10,000 years, which made human civilization possible, is apparently untypical. There have been long periods of both much hotter and much colder climates. The significant new discovery is that past changes from one climate pattern to another were quite abrupt – within just a few decades.[263,266]

It is not known what caused the climate to flip suddenly from one relatively steady state to another. One theory is that a change in ocean currents triggered the sudden shift. If so, the recent failure of the Odden Feature might portend a change in currents leading to a dramatic climate shift – either a runaway greenhouse effect leading to a much hotter world, or a shift in the other direction to a new ice age.

Of more specific concern to Britain is the possible effect of global warming on the Gulf Stream, which IPCC scientists suggest could reduce in strength and become less stable and more unreliable.[251] At present, the Gulf Stream provides Britain with heat equivalent to 30 per cent of that coming from the sun, giving a climate 6°C warmer than it would be without it.[266] If the Gulf Stream failed altogether, Britain's climate would become more like that of Labrador.

Greenhouse negotiations

Since the consequences of global warming are potentially so serious, it is clearly important to reduce the emissions of greenhouse gases that are causing it. IPCC scientists estimate that, to stop global warming, it will be necessary to cut global greenhouse gas emissions by about 60 per cent, while at the same time preserving the forests which, along with the oceans, at present absorb much of the carbon dioxide produced.

The greenhouse gases each country generates affect the climate of all. To control global warming it is necessary to get all countries to cooperate in reducing emissions and preserving forests. Securing voluntary agreements from more than 160 sovereign governments is no easy task.

There was a similar problem with ozone depletion and adequate global cooperation was secured to deal with it. But, the problem of chlorofluorocarbons (CFCs) was easier because only a handful of companies in a few countries were making them; adequate substitutes were readily available; and many of the companies that had been making them were in a position to switch profitably to making substitutes instead. Crucially, CFCs were not a major element in any national economy, or even in any major multinational company. Agreement on phasing them out could thus be reached without too many tears.

With greenhouse gas emissions, the situation is considerably more difficult. Economic expansion and population growth bring strong market pressure to use more and more energy (including more coal, oil and gas when they are the cheapest, most convenient and most profitable source) and to clear more and more forest when it is profitable to sell the timber or use the land for other purposes. Most countries are being pulled in the opposite direction because:

- energy, including fossil-derived energy, is a major element in *all* economies;

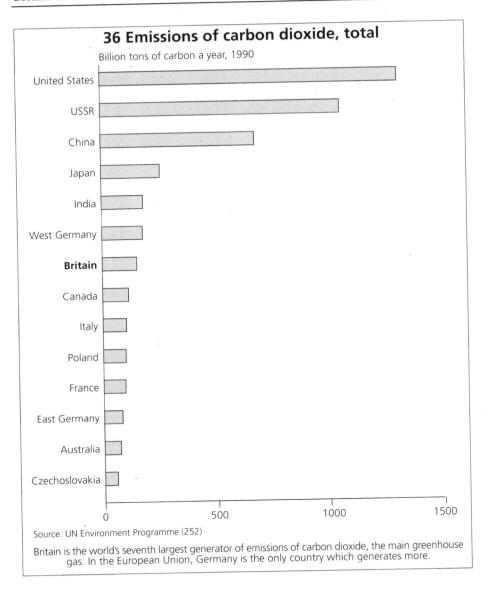

36 Emissions of carbon dioxide, total

Billion tons of carbon a year, 1990

Source: UN Environment Programme (252)

Britain is the world's seventh largest generator of emissions of carbon dioxide, the main greenhouse gas. In the European Union, Germany is the only country which generates more.

- expansion of energy use is assumed to be essential for economic expansion;
- cheap sources of energy are often regarded as a key factor in international competitiveness;
- both the energy industries and heavy user industries such as vehicles, steel and chemicals are major employers and influential lobbies; and

- domestic use in homes and vehicles is a sensitive matter in the minds of many voters.

It is difficult to get any government to take effective action to curb emissions. To get the required action by *all* governments is bound to be very much more difficult, and is certain to require skilful diplomacy and hard bargaining over a long period.

A start was made at the United Nations Conference on Environment and Development at Rio de Janeiro in 1992, when world leaders agreed in principle to bring emissions back to 1990 levels by the turn of the century – but in practice did nothing to bring it about. The agreement in Rio was followed by further meetings in Geneva and Berlin, leading up to a meeting in Kyoto in 1997 to confirm specific targets, measures for reaching them, and mechanisms for enforcing them.

The wide range of attitudes, circumstances and interests between countries made for long and acrimonious arguments at Kyoto. The agreement that was eventually reached was disappointing. The date for achieving the target reductions was not 2005, or 2010, but 2012. The effective overall reduction on 1990 for the industrialised countries was only about 5.3 per cent,[267] achieved through agreement on different nominal targets for different countries: 8 per cent for the EU, 7 per cent for the US and 6 per cent for Japan, with no cut for Russia and Ukraine, and an increase of 8 per cent for Australia. Because the targets did not apply to developing countries, whose emissions are increasing rapidly, by 2012 total global emissions are likely to be about 30 per cent *higher* than in 1990[267] – a long way from the 60 per cent global reduction considered necessary by the IPCC scientists. Finally, several contentious issues were left over to be settled later, and there are still serious doubts about ratification by the US Senate.

But, for all its serious deficiencies, the Kyoto agreement was a remarkable and momentous achievement; it brought hope for the future. A unanimous consensus was reached by more than 160 participating governments. All the industrialised countries are committed to legally binding targets for all six main greenhouse gases, along with provisions for the machinery needed for practical implementation. It should therefore be possible in the coming years, as the evidence gets firmer and public opinion gets more sympathetic, progressively to tighten the targets until they accord more closely with the requirements of the situation – as indeed happened with the Montreal protocol for phasing out ozone-depleting gases. It must be remembered that global warming is a *long-term* problem. While early action is preferable, and

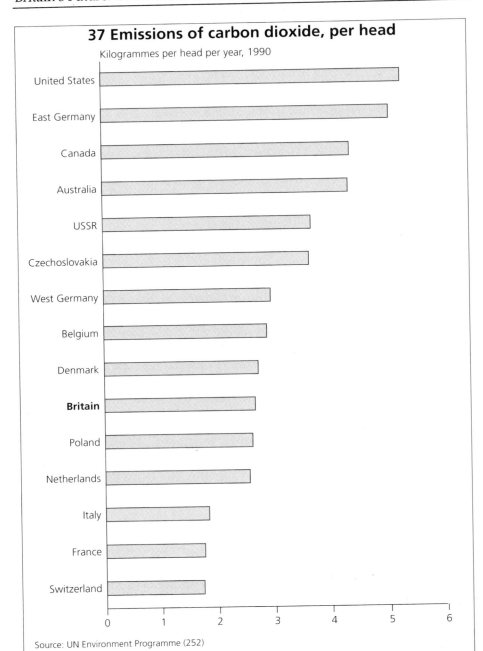

37 Emissions of carbon dioxide, per head

Kilogrammes per head per year, 1990

Source: UN Environment Programme (252)

In terms of emissions per head of carbon dioxide, Britain's emissions are lower than those of Germany, Belgium and Denmark, but higher than those of other EU countries. The shift of power stations from coal to natural gas will help Britain meet current modest international targets, but much larger reductions are likely to be required later.

while the changes eventually needed are likely to be considerable, it is over the coming *decades*, not the next few months, that they will need to be accomplished.

Countries in different circumstances and with conflicting interests were able to accept the Kyoto agreement because it was flexible. It made allowances for:

- different targets for certain countries with special situations;
- targets based on a 'basket' of all six main greenhouse gases (to allow for different mixes in different countries);
- 'bubbling' (a single overall target for the EU to allow different targets within it for individual member countries);
- forest carbon dioxide sinks (credits for afforestation and reforestation, debits for deforestation); and
- 'joint implementation' (credits for greenhouse gas-saving projects undertaken in other countries).

It also made provision, at US insistence, for internationally tradeable emission permits. This is a system under which firms are given permits for specific volumes of emissions, which they are free to buy and sell. Firms that find it easier to reduce their emissions do so by more than the amount required of them and sell their surplus permits to firms that find it more difficult. This means that the reductions are likely to be made where the costs of making them are least. A system of this sort has already been used in the US for cutting sulphur dioxide emissions, and the reductions were made in a much shorter time than expected and at 50 per cent lower cost to industry than would have resulted from traditional across-the-board regulatory measures.[268] The system was also easier and cheaper to enforce, and has given rise to less opposition.

What has made the system particularly controversial is that Russia and Ukraine have been set emissions targets of zero change from 1990, when in practice, because of the collapse of their economies, their emissions are likely to be well below the target levels, even without any special measures. They are therefore likely to have substantial 'hot air' surpluses available, which the US will be able to buy, thereby reducing the pressure on it to cut its own emissions.

The most serious deficiency in the Kyoto agreement is that it excluded all developing countries. The Americans insisted (as a prerequisite for Senate ratification) that developing countries, particularly China and India, as potential big emitters, should be required to make similar reductions in emissions. This outraged the developing countries, which see global warming as a problem brought about by the excessive energy use of the developed countries, particularly the US, which should be expected to make the adjustments needed to clear up the mess they had created. They argued that they needed to increase their energy use and emissions to achieve a reasonable pace of economic development, and that they lacked the technological and financial resources to restrain emissions without substantial help from the more developed countries.

The US was right to want to bring the developing countries into the emissions control system, particularly large ones like China. China's emissions per head are still low, but it is a huge country experiencing rapid economic development. It has large reserves of coal, which it intends to use, much of it in inefficient plants – China's emissions per unit of GDP are about seven times as high as the US's.[252] China is already the world's second largest emitter of greenhouse gases, and the World Bank estimates that between 1995 and 2020 its emissions of carbon dioxide will treble – equivalent to 40 per cent of the 1995 world total.[269] It is imperative to bring China and other developing countries into the system, so that they too curb their emissions in the future.

It is also important to include developing countries because the credits they would get against their internationally tradeable emission quotas would give them a strong economic incentive to preserve the tropical forests, which at present soak up some of the carbon dioxide generated by human activities. The World Bank has estimated that the world's remaining tropical forests are disappearing at the rate of nearly 1 per cent a year.[270] Other studies claim that, in Brazil alone, an area of forest three times the size of Wales is cleared *each year*.[271] The rapid clearance of forests is not only adding to global warming – it is also causing damage in the form of soil erosion, floods, droughts and air pollution from smoke, as when the recent forest fires in Indonesia spread a pall of smog over several neighbouring countries.

Forest clearance is also causing the extinction of species at more than 100,000 times the 'natural rate'.[272] If it continues, at least a quarter of all species of organisms on earth could be eliminated within 50 years.[273] There are reasons to preserve biodiversity other than sentimentality. About a quarter of all medicines,[273] with a total value of $40 billion a year,[272] are derived from plants and microorganisms – the results of research on fewer than one in a hundred of the earth's plant species. The loss from large-scale future depletion of species is hard to calculate, but is likely to be very large indeed.

No developing country will agree to join a system using 1990 emissions as the base year for national targets. In 1990, emissions per head were very low in most developing countries (in China about one-eighth of the US level). They see it as manifestly unfair that they should be expected to make cuts that would prejudice their future economic development in order to allow the richer countries to carry on with very much higher emissions rates than their own.

The only basis that would be likely to be acceptable as ethical, logical and appropriate for all countries, whatever their stage of development, would be a system of national quotas based on population. Energy is almost as basic a human need as food, air and water. If global emissions have to be restricted, it is fair that the limited amount available should be rationed on the basis of an equal entitlement for everyone. Though at first sight this might seem to be too idealistic to be practical, it is likely to be the only basis that *is* practical, for it will probably be the only feasible way of bringing in the developing countries, whose cooperation is essential.

With equal quotas per head, combined with trade in emissions entitlements, developing countries would have a strong incentive to join the scheme. It would enable them to continue their economic growth without being impeded by emissions constraints. Also, at least initially, it would give them substantial surplus quotas available for sale. The foreign exchange from these could be used for development and technical cooperation to help improve energy efficiency. At the same time, from the start, they would have an incentive to use energy efficiently and economically so as to maintain the saleable surpluses for as long as possible, and also an incentive to preserve their carbon dioxide-absorbing forests.

Industrial countries would gain from the inclusion of developing countries because their cuts would no longer be offset by rising emissions elsewhere. However, their quotas would inevitably be well below their current consumption levels, which would give them a strong incentive to make the serious cuts in their emissions that are needed. Meanwhile, they would be able to cushion the transition by buying surplus quotas from developing countries.

Organising the shift from the present quotas, based on 1990 emission levels, to the new basis of equal quotas per head, may present problems. Some, however, would diminish of their own accord. For example, with the industrialised countries making cuts and the developing countries continuing to expand their energy use, the gap between the emission levels of the two groups would narrow, thereby reducing the differences between the quotas under the alternative systems. A transitional period, with quotas based on combinations of both systems, might be necessary.

Sources of energy

For a high energy consuming country like Britain, the introduction of equal quotas per head would imply cuts in greenhouse gas emissions far more severe than the 60 per cent the IPCC urged for the world as a whole. Such cuts would require considerable changes in many areas. However, the problem is a long-term one, and it will be many years before cuts on anything like that scale would be required. Meanwhile, as part of the agreement at Kyoto, Britain is legally bound to cut emissions to 12.5 per cent below 1990 levels by 2010, but has set itself the higher voluntary target of 20 per cent. New sources of energy and changes in the ways in which it is used, should make it feasible to achieve these and even larger reductions without undue difficulty or hardship.

Britain's economy has been growing and energy consumption rising over a long period, yet emissions of greenhouse gases have been *falling*. Emissions of carbon dioxide, the main one, fell by 14 per cent between 1970 and 1990 and by a further 7 per cent between 1990 and 1995.[253] This was the result partly of more efficient use of energy, and partly of changes in the sources of energy, both of which are likely to continue.

Coal's share of total primary energy use in Britain has declined from 74 per cent of the total in 1960 to only 32 per cent in 1990 and 20 per cent in 1996,[274] and is expected to fall further still in the next few years. Natural gas, in contrast, was negligible as a source of energy in 1960, but has come to account for 24 per cent of the total in 1990, and 36 per cent in 1996,[274] and is expected to take an even bigger share in the years immediately ahead. Nuclear power, also negligible in 1960, has grown to account for 8 per cent in 1990 and 10 per cent in 1996. The share of petroleum has risen from 26 per cent in 1960 to 37 per cent in 1990, but has fallen back a little to 34 per cent in 1996. The significance of the changing shares of energy sources for greenhouse gas emissions is that, typically, petroleum gives off only about three-quarters as much carbon dioxide as coal for each unit of energy, and natural gas only a little over half as much, while nuclear power gives off none at all.

There are a number of reasons for the changes in sources of energy. Consumption of petroleum has risen steadily with the increase in motor transport, although this has been partly offset by reduced use of fuel oil for domestic and commercial heating, and in industrial processes and power

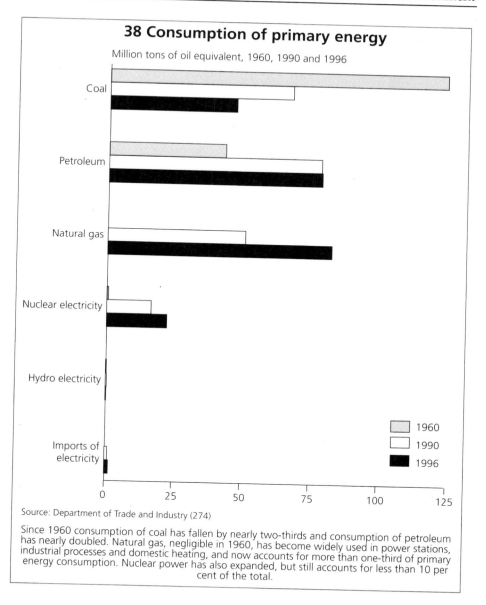

38 Consumption of primary energy

Million tons of oil equivalent, 1960, 1990 and 1996

Coal

Petroleum

Natural gas

Nuclear electricity

Hydro electricity

Imports of electricity

Legend:
- 1960
- 1990
- 1996

0   25   50   75   100   125

Source: Department of Trade and Industry (274)

Since 1960 consumption of coal has fallen by nearly two-thirds and consumption of petroleum has nearly doubled. Natural gas, negligible in 1960, has become widely used in power stations, industrial processes and domestic heating, and now accounts for more than one-third of primary energy consumption. Nuclear power has also expanded, but still accounts for less than 10 per cent of the total.

stations. Use of nuclear power has increased as more power stations have come on stream, most recently the large Sizewell B one. The availability of abundant and relatively cheap supplies of natural gas has led to its increasing use in domestic and commercial heating and in industrial processes.

Natural gas

The most spectacular recent change has been in the use of natural gas in power stations. In only six years, 1990 to 1996, the use of gas grew from less than 1 per cent to 21 per cent of the total. If plans for further new gas-fired power stations go ahead, within a few years the share of gas could rise to 50 per cent and that of coal could fall to only 15 per cent.

The reasons for the 'dash for gas' are partly political and economic and partly technical. As a monopoly supplier, the Central Electricity Generating Board had low risks and access to cheap capital. It could use a low discount rate, accept a lead time of up to ten years for the construction of power stations, and amortise the investment over two or three decades beyond that. It therefore sought to get economies of scale by concentrating on large, efficient power stations centrally located near major coal fields and on large, sophisticated nuclear installations.

After privatisation, the industry faced higher risks, dearer capital and a need to seek greater flexibility and quicker returns on investment. It therefore saw attractions in taking advantage of the greatly increased availability of natural gas and of technical advances in gas-fired plants. Modern combined-cycle units (which increase efficiency by using exhausts from gas turbines to heat water for steam turbines) can be built in only three years, require less capital investment per unit of output, can be economic on a smaller scale and, being easier to site, can be nearer to users.

Flexible siting of small-scale plants increases the scope for combined heat and power schemes. Heat that would otherwise be wasted is used for industrial, commercial or domestic heating, thereby further increasing efficiency – and bringing down greenhouse gas emissions to about one-third of those produced by coal-fired power stations.[275] At present, combined heat and power schemes represent only about 6 per cent of electricity used in Britain,[274] but they are more widely used in other countries and the switch to gas offers scope for more widespread use in Britain.

The switch from coal to gas has, however, had a serious downside. The premature phasing out of expensive mines and power stations has brought greater reliance on unreliable imports and environmentally damaging open-cast operations for remaining coal needs. The loss of 90 per cent of the remaining jobs in mining in a single decade, between 1985 and 1995, with devastating social effects on mining communities, has also brought high economic costs in unemployment and job creation.

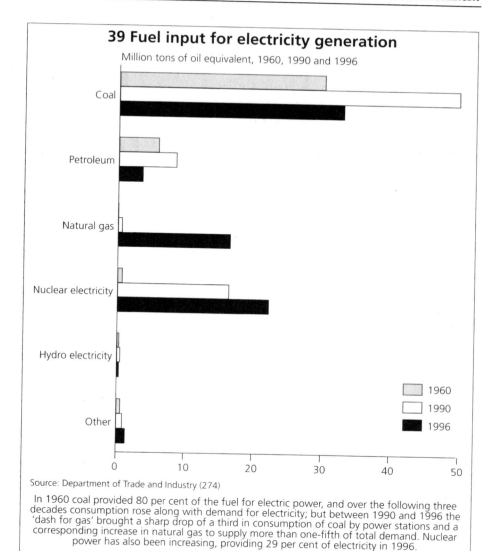

39 Fuel input for electricity generation
Million tons of oil equivalent, 1960, 1990 and 1996

Source: Department of Trade and Industry (274)

In 1960 coal provided 80 per cent of the fuel for electric power, and over the following three decades consumption rose along with demand for electricity; but between 1990 and 1996 the 'dash for gas' brought a sharp drop of a third in consumption of coal by power stations and a corresponding increase in natural gas to supply more than one-fifth of total demand. Nuclear power has also been increasing, providing 29 per cent of electricity in 1996.

Nuclear power

In the years immediately ahead, most of the reduction in greenhouse gas emissions will be achieved by shifting from high-emission to lower-emission energy sources. Later, it will be necessary to rely more on zero-emission sources.

Nuclear power stations emit no greenhouse gases at all and were seen after the war as a source of almost unlimited safe, clean and cheap energy. In the event, problems with safety, waste disposal, decommissioning and costs have belied the early promise.

The risk of catastrophic accidents in British power stations is probably very small, but difficult to quantify. The enquiries into the Chernobyl and Three Mile Island accidents both put the blame on human error – something that can happen anywhere and against which there can be no absolutely certain protection.

The International Atomic Energy Agency claims that many of the reactors in former Soviet bloc countries are unsafe and should be shut down. Though reactors in western countries are of safer design and are more reliably maintained and controlled, there have still been expressions of concern by well-informed experts. France's chief inspector for nuclear safety has estimated that there is a 1 in 20 risk of a serious nuclear accident in France in the next 20 years.[276] The former director of safety at Scottish Nuclear has warned of pressures on safety following privatisation.[277] And the former director with responsibility for safety at British Nuclear Fuels has written a book in which he claims that there is secrecy and complacency at the Sellafield reprocessing plant, where there have been numerous leaks and accidents, one of which came near to causing a 'critical incident'.[278]

Scientists at CERN (Conseil européen pour la recherche nucléaire) claim to have designed a new type of reactor which would be completely safe. However, even if it works, it is still many years away from commercial use; and the ultimate in safety, the fusion reactor, is even further off – after four decades of research, it appears still to be at least half a century away.

The second problem with nuclear power is that it generates waste. Some is highly toxic and remains so for many years, and some can be processed for use in nuclear weapons. With a view to dealing with this problem, £2.8 billion was invested in the Thorp reprocessing plant in Cumbria. It had been hoped that spent nuclear fuel could be reprocessed into uranium for reuse in power stations, and into plutonium for use in nuclear weapons programmes and in a new kind of fast-breeder nuclear power station. However, the economic justification has been undermined by cheaper alternatives for disposal of nuclear waste, by the continuing plentiful availability of uranium, and by greatly reduced demand for plutonium as a result of the scaling down of nuclear weapons programmes and the cancellation of all the fast-breeder reactor programmes as unsafe and uneconomic. Consequently, throughput at the plant has so far been far below the volumes projected.

And, in view of problems in cutting discharges of radioactive waste to 'near-zero', and doubts about the wisdom of building up stockpiles of plutonium, which could be a target for nuclear terrorists, the most appropriate future for the plant would seem to be early closure.

The third problem is that, as nuclear power stations get older, they become more prone to accidents and stoppages, need more maintenance, become less economic to run and, ultimately, need to be decommissioned. The dismantling and disposal of radioactive components is a difficult and costly process.

And the fourth problem, which in Britain has proved decisive, is costs. Despite four decades of heavy investment in research and development, power from nuclear reactors in Britain has turned out to be much more expensive than power from conventional coal-fired stations – so much so that when the rest of the electricity industry was privatised, the nuclear power stations had to be kept aside because no private investors were prepared to buy them.

When the nuclear sector was finally sold seven years later, it was only possible to get rid of it by:

- excluding the older stations with their earlier decommissioning costs;
- cancelling plans for two additional power stations, which would have cost £5.4 billion;[279]
- writing off half the debt;[280]
- adopting a higher discount rate to cut liabilities by a third;[281] and
- allowing only £16 million a year for decommissioning – less than a tenth of the amount originally considered necessary.[282]

Even then, the eight power stations in the sale together raised only £1.4 billion[283] – barely half the cost of a single power station, the most recent Sizewell B one.[283]

These problems make it unlikely that additional nuclear power stations will be built in Britain or in other western countries. The existing nuclear power stations will continue to make a useful and greenhouse gas-free contribution to energy needs for several decades to come, but their share of the total will gradually decline as older plants come to the end of their lives and are taken out of service.

Renewable energy

In the decades ahead, it will be necessary to look for an increasing contribution from renewable sources of energy. In the EU, renewables accounted for 5.3 per cent of total primary energy consumption in 1995; the European Commission has put forward proposals to increase the share to 12 per cent by 2010.[284] The World Bank postulates that, by 2050, renewables could be supplying more than 60 per cent of total world energy demand.[270]

In Britain in 1995, renewables' share of energy was only 0.7 per cent, one-seventh of the European average and the lowest of any country in the EU.[284] There is scope for substantial increases, although prospects vary greatly for different kinds of renewable energy.

Biomass

Biomass is a versatile source of energy. It can be derived from many sources, including energy crops, agricultural residues, manure, wood and wood-working residues, municipal and household waste and sewage sludge. It can be used for electric power, heat and vehicle fuel. It can be stored and production units do not need to be large to be efficient. It is at present the largest single source of renewable energy, both in Britain and the EU.

The European Commission envisages a trebling of biomass energy use in Europe by 2010, half of it from short rotation forestry and energy crops, and there appears to be scope for considerable further increases in Britain. In 1994, Austria, though much smaller than Britain, produced three times as much biomass energy, while Germany and Spain produced four times as much, Finland five times as much, Sweden seven times as much and France twelve times as much.[285]

Hydroelectricity

Hydroelectricity at present accounts for the bulk of the remainder of renewable energy both in Britain and in the EU as a whole. It is a well established and fully competitive technology. However, most of the sites suitable for large-scale schemes are already exploited and, although there is scope for wider use of small-scale projects, they are unlikely to constitute a major source of additional energy.

Britain has some of the best sites in the world with potential for tidal power, but the scale of investment needed would be very large, the payback slow and the environmental problems serious. It is unlikely to figure in any early programmes to develop renewable energy.

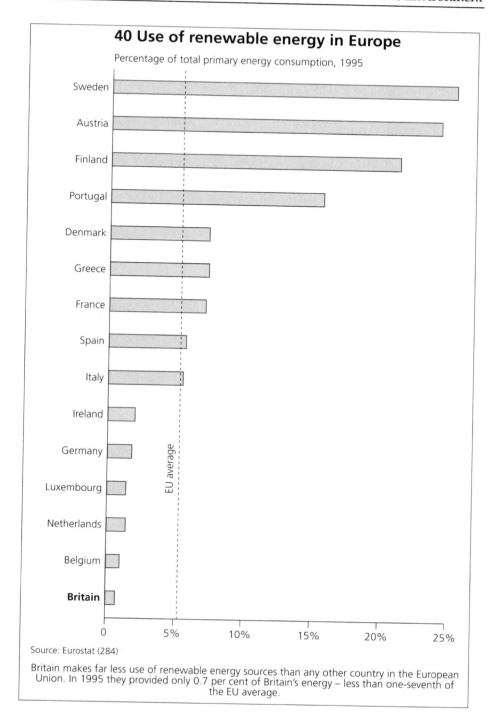

40 Use of renewable energy in Europe

Percentage of total primary energy consumption, 1995

Source: Eurostat (284)

Britain makes far less use of renewable energy sources than any other country in the European Union. In 1995 they provided only 0.7 per cent of Britain's energy – less than one-seventh of the EU average.

Windpower

The efficiency of windpower systems has been improving rapidly. Their costs have been falling sharply and, on favourable sites, they are now competitive with nuclear and coal-fired power stations, although not yet with gas. Installations in Europe have been increasing at more than 30 per cent a year.[284]

Britain has many of the best sites in Europe, and about 40 per cent of the total windpower potential of the EU.[286] If fully exploited, windpower sites in Britain could supply the whole of electricity consumption.[286] Many sites will not be exploited because of difficult access, noise, or visual intrusion on areas of natural beauty. Britain also has many excellent offshore sites and it is estimated that, after allowing for shipping and fishing, sites in water less than 30 metres deep have the potential to supply further power equivalent to total electricity demand.[286]

Wavepower

Britain also has many of Europe's best sites for wavepower and, ultimately, this could become a major energy source. However, much further research and development work is needed to establish the most efficient system. This is an area of research in which Britain had a world lead until the programme was cut back on the grounds that costs would be too high – although it subsequently transpired that costs are lower than for nuclear energy.[287]

Other renewable sources

Geothermal energy seems unlikely to become important in Britain unless new sites are discovered, and solar energy is likely to become economic first in countries with more sunshine. The costs of photovoltaic systems (in panels on walls and roofs of buildings) fell by 80 per cent between 1978 and 1991,[288] and British Petroleum (BP) scientists estimate that a further 80 per cent fall could be achieved if solar panels were produced in greater volume.[289] Even then, photovoltaic electricity would still be more expensive than electricity from conventional power stations. However, even in Britain, there is likely to be increasing scope for photovoltaics in special applications and remote locations.

There should also be scope for getting more benefit from passive solar energy. At present about 40 per cent of the heating in domestic and commercial buildings is provided by sunshine through windows,[284] and this proportion could be increased substantially at little cost, particularly in new buildings, by the use of new types of heat-retaining glass and wall materials.[284]

Changing cost differentials

The main disadvantage of most renewable sources of energy is that their costs are at present higher than for energy from gas-fired power stations, in some cases several times higher. However, with any new technology, efficiency tends to improve and costs to fall as a result of continuing research and development and large-scale use. Current cost levels for coal, gas and oil energy are the result of a century of continuous investment and considerable economies of scale.

For several of the renewables, costs have already fallen greatly, even though the investment put into their development has been on a very small scale and over a relatively short period – the World Bank estimates that total R&D expenditure on all the renewables combined has been only about one-tenth of that invested in nuclear power.[270] There seems little doubt that higher investment in developing renewables will greatly accelerate the fall in costs to more competitive levels.

Energy conservation

The shift from coal and oil to natural gas will not, in itself, be enough. The development of renewables will take time and, anyway, will have only a limited impact on the three-quarters of energy consumption that is not in the form of electricity. It will be important also to use energy more economically and in smaller quantities. There are plenty of ways in which this can be done – and some of them are likely to bring quick results at little cost.

Road transport is an area of particular importance, accounting in 1995 for 20 per cent of total carbon dioxide emissions in Britain.[253] Between 1970 and 1990, when total emissions in Britain were falling, road transport emissions doubled in line with the rise in traffic and have remained steady subsequently.[253] This is because low-emission fuels have not been generally available and because improvements in the engine efficiency of cars have tended to be offset by the fuel-increasing consequences of higher speed and performance, greater comfort and extra features, improved safety standards and more stringent environmental requirements.

Measures to reduce traffic congestion and air pollution by encouraging the use of alternatives to cars will help reduce greenhouse gas emissions – buses and trains typically have carbon dioxide emissions (per person carried) of less than half those of cars,[290] while walking and cycling generate no greenhouse gases at all. However, cars will continue to be widely used and it will be important to reduce emissions from them.

Hydrogen-powered fuel cells and other kinds of emission-free energy for vehicles may make a decisive difference – but not for many years to come – and some contribution may be expected from vehicles driven by compressed natural gas or ethanol. However, in the more immediate future, the main emphasis will need to be on reducing emissions from petrol-engined cars – for which, fortunately, there is considerable scope.

There can be savings from:

- improvements in transmission and in aerodynamics;
- smaller size – new micro city cars coming onto the market have half the petrol consumption of ordinary cars;
- lighter weight – savings of 30 per cent or more are possible from the use of new steels, new plastics and aluminium;[291]
- more efficient engines. The UK Energy Technology Support Unit estimates that a 20–30 per cent gain in average fuel efficiency could be achieved by the general use of the best engine technology currently on the market;[292] and
- new technologies. A Japanese petrol-electric hybrid car, which is already on the market, has double the fuel efficiency of similar cars with conventional engines.[291]

It may be possible to obtain more energy efficiency improvements in aviation than in road transport. It is estimated that by 2020, the fuel efficiency of new designs of aero engines may be improved by 50 per cent, and that similar savings may be achieved by advances in airframe design and by use of larger aircraft.[293] It is particularly important to ensure that these gains are achieved. Recent research suggests that, because of the different chemistry at high altitudes, the greenhouse effect of jet engines in flight is many times greater than at ground level. It now seems that aircraft may be responsible for as much as 15–20 per cent of the total global warming effect – more than road vehicles – and also that their high altitude emissions of nitrous oxides may be doing serious damage to the ozone layer.[293] It is anomalous that, while petrol and diesel fuel for road vehicles are taxed, aviation fuel for international flights is not. Ironically, the mode of transport that is most costly in terms of greenhouse gas emissions is at present given a cost advantage relative to other forms of transport.

Domestic and commercial heating also offer considerable scope for more efficient energy use. Many buildings have low-efficiency, poorly controlled heating systems. A House Condition Survey for the Department of the Environment showed that the majority of homes in Britain were inefficiently heated and badly insulated, resulting in much avoidable discomfort, ill health and waste of energy. Uprating the housing stock to the standard required by Danish building regulations would reduce total carbon dioxide emissions in the UK by 7 per cent.[294]

Household appliances also offer scope for better energy efficiency. A study by the Department of Energy[295] found that the best larder freezer, fridge freezer and chest freezer were all twice as efficient as the average on the market. Tests on fridge freezers, dishwashers, washing machines and tumble dryers by the Consumers' Association[296] found that a consumer buying the most, instead of the least, energy-efficient model of each would use less than half the energy and save more than £100 a year. A Dutch study[297] showed that, for domestic appliances in general, those using the best available technology used 40–50 per cent less electricity than the current average.

There is also scope for substantial energy savings in other areas, for example in:

- greater efficiency in industrial machinery and heat-using processes;
- the use of less energy-intensive materials;
- more extensive recycling of used products and materials;
- less intensive use of chemical fertilisers in agriculture; and
- the use of more energy-efficient lighting. Compact domestic fluorescent light bulbs are four times as efficient as traditional ones, and cost less to run.

Taken together, the various opportunities for saving energy could make a great difference at relatively little cost. A major international study[298] has estimated that if all the various energy-conservation possibilities were adopted, it would be possible for countries such as Britain to halve their consumption of energy, while maintaining current living standards.

Ensuring implementation

Thus, it is clearly possible to meet targets for reductions in greenhouse gas emissions (even ones more stringent than those contemplated at present) by a combination of using energy more economically and getting more of it from low-emission or zero-emission sources. However, the potential for improvement will not be realised in practice unless specific measures are taken to modify the normal working of market forces.

Global costs, such as those that arise from greenhouse gas emissions, are normally external to the bottom line calculations of both energy suppliers and energy consumers. Market pressures and environmental needs only occasionally and coincidentally move in the same direction, as with the 'dash for gas'. More generally, market forces push for *higher*, not lower, emissions of greenhouse gases.

Energy suppliers normally seek to maximise their profits by selling *more*, not less, and their marketing strategies, tariff structures and staff incentives are all designed to bring this about. They seek to supply their customers at the lowest possible cost to themselves, which normally means using established fuels and technologies, and keeping away from renewables, which involve more investment in R&D, a slower return, higher risks and higher initial costs.

The same applies to energy consumption. Manufacturers competing in the market aim to sell *more*, not fewer, cars, washing machines, or whatever, and plan their marketing strategies, advertising and prices accordingly. Moreover, they tend to see a competitive advantage in gearing their design and promotion to emphasise qualities such as speed, performance, luxury and size – which tend to go with higher energy consumption. Energy *economy* is seldom regarded as a selling feature.

While many consumers are concerned about environmental issues and are interested in lower energy costs, they seldom make energy economy a prime factor in their purchases, either because other considerations seem more important, or they have no information on relative energy costs, or they are not offered a choice of more energy-efficient products.

In a free market situation, suppliers and consumers tend to ignore the implications of greenhouse gas emissions. This is not because they are indifferent to environmental needs, but because environmental costs are external to the factors that weigh in market decisions. The factors that *do* carry weight normally pull in other directions. Leaving things to 'business as usual' is likely to increase greenhouse gas emissions. Bringing them down will require deliberate government measures to override the pressures of the market.

Now that electricity has been privatised, the government can no longer simply issue an instruction to change policy. However, there is much that it can do to achieve a similar outcome. It can use tradeable permits to get generators to reduce greenhouse gas emissions; it can use the powers of the regulators to get distributors to encourage economy in consumption; and it can use the fossil-fuel levy to increase investment in different kinds of renewable energy instead of subsidising a high-cost nuclear industry.

Probably the most important general measure would be a system of escalating energy taxes. There is already provision for an automatic increase in road fuel taxes of 6 per cent each year, which will double prices over a 12-year period. It has been calculated by Cambridge Econometrics[299] that if the escalator were increased to 10 per cent a year, it would reduce greenhouse gas emissions by 8 per cent over ten years; while a more broadly-based carbon tax would bring a reduction of 16 per cent. Either would bring in more than £30 billion in extra government revenue, which could be used to cut other taxes.

'Green taxes' work best if they are supplemented with regulatory measures and better information.[300] Much energy could be saved by setting minimum energy efficiency standards for industrial equipment and domestic appliances; by raising energy efficiency standards for new buildings; and by encouraging improvements in the energy efficiency of existing buildings – a start has been made with the recent lowering of VAT on insulating materials.

There are already many 'green consumers'. They would be more effective if they had better information on the energy performance of products – particularly on the energy costs per year of cars and domestic appliances. There are already many 'green companies' that undertake energy audits and consciously strive to follow best environmental practice.[301] More would be encouraged to follow suit if they had better information on the cash benefits of more energy-aware operations, and of the scale of opportunities in the environment market itself – the provision of environmental equipment and services is estimated to have amounted to about $210 billion worldwide in 1992, and is expected to grow to more than twice that size by 2010.[302]

It is important to appreciate that the adoption of the various kinds of measures needed should not involve a halt, or even a slowing down, in the pace of economic growth. A number of studies[1,299,303] have shown that total GDP would grow at almost exactly the same rate, but would change to a less energy-intensive pattern. Costs and prices in the more energy-intensive industries (particularly metal production and heavy chemicals) would be increased, bringing a fall in consumption. Costs and prices in the less energy-intensive industries (by and large the industries of the future) would be reduced, bringing an offsetting *rise* in consumption of them. This should not have much effect on the balance of payments. If, as would be likely, similar changes were being made throughout the EU, then changes in Britain would be matched by changes in our main trading partners. Even if Britain introduced higher energy taxes unilaterally – as Sweden, Norway, Finland, Denmark and the Netherlands have done already – the effect should not be great, with reduced competitiveness in some areas being largely offset by increased competitiveness in others.[303] Indeed, Britain would be exceptionally well placed to act unilaterally if other countries continued to increase their energy consumption. Falling domestic petroleum consumption would release additional North Sea oil for export, the earnings from which, it has been calculated, would be enough to offset the reduced export earnings from the energy-intensive industries.[1]

Finally, we should not suppose that 'green taxes' would necessarily be unpopular. On the contrary, people would see the point of tax changes that benefited the environment, especially if they also brought higher employment and lower taxes elsewhere. It has been calculated that, over ten years, an escalating carbon tax could generate nearly half a million extra jobs and enough revenue to halve income tax.[299,303]

7 World Population

What will be the impact of the rise in world population, and can it be averted?

In the countries of Europe there is a problem with *ageing* population as a result of *low* fertility rates. In some of the developing countries there is a problem with *rising* population as a result of *high* fertility rates. If 1990 fertility rates continued, world population would in theory quadruple by the middle of the twenty-first century. In practice, fertility rates in most countries have been falling, but even if they continue to fall, world population is likely to nearly double by 2050. This could give rise to serious shortages of food, water, minerals and energy and make it more difficult to narrow the fivefold gap in living standards between the industrial countries and the developing ones. The countries most at risk are the poorest ones with the fastest rates of population increase; but Britain and other European countries are also likely to be affected, for example through increasing immigration pressures.

In the past, in all the industrial countries rising prosperity has brought falling birth rates. Ultimately this will happen in the developing countries also, but for some of them it has not been happening fast enough. What is needed is a special programme to speed up investment in human development. Fortunately, the resources needed for this are not beyond reach – they could be mobilised by a manageable increase in the size of international aid programmes, or a better targeting of existing ones.

Population growth

Between 1650 and 1950 world population doubled twice over; between 1950 and 1990 it doubled again – the fastest rate of growth in human history. Currently, total world population is increasing by more than 80 million people (another Britain and a third) *each year*; and by more than 850 million people (another Europe and North America) each decade.[304]

UN demographers have calculated that if recent fertility rates were to continue indefinitely, total world population would, in theory, rise from 5.3 billion in 1990 to 11 billion in 2025, 21 billion in 2050, and 109 billion in

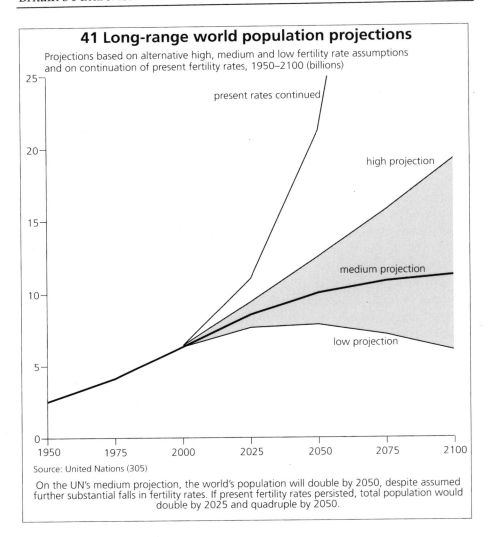

41 Long-range world population projections

Projections based on alternative high, medium and low fertility rate assumptions and on continuation of present fertility rates, 1950–2100 (billions)

present rates continued

high projection

medium projection

low projection

Source: United Nations (305)

On the UN's medium projection, the world's population will double by 2050, despite assumed further substantial falls in fertility rates. If present fertility rates persisted, total population would double by 2025 and quadruple by 2050.

2100.[305] There can be little doubt that such a twentyfold increase in population could not in practice happen. At some point, the increase in numbers would exceed the earth's maximum carrying capacity and be brought to a catastrophic halt.

Fortunately, there is no need to expect such a runaway rate of growth, since average world fertility rates are most unlikely to remain at recent levels. Fertility rates have already fallen to around the replacement level (a little more than two children per woman) in the industrial countries; and

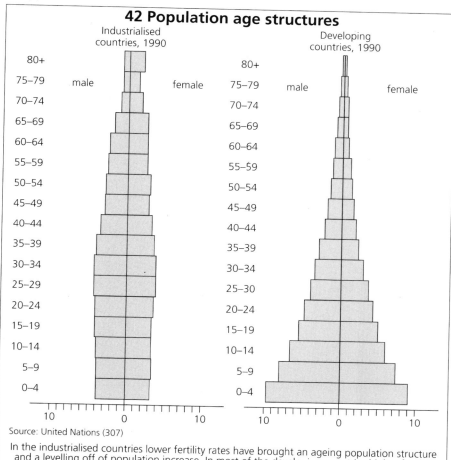

42 Population age structures

Source: United Nations (307)

In the industrialised countries lower fertility rates have brought an ageing population structure and a levelling off of population increase. In most of the developing countries higher fertility rates have brought a young population structure which gives a momentum to further population increase – even if fertility rates drop, for a time population will go on increasing as the disproportionate number of young people reach child-bearing age.

they have been falling also in many of the developing countries.[306] The crucial question is, in the countries where they are still high, how far and how fast are they likely to fall in the decades to come? A great deal will depend on the answer.

United Nations demographers have prepared three long-term projections[305] of future world population on the basis of alternative assumptions about future declines in fertility rates. They show world population rising from 5.3 billion in 1990 to either 7.8, 10 or 11.5 billion in 2050.

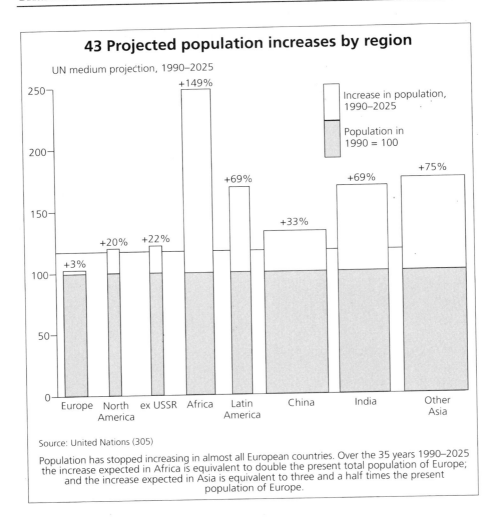

43 Projected population increases by region

UN medium projection, 1990–2025

Legend:
Increase in population, 1990–2025
Population in 1990 = 100

Bars with percentage increases:
- Europe +3%
- North America +20%
- ex USSR +22%
- Africa +149%
- Latin America +69%
- China +33%
- India +69%
- Other Asia +75%

Source: United Nations (305)

Population has stopped increasing in almost all European countries. Over the 35 years 1990–2025 the increase expected in Africa is equivalent to double the present total population of Europe; and the increase expected in Asia is equivalent to three and a half times the present population of Europe.

The low projection is based on the improbable assumption that over three decades average world fertility rates will fall by more than a third to substantially below replacement level. The high projection, although based on a 'reasonable' looking ultimate average family size of 2.5 children, gives a population increase to 28 billion by 2150, which is almost certainly more than the earth could support.

The most probable outcome is somewhere near the medium projection. Even this gives a very large increase in total population. This is because the young age structure in many developing countries,[307] with a high proportion

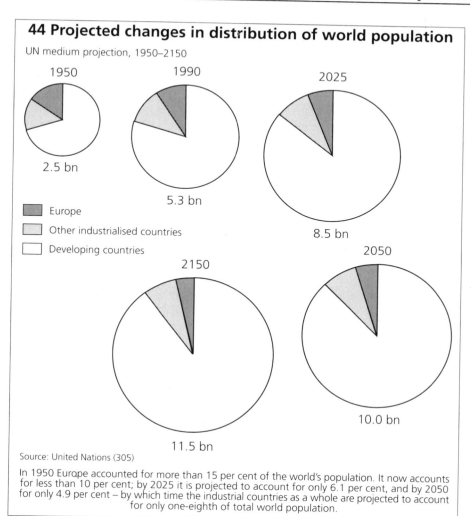

44 Projected changes in distribution of world population

UN medium projection, 1950–2150

1950 — 2.5 bn

1990 — 5.3 bn

2025 — 8.5 bn

Legend:
- Europe
- Other industrialised countries
- Developing countries

2050 — 10.0 bn

2150 — 11.5 bn

Source: United Nations (305)

In 1950 Europe accounted for more than 15 per cent of the world's population. It now accounts for less than 10 per cent; by 2025 it is projected to account for only 6.1 per cent, and by 2050 for only 4.9 per cent – by which time the industrial countries as a whole are projected to account for only one-eighth of total world population.

of people in or approaching the ages of highest fertility, means that even when fertility *rates* drop, the *size* of total population goes on rising for a while. The UN demographers have calculated that, even if from 1995 fertility rates dropped *immediately, everywhere,* to replacement level, and stayed there, the momentum built into the age structure would still push total world population up by about 2 billion by the middle of the next century.[305]

On the medium projection, world population rises from 5.3 billion in 1990, by about 3.2 to 8.5 billion in 2025; by a further 1.5 to 10 billion in 2050; and, more slowly, by a further 1.5 to 11.5 billion in 2150, when it finally stabilises – at about double its present size.[305]

These projected increases are very large and very unevenly distributed. In Europe, where fertility rates in almost every country are already around or below replacement level, the increase in population projected between 1990 and 2025 is only 3 per cent. The increases projected for North America and the former Soviet Union are only 20 and 22 per cent. In China, where earlier sharp reductions in fertility rates are expected to be maintained, the population increase by 2025 is projected to be relatively small in percentage terms (about 33 per cent), but still large in absolute numbers – more than 370 million people, an *increase* the size of the present *total* population of the EU. In other regions, fertility rates, although falling, are expected to be much higher, resulting in projected increases in population by 2025 of more than two-thirds in India, the rest of Asia and Latin America, and of nearly 150 per cent in Africa.[305]

These differential rates of increase imply major shifts in the geographical balance of world population. Between 1990 and 2025 the *increase* in population of the developing countries is projected to be nearly three times as great as the present *total* population of the industrial countries.[305] Europe's share of total world population is projected to fall from 9.4 per cent of the total in 1990 to 6.1 per cent in 2025, 4.9 per cent in 2050 and 3.7 per cent in 2150.

These changes in relative population sizes imply significant shifts between regions in the consumption of resources and in the balance of power. The great size of the total increase in population implies extra pressures on food supplies and other resources that pose a particularly serious threat to the countries with the fastest population increases.

Pressures on resources

Over a long period there have been repeated warnings that further increases in population would put excessive pressure on limited material resources and bring catastrophe. And, over a long period, the warnings have proved to be unfounded – available resources have increased to meet the needs of rising population, so far.

Food

Two centuries ago, Malthus predicted that rising population would be checked by the harsh imperative of starvation – there would be no possibility of raising food production enough to feed the extra people.[308]

Since then, he has been proved wrong twice over – world population has doubled, and doubled again, and living standards, including nutrition standards, have gone *up*, not down.

In the nineteenth century, the rise in population was mainly in Europe. The Industrial Revolution greatly increased productivity in manufacturing, and higher food production was made possible by European exploitation of previously under-used land in other continents.

Since the Second World War, world population has again doubled, this time with the increase predominantly in the developing countries. But food output has more than doubled, mainly as a result of higher productivity in agriculture.[309] In the past four decades there have been famines in particular regions where wars, political actions or natural disasters have prevented food supplies reaching the people in need of them. But there has been no *general* shortage of food – indeed, worldwide, there has been some *improvement* in average levels of nutrition.[310]

The question now is, if world population doubles again between 1990 and 2050, will it be possible to double food output again to feed the extra people? Or is there a risk that, after two centuries, Malthus's gloomy predictions will finally be fulfilled?

Area under cultivation

In previous centuries, higher food output was achieved mainly by increasing the area under cultivation. This still amounts to only about 11 per cent of the total land area of the planet.[311] However, the majority of the earth's surface is too cold, too dry, too wet, too steep or too rocky to be suitable for cultivation. Of the remainder, some is covered in forest, or in grass used for grazing, and some is used for houses, factories, mines, roads and other human developments. Of the cultivated area, some is used for non-food crops.

Much of the land not at present under crops is of poor quality, would be difficult and expensive to use, and would be likely to give much lower yields than the land already under crops. In practice, the amount of new land that has been brought into production in recent decades is relatively small and falling: an extra 4.4 per cent in the 1960s, an extra 3.3 per cent in the 1970s, and an extra 2 per cent in the 1990s.[312] The most important part, the area under grain, has actually *fallen* since 1976.[313]

In recent years, most of the increase in land under crops has been achieved by clearing land previously covered in forest.[309] Net deforestation has been clearing an area bigger than England *each year*.[314] This is presenting problems in the form of loss of future harvests of timber and other forest products; reductions in biodiversity; soil erosion; disruption of local weather patterns; and contributions to global climate change through reducing the earth's absorption capacity for greenhouse gases. It will therefore be desirable to stop reducing the area under forest and, if possible, to start *increasing* it (see Chapter 6).

At present, about 32 per cent of the earth's land surface is still not used for agriculture, pasture or woodland. However, the World Bank estimates[309] that in the period 1965–89, this 'potentially available' area was not reduced *at all* – despite the increasing demand for food.

There is also loss of quality in the land that *is* used as a result of deforestation, overgrazing, overcropping and other unsuitable practices. An area equivalent to 6 per cent of total world crop and pasture land has become severely degraded (largely destroyed) and a further 19 per cent has become moderately degraded.[315] Nearly one-third of all arable land is affected by elevated salt concentrations and new areas are being degraded faster than other soils are being rehabilitated.[309] Each decade, between 6 and 12 million hectares of cropland (an area greater than the total cropland of the United Kingdom) is lost to desertification.[316-17]

Crop yields

In the coming decades, as in the recent past ones, it seems likely that increased food output will have to come mainly from higher output from the land already in use.

Between 1950 and 1989, world grain output increased by nearly 170 per cent.[309] A major factor in that was the tenfold increase in world fertiliser consumption over the same period;[318] but since 1989, fertiliser consumption has dropped back a little, partly due to diminishing returns from additional use. In the future, there are likely to be increasing water pollution problems from high use of fertilisers and pesticides, and also from constraints on energy use – in modern high-tech grain production, for every calorie of solar energy used, there are several calories of fossil fuel energy in the form of fertilisers, irrigation, machinery, vehicles and fuel.[312]

The other main element in the 'green revolution', which saw greatly increased yields in the 1960s and 1970s, was the introduction of better varieties of plants and livestock. Higher yielding varieties of rice and wheat have been particularly important in providing food for increasing populations in Asia. However, in some of the least developed countries in Africa, root crops are the staple food, and for them the increase in yields has only been one-third as great as for grains.[309]

The scope for further major increases in yields is uncertain. Conventional methods have increased the ratio of grain to roots, stalks and leaves in plants, and produced animals that use a higher proportion of their feed to produce meat. Since plants must have *some* roots, stalk and leaves, and animals must use *part* of their feed for their general maintenance, there are limits to the further gains that can be expected from conventional breeding techniques.

With the use of biotechnology, more fundamental changes may produce more spectacular changes, but the gains are further away, more uncertain and will require substantial investment in R&D. The prospect of producing synthetic food is even more remote.

The overall impact of these developments on future food output is uncertain. One forecast,[319] made for the World Bank, suggests that average yields will continue to rise steeply in the coming decades, and in due course will probably double – but not until after the middle of the twenty-first century.

Fish

There is also the possibility of getting more food from the sea. The total world fish catch quadrupled between 1950 and 1989;[320] but since then, it has fallen back a little, and most of the main fishing grounds are already fully exploited, with yields at or near the sustainable limits.[321] In most fishing grounds within easy reach of Europe, yields have been falling because of overfishing.[321]

It may be possible to make more use of less popular species, to take more krill from polar waters and, eventually, perhaps to get food directly from plankton in surface waters. It is also probably possible to get more output from aquaculture, which already accounts for about one-eighth of the total fish catch, but further expansion may give rise to environmental problems.[322]

All in all, unless international action is taken to preserve fish stocks, the supply of food from the sea is probably more likely to decline than to increase. Moreover, fish, while rich in protein, are a poor source of *calories*, and it looks as though in the future it will continue to be necessary to rely on grains grown on land as the main source of energy for humans.

Vegetarianism

It has been suggested that the potential problem of insufficient food for rising population numbers could be avoided if everyone adopted a vegetarian diet. Only about 10 per cent of the calories in the grain fed to animals is converted into calories in the meat. Hence, if people ate the grain instead of feeding it to animals to be turned into meat, the land could then be used more efficiently, and could support far more people.

While this is true in principle, the actual advantages to be gained are in practice much less than it might at first seem. Only part of the meat consumed is produced by feeding animals with grains. Much is produced from leaving the animals to graze on pasture, often on low grade land, which, if suitable for cultivation at all, would mostly provide much less than a tenfold improvement in calorie output.

Vegetarianism has been increasing in Britain in recent years, and in some other European countries. If everyone in the industrial countries adopted a vegetarian diet, it would probably postpone the time when world food supplies would become insufficient by about 15 years.[312] On the other hand, many people in developing countries are vegetarian already through poverty; they would eat more meat if they were able to afford it. If they all adopted a Northern diet, a world food crisis would come much sooner. On current trends, the latter influence appears to be the stronger. Since 1950, world meat consumption has been rising nearly three times as fast as grain consumption.[323]

Total carrying capacity

With considerable uncertainties about long-term changes in agricultural yields, crop areas, fish supplies and diet patterns, assessments of how big an increase in world population it would be possible to feed vary greatly.[310,312,324-5]

In some ways, particularly worrying is a study[326] undertaken by scientists at Stanford University. This estimated the fundamental capacity of the planet to make use of the basic source of energy for all life – the photosynthesis that converts sunlight into living tissue in green plants, which in turn are eaten by other creatures further up the food chain. The study calculated that humans consume directly, through food, animal feed and firewood, about 3 per cent of the total photosynthetic product of the earth's land area, and also control indirectly, through the impact of our activities, a further 36 per cent. The implication is that, with a doubling of world population, we would be likely to control something more like four-fifths of it. Since there is no way to increase the total amount of sunshine, or to use more than 100 per cent of it, the possibility arises that we may be approaching the absolute limits of the earth's carrying capacity – at any rate on the present pattern of resource use.

Water

Food is not the only area in which rising world population is likely to bring problems. Another is water.

At present, available water supplies total about three times current world consumption levels.[327] This might seem a comfortable margin, bearing in mind that there is still scope for more dams and for drawing on underground supplies. However, average consumption per head has been rising, with total water consumption increasing more than twice as fast as population.[325] The amount of water made unusable by pollution is growing rapidly, and is now nearly as great as the amount of water actually used.[325] If recent trends in population, consumption and pollution continue, the global balance of fresh water will become much tighter during the next century.

Because water is expensive to transport, it is not the global balance but regional and local situations that matter most. The position is already getting difficult in some regions, particularly in the Middle East and North Africa, where annual water withdrawals already amount to more than 70 per cent of the region's total water resources.[309] A few small and rich, but lightly populated, countries – Qatar, Libya, United Arab Emirates, Yemen and Saudi Arabia[322] – are actually consuming *more* than 100 per cent of their indigenous water resources by the use of imports and desalination plants – but this way of getting round local difficulties is far too expensive for most countries.

Some countries already have a serious national water problem. Israel, for example, already uses 86 per cent of its water resources; and Egypt uses 97 per cent.[314] Many other countries have regional or local water problems – mainly difficulties providing water to fast growing cities. UN reports have warned that, by 2025, two-thirds of the world's population may be living under water stress conditions. With more than 300 major river basins crossing national boundaries, conflicts over water could replace conflicts over oil as a major cause of wars in the twenty-first century.

In most countries, the bulk of water consumption is for agricultural irrigation and industry. In Egypt, for example, only 7 per cent of total water consumption is for domestic use and, in Pakistan, only 1 per cent.[314] The main constraint on water for domestic use is in transport and in the treatment plant, not the total water resources available to draw on. When water shortages become more serious, they will be felt most strongly in agriculture, where they will act as a constraint on the further spread of irrigation. Typically, irrigation makes land two to four times more productive. Any constraint on its use will thus impede the needed increases

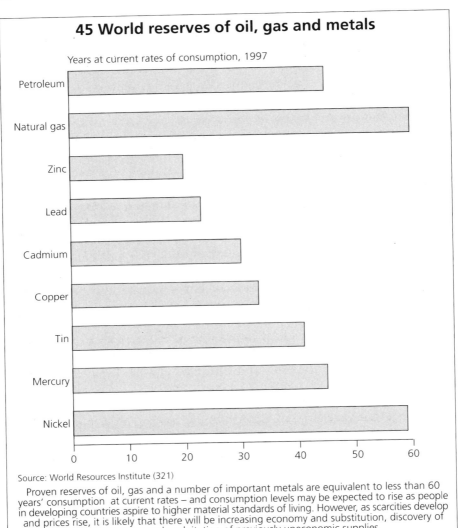

45 World reserves of oil, gas and metals

Years at current rates of consumption, 1997

Petroleum	
Natural gas	
Zinc	
Lead	
Cadmium	
Copper	
Tin	
Mercury	
Nickel	

0   10   20   30   40   50   60

Source: World Resources Institute (321)

Proven reserves of oil, gas and a number of important metals are equivalent to less than 60 years' consumption at current rates – and consumption levels may be expected to rise as people in developing countries aspire to higher material standards of living. However, as scarcities develop and prices rise, it is likely that there will be increasing economy and substitution, discovery of new reserves and exploitation of previously uneconomic supplies.

in food production. However, much of the water used for irrigation is wasted and, as water gets scarcer, there will often be scope for increasing the efficiency of use for irrigation.

Non-renewable resources

There are also likely to be problems in the longer term with some non-renewable natural resources. Proven world reserves of natural gas are equivalent to about 60 years' use at current rates of consumption, and reserves of petroleum to about 45 years.[321] Reserves are also limited for some important metals – tin 41 years, copper 33 years, cadmium 30 years, lead 23 years and zinc 20 years.[321] These periods become shorter if allowance is made for rising consumption in the industrial countries; shorter still if allowance is made for the efforts of developing countries to bring their standards of living up to those of the industrial countries; and yet shorter still if allowance is made for the expected increases in world population.

These figures almost certainly underestimate the full extent of eventual reserves. Oil and mining companies do not normally bother to explore resources for use in the distant future. Only when consumption rises are companies encouraged to explore new areas, to develop improved recovery technologies and to consider using lower grade or higher cost sources previously regarded as uneconomic. Reserves of both natural gas and oil, for example, have not only increased, but have increased even faster than consumption, so that they now represent *more* years of consumption than they did ten years ago.[328]

Prices tend to go up when a resource becomes scarce. This encourages the development and use of substitutes, greater economy in use, or, in some marginal cases, managing without altogether, thus leading to a decline in consumption. In the past, the market system has been remarkably resilient, repeatedly turning shortages into surpluses.

With an increasingly open global market economy, it is likely that the market system will keep scarcity at bay for several decades – but not indefinitely. Where world resources are finite and, with rising population and consumption levels, are being depleted at increasing rates, shortages of natural resources will at some point become a serious and intractable problem.

Living space

A further problem accentuated by rapidly rising population is urbanisation. With lack of extra land in rural areas and perceptions of opportunities in urban areas, people are moving from the countryside to the towns. In developing countries, the proportion of people living in towns has risen from 17 per cent in 1950 to 37 per cent in 1994 and a projected 41 per cent in 2000.[306,329] By 2000, there will be more than 300 cities in developing countries with populations of more than 1 million, including 17 of the largest 20 in the world.[330] In 1950, London was the second largest city in the world. Today it is not even in the top 20.[330]

Partly because of in-migration from rural areas, population in the cities in developing countries is growing at more than double the rate of total population, and accounts for 83 per cent of the total increase – currently equivalent to about 10 extra Londons *each year*.[330] According to the UN's medium projection, total urban population in developing countries is expected to increase sixteenfold between 1950 and 2025.[305,330] This compares with a fivefold increase in the urban population of the industrial countries between 1840 and 1914.[330] With a rate of increase three times as fast as in Europe after the Industrial Revolution in countries with a lower standard of economic development, there has been little time to make the necessary adaptations and build up the infrastructure and institutions required.

For people in rural areas, food, water, fuel, housebuilding materials and work are all available within walking distance. When they move to the big city, all these things have to be brought in from outside, sometimes over considerable distances. More elaborate arrangements need to be made for water treatment, sanitation, transport and other public services. With large increases in needs, and meagre resources available to meet them, provision is often inadequate. Hundreds of millions of people live in primitive shanty dwellings, crammed close together with poor services. Population density per square kilometre in Cairo is six times as high as in Birmingham, ten times as high as in Manila, and 20 times as high as in Calcutta.[329]

Global poverty

Rapidly rising population makes it difficult to raise living standards. This is a major factor in the persistence of extreme poverty for very large numbers of people. About one-quarter of the world's population subsist on incomes of less than $1 a day, do not have safe water or sanitation, do not get enough to eat, and do not have access to health services.[306] Six million children a year die of malnutrition,[331] and a further six million die from preventable diseases.[332] Some 850 million adults are illiterate[306] and 500 million people are not expected to survive to the age of 40.[306]

The North–South gap

The gap between the poverty of many developing countries and the relative affluence of many industrial countries is huge. In developing countries as a whole, average income per head (on the purchasing power parity basis) is only 18 per cent of that in industrial countries as a whole, and in the 48 least developed ones it is only 6 per cent.[306]

46 Extent of world poverty

Number of people and proportion of world total

160 million –
undernourished children

750 million – no access
to health services

840 million – adult
illiterates

1,200 million – no access
to safe water

1,300 million – living on less
than $ a day

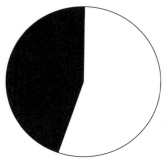

2,500 million – no sanitation

Source: United Nations (306) (331)

About one-quarter of the world's population still lives in extreme poverty.

47 The North–South gap

South as a percentage of North

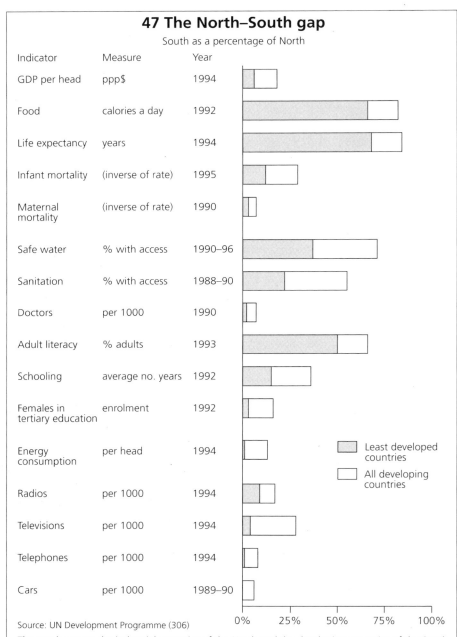

Indicator	Measure	Year
GDP per head	ppp$	1994
Food	calories a day	1992
Life expectancy	years	1994
Infant mortality	(inverse of rate)	1995
Maternal mortality	(inverse of rate)	1990
Safe water	% with access	1990–96
Sanitation	% with access	1988–90
Doctors	per 1000	1990
Adult literacy	% adults	1993
Schooling	average no. years	1992
Females in tertiary education	enrolment	1992
Energy consumption	per head	1994
Radios	per 1000	1994
Televisions	per 1000	1994
Telephones	per 1000	1994
Cars	per 1000	1989–90

Least developed countries

All developing countries

0%   25%   50%   75%   100%

Source: UN Development Programme (306)

The gap between the industrial countries of the North and the developing countries of the South is still very large. On average people in the developing countries die 16 years younger, have one-sixteenth as many doctors, have one-third of the years' schooling, have less than one-sixth of the income, use one-eighth of the energy and run one-sixteenth as many cars.

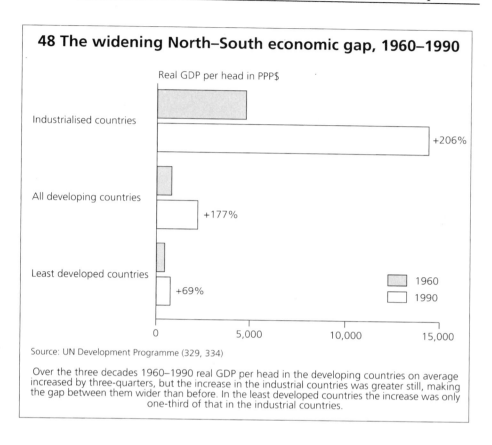

48 The widening North–South economic gap, 1960–1990

Real GDP per head in PPP$

Industrialised countries — +206%

All developing countries — +177%

Least developed countries — +69%

Legend: 1960 / 1990

(horizontal axis: 0, 5,000, 10,000, 15,000)

Source: UN Development Programme (329, 334)

Over the three decades 1960–1990 real GDP per head in the developing countries on average increased by three-quarters, but the increase in the industrial countries was greater still, making the gap between them wider than before. In the least developed countries the increase was only one-third of that in the industrial countries.

These disparities are reflected in health prospects. In developing countries, average food consumption is 18 per cent lower, access to safe water 30 per cent lower, access to sanitation 45 per cent lower, and there are 12 times as many people per doctor.[306] Infant mortality is over three times as high, maternal mortality 15 times as high and average life expectancy is 16 per cent lower.[306]

Similarly with education; the average number of years in school is one-third of that in the industrial countries, and the proportion in tertiary education is only one-seventh.[306]

And similarly with material possessions. On average, people in developing countries have only one-quarter as many television sets, one-twelfth as many telephones and one-seventeenth as many cars.

The most recent and most dramatic disparity is in AIDS. About 90 per cent of HIV-positive people are in developing countries. New drug treatments, which now help most of those infected in Europe and North America, are far too expensive for almost everyone in the developing countries, where more than 2 million people died of AIDS in 1997.

These comparisons are between two broad groups of countries that are by no means homogeneous. The countries the UN has classified as 'industrial' include not only rich countries such as Switzerland and the US, but also very poor ones from the former Soviet bloc such as Albania and Tajikistan. Those classified as 'developing' include not only some very poor ones, but also some very rich oil states and some rapidly developing countries in east Asia, where income per head is now higher than in many 'industrial' countries. Differences between the averages of industrial and developing countries are sometimes smaller than the differences between individual countries within each group.

There are also important differences *within* countries. In many developing countries, thriving industrialised sectors give some people quite high living standards in the main towns, while in the much less developed rural hinterlands living standards remain very low.

The gap between better and worse off *individuals* is thus greater than the gap between better and worse off *countries*. If allowance is made for differences in living standards *within* countries, it can be calculated that the richest 20 per cent of the world's population (living predominantly in the North) has more than 50 times the real income per head of the poorest 20 per cent (living mainly in the least developed countries of the South).[329]

Moreover, the poorest 20 per cent account for barely 1.5 per cent of world GDP, an estimated 1 per cent of world trade, 1 per cent of domestic savings, 1.3 per cent of domestic investment and 0.2 per cent of commercial lending.[329] They are therefore poorly placed to improve their situation.

Narrowing the gap

In the long term, more important than the size of the North–South gap at present is whether it is narrowing or widening. Between 1960 and 1990, the gap narrowed for nutrition levels, life expectancy, under-five mortality, literacy, and the proportion of people without access to safe water.[306] It *widened* for average numbers of years of schooling, enrolment in tertiary education, numbers of scientists and technicians, and expenditure on research and development.[306]

If GDP per head is taken as a general measure of economic standards, World Bank figures suggest that in 1989 developing countries as a whole got slightly nearer the level of industrial countries than they had been in 1950 –

but slightly further away than in 1913.[333] If the better measure of real GDP per head on the purchasing power parity basis is taken, UNDP figures suggest that between 1960 and 1990 the industrial countries as a whole increased their GDP per head by 206 per cent, but the developing countries increased theirs by only 177 per cent and the least developed countries increased theirs by only 69 per cent.[329,334] On these figures, then, it seems that the gap between the industrial countries and the developing ones has been widening slightly, while the gap between them and the *least* developed countries has been widening substantially.

Implications of the gap

If continuing increases in world population make it difficult to narrow the North–South gap, it is in developing countries that the consequences will be felt most through the continuation of widespread poverty. It is there that problems of urbanisation will be the most acute, water shortages the most serious, and any future world shortages of food the most disastrous. It is in the poorest developing countries that population is growing fastest, the limits of agricultural expansion are nearest and the need for imports of food may come soonest. These countries are the least well placed to raise agricultural productivity or pay for imports of food. For them, the consequences of continued high fertility rates could be calamitous.

For industrial countries, the implications of further rises in world population would be less extreme. They already have relatively high living standards, are largely self-sufficient in food and could afford to pay for more food imports if they needed them.

They will, however, be affected in three ways. They will have to pay more for their raw materials as non-renewable resources become scarcer. They will need to spend more on defence and peace-keeping in response to increasing conflicts over scarce resources and living space. And, as they are finding already, they will encounter increasing immigration pressures as people seek to escape from poverty and conflict in the worst afflicted parts of the developing world.

There are already about 100 million international migrants of all kinds around the world,[335] including about 17 million refugees.[336] It is estimated that during the 1980s, 7–10 million migrants entered the US and that between 1980 and 1992, 15 million migrants entered western Europe.[330]

Remittances home from migrants total about $70 billion a year globally – second only to oil in value in international flows.[330] They are an important source of foreign exchange to many countries. In 1987, they were worth more than total development aid to Colombia, Morocco, Egypt, Jordan, Tunisia and India, and paid for more than one-fifth of imports in Jordan, Pakistan, Bangladesh, Morocco and Egypt.[334]

Each year, more than 30 million extra people join the labour force in the developing countries, in addition to the 700 million already unemployed or underemployed. Each year, more people hear about life in the industrialised world through the media or from friends and relatives already there. And, each year, improvements in long-haul transport make it easier and cheaper to make the journey. Already, migration from South to North involves millions of people and is a significant item in the global economy. If population continues to grow, and this causes disparities in living standards to persist, or even become larger, pressures for migration will also grow, with ever greater numbers of people with ever greater urgency of purpose.

In most countries in western Europe and North America, immigration rules have been made much stricter, but that is unlikely to prevent an increasing volume of illegal immigration. Western Europe, with a long land frontier to the east and a narrow sea to the south is particularly easy to enter – and once into any EU country, there are increasingly few barriers to stop migrants moving on to others.

If migration pressures increase, and the policing of external frontiers proves increasingly difficult, there is the risk that the removal of the old Iron Curtain intended to keep people *in* eastern Europe may be replaced by a new Iron Curtain to try to keep people *out* of western Europe. If even that fails, there may be increasingly rigorous internal police checks to detect illegal immigrants *after* they have arrived, with damaging consequences for civil liberties and community relations.

Rising world population may be expected to hit the least developed countries hardest, but it will also seriously affect industrial countries. What are the chances of addressing the problem at its source?

Economic development

There is a clear, inverse relationship between rising population and rising living standards. In industrial countries, average fertility rates are low and living standards are high; in developing countries as a whole, average fertility rates are twice as high and average living standards much lower; and in the least developed countries, average fertility rates are more than three times as high and average living standards are much lower still.[306] A study of 82 developing countries for the United Nations Population Fund[337] found that in the 41 countries with slower population growth, incomes grew in the 1980s by an average of 1.23 per cent a year, but in the 41 countries with faster population growth, they *fell* by an average of 1.25 per cent a year.

However, the relationship between population and prosperity is a two-way one. When fertility rates are high and population is rising rapidly, it is very difficult to establish the kind of economic development that would bring higher standards of living and lower fertility rates. But, when economic development brings higher living standards, fertility rates fall and populations stop growing. This has happened in all the industrial countries and is also happening in newly-industrialising countries such as Singapore, Thailand and South Korea. What scope is there to achieve faster economic development in the developing countries so as to raise living standards and check the rise in population?

Any free market system tends to work in ways that favour economies that are already strong and make difficulties for those that are weak and in need of development. The global market system also works in a number of ways that directly impede economic development in the developing countries. Establishing a more level playing field in which to compete would greatly help their chances of breaking out of the mould of rising population and depressed living standards.

Trade

Higher exports would help pay for development. About half the export earnings of developing countries come from the sale of primary products. The prices of these have fluctuated erratically and, by 1993, had fallen to less than one-third of the peak level reached in 1951.[338] Food commodity exports are subject to import restrictions, subsidies and price support systems, such as the EU's Common Agricultural Policy. These have been costing developing countries $182 billion a year,[306] but with the reductions agreed to in the GATT Uruguay Round, will cost less in the future.

Exports of manufactures from the developing countries have increased from about 4 per cent of the world total in 1955 to 19 per cent in 1989. However, more than half these exports come from only five countries, all of them in east Asia.[329] Here too, exporters have faced unfavourable price movements. Rising tariff barriers have cost them at least $40 billion a year in lost exports and $75 billion a year (3 per cent) in lost GNP.[329]

Non-tariff barriers present an even greater problem. They affect about half the manufactured exports from developing countries, costing them an estimated $24 billion a year in lost export earnings.[329] The most important

191

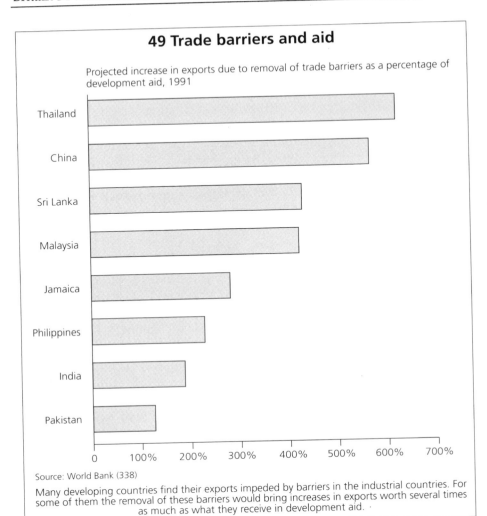

49 Trade barriers and aid

Projected increase in exports due to removal of trade barriers as a percentage of development aid, 1991

Thailand
China
Sri Lanka
Malaysia
Jamaica
Philippines
India
Pakistan

0   100%   200%   300%   400%   500%   600%   700%

Source: World Bank (338)

Many developing countries find their exports impeded by barriers in the industrial countries. For some of them the removal of these barriers would bring increases in exports worth several times as much as what they receive in development aid. ·

barrier has been the Multi-Fibre Arrangement (MFA), which limits exports of textiles and clothing. The phasing out of this and other changes agreed to in the GATT Uruguay Round will probably increase manufactured exports from developing countries by around $35 billion a year[329] – equivalent to more than half the bilateral aid from all the OECD countries combined.[339]

If *all* trade barriers were removed, there would be substantial increases in exports of manufactures. It is estimated that exports from South Korea, Jamaica, Thailand, the Philippines and India would be likely to rise by more than one-third; from Pakistan by more than a half; and from Bangladesh and Sri Lanka by more than 100 per cent.[338] For a number of countries, the increase would be worth more than the total development aid they receive.[338]

Investment

There has been very little private foreign investment for much of the postwar period, but it has increased greatly in recent years. In 1995, it rose to a total of $184 billion,[314] equivalent to more than three times the total of aid from OECD countries in that year.[339] In 1995, however, 63 per cent of private investment went to just seven countries – all of them, except China, among the more developed ones – and only 5 per cent went to the least developed ones.[314] In many countries, the benefits of direct inward investment have been more than offset by the drain of personal flight capital. Total outward flows averaged more than double the rate of inward direct private investment between 1977 and 1988, when they reached a peak of $80 billion.[338]

Interest and debt

Most developing countries greatly need more capital, but industrial countries dominate world market finance. Developing countries have to pay much higher interest rates on what they borrow – at a cost to them that is estimated to be about $120 billion a year, which is more than double the value of total development aid.[329] On average, debt servicing costs mop up 20 per cent of their export earnings.[306]

High interest rates, unwise lending and unwise (or corrupt) borrowing have combined to cause a dramatic build-up of the international debts of developing countries. These have risen from $100 billion in 1970 to $1444 billion in 1994 – equivalent to 38 per cent of their GNP, and for the least developed ones 106 per cent.[306] In 31 countries the total debt is greater than a whole year's GNP, and in five of them greater than three years' GNP.[306]

Reduced lending and increased debt servicing costs transformed average net transfers from richer to poorer countries of $21 billion a year between 1972 and 1982 into average net transfers *from* poorer countries *to* richer ones of $21 billion a year between 1983 and 1990.[329] Subsequently, net transfers have become positive again, but for many countries high debt interest payments remain a crippling burden. In 1995 developing countries paid out three times as much in debt interest payments as they received in international aid.[340]

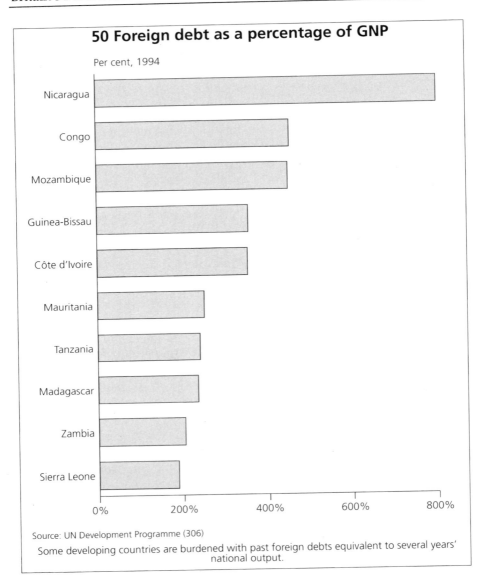

50 Foreign debt as a percentage of GNP

Per cent, 1994

Source: UN Development Programme (306)

Some developing countries are burdened with past foreign debts equivalent to several years' national output.

Other market factors

In addition to problems with terms of trade, trade barriers, capital flows, interest rates and debt, developing countries have also been disadvantaged in their trade in services, estimated to cost them $20 billion a year;[329] in technology transfer, estimated to cost them a further $20 billion a year;[329] and

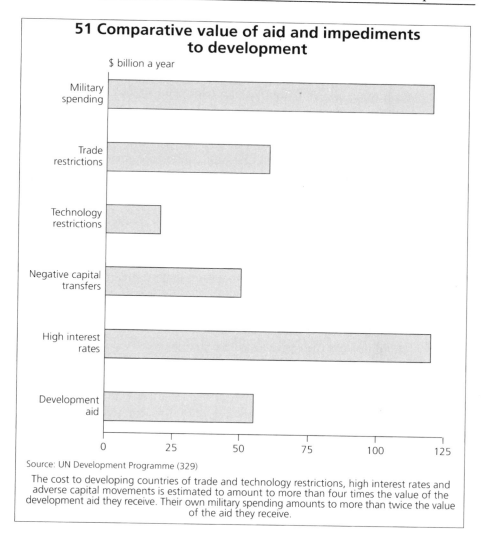

51 Comparative value of aid and impediments to development

$ billion a year

- Military spending
- Trade restrictions
- Technology restrictions
- Negative capital transfers
- High interest rates
- Development aid

0   25   50   75   100   125

Source: UN Development Programme (329)

The cost to developing countries of trade and technology restrictions, high interest rates and adverse capital movements is estimated to amount to more than four times the value of the development aid they receive. Their own military spending amounts to more than twice the value of the aid they receive.

in restrictions on the free movement of labour, which, on UNDP estimates, costs them as much as all the others combined.[32]

The world free market is not as 'free' as it might be. The various barriers and distortions operate to the serious disadvantage of the developing countries struggling to achieve faster economic growth. The total cost of these imperfections in the market is reckoned to be at least four times as great as the total value of international development aid.[329] If they could be reduced, the pace of development would be materially speeded up.

Governance

Even more important than removing the anomalies in the world market system that impede economic development, would be the removal of impediments within the developing countries themselves. The quality of governance is the key factor in any country's development.

The first and most obvious need is for stable, competent government. Studies have shown that stable government is the most important single requirement for inward private investment and subsequent expansion.[341] The claim that 'stability' demands authoritarian governments to give a 'firm lead' and make 'hard choices' is, in the words of the World Bank, 'patently false'. The evidence from many different countries does not endorse the notion that despotic governments are more successful in achieving economic growth, or that democratic rights and civil liberties present an obstacle to growth.[333] On the contrary, longer term stability and deeply based growth require the popular support and participation that go with a free society.

Nor are the extreme disparities in income distribution the price that has to be paid for rapid economic growth. On the contrary, World Bank studies have shown that, 'if anything, it seems that inequality is associated with *slower* growth'.[333] Many of the countries with the *fastest* economic growth – South Korea, Singapore, Taiwan and Hong Kong – are among those with the *least* income inequality, and many of those with the *slowest* growth – Venezuela, Peru, Ivory Coast – are among those with the *most* income inequality.[333]

The most important features of good governance are sensible economic policies and fair and efficient administration. In some countries, corruption is endemic at every level, particularly at the top. Huge sums have been spent on royal palaces and presidential yachts, and substantial parts of the wealth of several nations have been diverted to private foreign bank accounts. Under these conditions, whatever development resources are poured in tend to flow out through the holes in the sieve and leave little lasting benefit.

The misuse of resources is not confined to corrupt dictatorships. In other countries, too, resources are not necessarily used to best advantage. Administrations can be inefficient because of poor organisation, unclear objectives or lack of adequately trained staff. Even in the most democratic countries (in aid donor countries too), weak politicians have been known to favour 'prestige' projects – big, spectacular, state-of-the-art developments that can be seen and admired, and where the politicians commissioning and opening them can be seen and admired with them. There is a chronic temptation to put funds into international airports rather than rural roads, into huge hydroelectric schemes rather than village-level power and irrigation projects, into world-

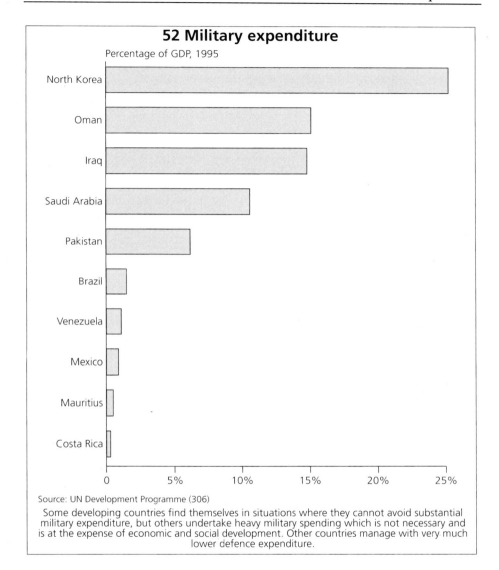

52 Military expenditure

Percentage of GDP, 1995

Source: UN Development Programme (306)

Some developing countries find themselves in situations where they cannot avoid substantial military expenditure, but others undertake heavy military spending which is not necessary and is at the expense of economic and social development. Other countries manage with very much lower defence expenditure.

class university departments rather than primary education, into high-tech hospital facilities rather than local clinics, and into 'modern' industry rather than unglamorous agriculture.

One of the most important considerations of all is the allocation of resources in government budgets. In some countries, public expenditure on health and education accounts for more than 10 per cent of GDP, in others for under 5 per cent.[306] In some countries, less than 1 per cent of GDP goes into military expenditure, while others spend more than 10 per cent, and some spend more on defence than on health and education combined.[306]

Human development

Fertility rates in some developing countries have dropped by as much as two-thirds over the past three decades, yet in others they remain as high as three times replacement level. The need is to bring fertility rates down and living standards up in this second group of countries as well. General economic development will eventually bring these down, but that will take too long. What is needed is a programme that focuses specifically on investment in *human* development.

The UNDP – a highly experienced operator in this field – has identified four key areas in which carefully targeted investment will bring disproportionate benefits in terms of improving welfare and lowering fertility rates. They are family planning, girls' education, water and sanitation, and basic health services. The specific proposals for what investment is needed and what it will cost have been put forward by the world's leading development financier – the World Bank. Its hard-headed economists have prepared a package to show the most cost-effective way to invest development funds.

The World Bank's Human Development Package[309,342]

Additional investment proposed (in $US billion a year)	
7	Family planning
2.4	Education for girls
10	Water and sanitation
35	Primary health
54.4	Total

The four areas for investment constitute an interlocking programme for development, which will work in three different ways.

- They will address head-on the most acute human problems of the South (poverty, malnutrition, sickness and ignorance) and effectively narrow the North–South gap in areas where it is most painful and indefensible.
- They will bring a high, sure and early economic return.
- They will have a decisive effect on fertility rates and make it possible to stabilise world population sooner and at a lower level.

Family planning

Family planning is the most directly and obviously relevant way of achieving population stabilisation. However, even if it had no influence on population levels at all, it would still be enormously worthwhile for its benefits to the health and standing of women, to the health and education of their children, and to the income and living standards of their families.

Access to safe contraception is the most effective way of reducing the 200,000 deaths each year from abortions.[343] It also helps women avoid pregnancies too early or too close together – offering the possibility of cutting child mortality by a quarter and saving as many as 200,000 lives a year from maternal mortality.[344] Poor families with fewer and more widely spaced children spend more per child on food;[345] they have taller, healthier children who get more parental attention, go to school for longer and do better while they are there.[334,346] Families with fewer children in rural areas have the use of more land per head, and in all areas have more living space and more income per head, with all the advantages associated with these.[331,347]

The desired family size is declining in many countries,[343] and the use of family planning has grown from less than 10 per cent of married couples in developing countries in 1950 to more than 50 per cent today.[306] Many women, however, still do not have access to modern family planning services. It is estimated that they are available to only 9 per cent of women in sub-Saharan Africa and to only 13–25 per cent in the Arab states.[330,348]

Nearly all governments in developing countries now provide support for family planning.[343] This has been a major factor in bringing down fertility rates without recourse to coercive methods – by two-thirds between 1960 and 1990 in Hong Kong, South Korea, Mauritius and Thailand, and by a half in Guyana, Colombia, Cuba, Costa Rica, Jamaica, Sri Lanka and Mexico.[334]

At present, the governments of developing countries cover about 80 per cent of the costs of their family planning services. Overseas aid covers the remaining 20 per cent – which amounts to less than 2 per cent of all development aid. Even if the *whole* of the increase proposed by the World Bank were funded out of overseas development aid, the extra would represent only about 12 per cent of the present total aid budget.[339]

Education of girls

The second key priority area is education, particularly basic education, and particularly for girls. Education is one of the areas in which the North–South gap is widest, particularly in the least developed countries. Investment in

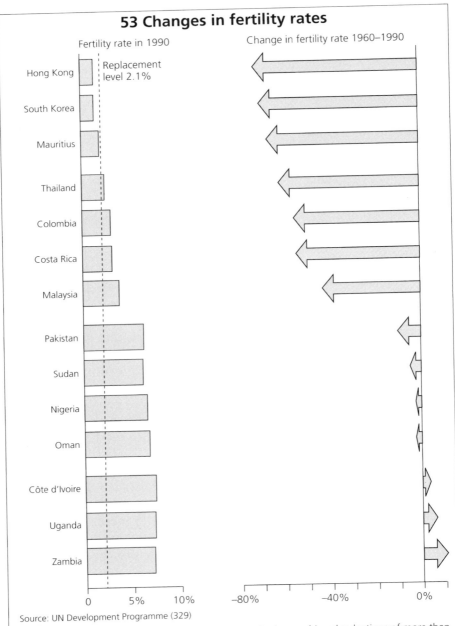

53 Changes in fertility rates

Fertility rate in 1990 — Change in fertility rate 1960–1990

Source: UN Development Programme (329)

Over the past three decades, some developing countries have achieved reductions of more than two-thirds in their fertility rates, bringing them down to below replacement level; and some have achieved reductions nearly as great, although their fertility rates are still somewhat above replacement level; but some countries have achieved no significant reduction, or even experienced a small increase, and their fertility rates are still at more than three times replacement level.

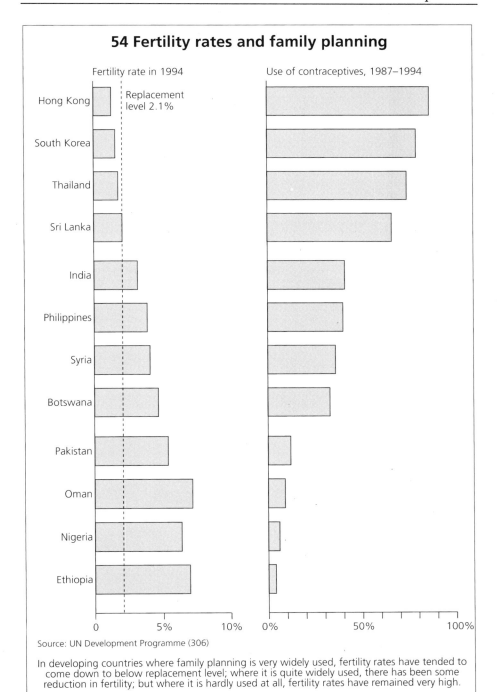

54 Fertility rates and family planning

Fertility rate in 1994

Use of contraceptives, 1987–1994

Hong Kong — Replacement level 2.1%

South Korea

Thailand

Sri Lanka

India

Philippines

Syria

Botswana

Pakistan

Oman

Nigeria

Ethiopia

0   5%   10%   0%   50%   100%

Source: UN Development Programme (306)

In developing countries where family planning is very widely used, fertility rates have tended to come down to below replacement level; where it is quite widely used, there has been some reduction in fertility; but where it is hardly used at all, fertility rates have remained very high.

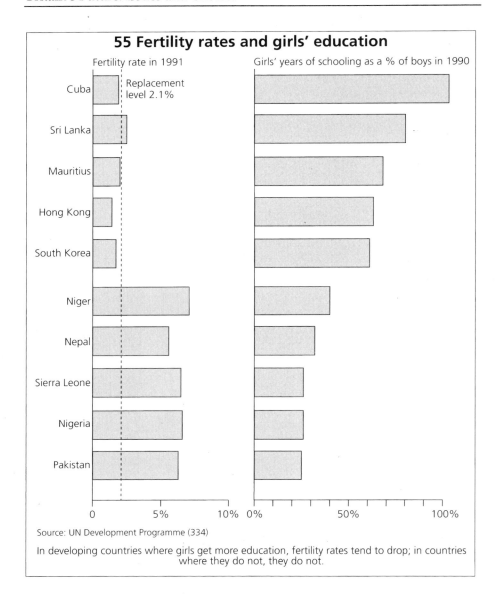

55 Fertility rates and girls' education

Fertility rate in 1991 — Girls' years of schooling as a % of boys in 1990

Cuba — Replacement level 2.1%

Sri Lanka

Mauritius

Hong Kong

South Korea

Niger

Nepal

Sierra Leone

Nigeria

Pakistan

0   5%   10% 0%   50%   100%

Source: UN Development Programme (334)

In developing countries where girls get more education, fertility rates tend to drop; in countries where they do not, they do not.

education is crucially important for improving life opportunities. It can also be expected to yield a high return in terms of economic development and population stabilisation.

Research for the World Bank suggests that GDP is raised by 9 per cent for each of the first three years of education of the labour force, and a further 4 per cent for each of the next three years, giving a total increase of 39 per cent in GDP for the first six years of education.[333] The World Bank concludes, 'The evidence that education promotes economic growth, and thus puts other goals of development within reach, is firm.'[333]

Of particular importance is education for girls, who in developing countries as a whole have an average of only 58 per cent of the years of schooling of boys, compared with 99 per cent in the industrial countries.[334]

Poor education is a major factor in women's low social and economic status in many developing countries. The International Labour Organisation has identified it as the 'single most important reason for the persistence of widespread poverty and continued high population growth'.[330,349]

Better education for girls helps them get jobs and makes them more productive. They are better paid in the work they do and so make a bigger contribution to the economy.[330,333] The higher incomes of educated women help them to afford to send their children, particularly their girls, to school, so that their children, and later their children's children, reap the rewards of a better education.[350] Reducing female illiteracy also has important social benefits. It enables women to read medicine labels, seed catalogues, equipment instructions, public notices and advertisements in shops and newspapers.[351]

The advantages to health are particularly important, for a better education for women is associated with lower infant and child mortality rates.[342,352] As the World Bank puts it:[33] 'The educational status of adult women is by far the most important variable explaining changes in infant mortality and secondary enrolments. An extra year of education for women is associated with a drop of 2 percentage points in the rate of infant mortality.'

The reduction in infant mortality associated with women's education, which might be expected to lead to higher fertility, in practice has the reverse effect – improvements in child survival increase the predictability of the family's life cycle and reduce pressures for additional births as insurance against children dying early.[353]

Finally, better education for girls has a marked impact on fertility. Better-educated women are more likely to be aware of the advantages of family planning, to understand contraception and to use it.[333] Girls who stay in education longer tend to marry later and to start their families later, thus reducing the length of their child-bearing life span.[353]

Educated women have better job opportunities and this too gives them an incentive to control the size and spacing of their families. Having an independent income, together with the knowledge and status provided by education, give women more say in family decisions, including decisions about how many children they should have and when.

The United Nations Population Fund has concluded that: 'Equal access to education for girls and women is one of the most critical components in efforts to reduce poverty and high fertility.'[30]

The World Bank, after a special study of the economic effects of investment in education, has claimed that: 'Improving education for girls may be the most important long-term environmental policy in the developing world.'[33]

The World Bank proposes that $1 billion should be invested to raise girls' enrolment rates to match those of boys in primary schools, and a further $1.4 billion in doing the same in secondary schools. The World Bank's former chief economist has calculated that this would bring a return of over 20 per cent – about four times the return on new power stations. He reckons that 'this may well be the single most influential investment that can be made in the developing world.'[54]

Water and sanitation

The third priority – to provide water and sanitation – addresses an area of particular deprivation in developing countries. The UNDP estimates that about 1.2 billion people still lack a safe water supply and about 2.5 billion have inadequate sanitation facilities.[306] While estimates here cannot be precise, there can be no doubt that these figures represent a huge burden of human suffering.

The United States Agency for International Development (USAID) has analysed the findings of about 100 studies on the impact on health of improvements in water supplies and sanitation, and found that they are associated with major reductions in the most common diseases.[355] The World Bank estimates that improvements in water supply and sanitation could result in 300 million fewer people with roundworm infection and 150 million fewer with schistosomiasis.[309] It would save 2 million deaths from diarrhoea each year among children under five.[309]

It would also bring economic gains in the form of lower demands on health services, higher productivity from a healthier labour force and more general economic savings. It would bring savings in supply costs – a study of 16 cities has shown that resort to vended water from private buyers typically costs 12 times as much.[309] It could end the regressive effects on income distribution that can arise from the lack of safe public water supplies. For example, poor people in Lima pay ten times as much per litre for contaminated water collected in buckets as do middle-class people with water piped into their homes by the publicly subsidised water company.[342]

The World Bank estimates that investment of an extra $10 billion, combined with efficiency reforms, would give everyone safe water and reduce by 2 billion the number without adequate sanitation.[309] This investment is equivalent to only 0.7 per cent of developing countries' gross investment,[309] and less than one-fifth of international development aid at present levels.[339] The World Bank commends it as offering 'high economic, social and environmental returns'.[309]

Health services

Improving basic health services is the fourth area for priority attention. Developing countries have 12 times as many people per doctor as OECD countries, and the least developed ones have 38 times as many.[306] Developing countries spend only 6 per cent as much per head on health as industrial countries, and the least developed ones spend less than 1 per cent as much.[342]

There is no immediate possibility of countries in the South being in a position to spend anywhere near as much per head on health as richer countries in the North – particularly since spending in the richer countries is still rising fast. Significant benefits can, however, be achieved by targeting health investment in developing countries on areas where it will make most impact. Primary preventive health care typically costs $100–500 per life saved, while curative treatment costs $500–1000.[356] Yet, many developing countries spend 80 per cent or more of their health budgets on expensive hospitals with sophisticated treatments, when investment in rural clinics would give better value for money.

The World Bank has made a major study[342] of the economics of investment in health in developing countries, with a systematic analysis of the disease burden, of its economic implications and of the cost effectiveness of different kinds of health investment. It has found that the two most cost-effective kinds of spending are in public health (programmes of inoculation, school health, tobacco and alcohol control, prevention of sexually transmitted diseases, provision of health and nutrition information, and so on), and in certain essential clinical services, mostly at the primary level (tuberculosis treatment, antenatal and delivery care, treatment of infections, and so on).

It considers that major improvements in health care can be achieved by increasing average expenditure on the former from a little over $1 per head per year to $5, and on the latter from about $5 a head to $10, at a total cost of $35 billion.[342]

Since *total* public health expenditure in developing countries is only about $21 per head, this would, if total spending were unchanged, leave only about $6 a head for all other public health expenditure. Such a large transfer would not in practice be possible, and therefore most or all of the extra expenditure would need to come from additional resources. If the *whole* of the cost of the proposed health improvements were additional, and if *all* of it were funded out of international development aid, the cost would be equivalent to more than half of total present spending on development aid.[339]

Development aid

If general economic development is too slow, can international aid fund the investment in human development needed to end world poverty and slow down the rise in world population? It so happens that the cost of the World Bank package of human development measures is almost exactly the same as the current value of the overseas assistance programmes of the OECD countries.[309,339,342] It follows that it would be possible, in principle, to fund a package of this kind, either by doubling the size of the present aid programme, or by devoting a programme of the existing size entirely to it, or by some combination of the two.

The target size of the OECD countries' international assistance was set many years ago at 0.70 per cent of their GNP. This was reaffirmed at the Rio de Janeiro conference in 1992. However, the target level has never been reached. During most of the 1980s and 1990s, international aid was running at a little below half the target level, and in 1996 it fell to barely more than one-third of it, at 0.25 per cent of GNP.[339]

The present level represents less than 2 per cent of government expenditure in the OECD donor countries,[357] and is small in relation to other kinds of expenditure. OECD countries spend three times as much on agriculture, ten times as much on defence, and many times more on supporting welfare in their own countries.[306] The agreed target of 0.70 per cent of GNP is by no means an impossible objective: four countries – Denmark, Norway, the Netherlands and Sweden – already exceed it, and have done so for many years.[339]

The difficulty is with the other countries. The largest contributions are from countries with the largest economies – Japan and the US – which provide 17 per cent and 16 per cent of the total respectively. As a percentage of GNP, however, their contributions are the lowest of all OECD countries – 0.20 per cent and 0.12 per cent respectively. If every country were to meet the agreed target of 0.70 per cent of GNP, large increases would be required from most countries, including an increase of 159 per cent from Britain. Japan would have to provide three and a half times as much as in 1996, and the US nearly six times as much. Increases of this order of magnitude, however desirable, do not seem likely to be provided in the years immediately ahead.

On the analogy of income tax, where richer people pay tax at higher rates, it has been suggested that it would be fairer to have a mildly progressive basis for international aid, with an average of 0.70 per cent of GNP, but with richer than average countries contributing a slightly higher percentage of their GNP, and less rich ones paying a slightly lower percentage. The effect of this (shown in the lighter, lower bars in the second chart) is that some countries, such as Britain and Italy, would not have to provide such large increases. However, for Japan and the US, the required increases would be greater than with a flat rate of 0.70 per cent. A progressive scheme of this kind, though fairer as an ultimate objective, seems even less likely to be achieved in the near future.

If all countries find it difficult quickly to achieve the target to which they have pledged themselves, there is more immediate scope for using the aid that is already being provided to better effect. Existing programmes mostly take forms that are ill suited to the objectives of improving welfare and reducing fertility.

Only about one-quarter of international aid goes to the least developed countries.[306] Some countries with moderately high living standards receive high levels of aid, while other countries that are exceptionally poor receive very low levels of aid.

Much aid is tied to the donor country's goods and services, which are not always the most suitable or the best value. This reduces the average value of the aid to the recipient country by about 15 per cent.[338]

Only a small part of total aid is spent on the most relevant projects. Less than 15 per cent goes on social development, and less than 7 per cent on the four areas the World Bank has identified as being of key relevance.[329]

Many aid programmes are seen partly, or even mainly, as vehicles for furthering the donor countries' interests in promoting exports, securing construction contracts, gaining military advantages, or furthering foreign policy objectives. It is not surprising that so much aid is spent on grandiose 'prestige' projects that offer scope for patronage, photo opportunities or political advantage, when smaller, more dispersed and less conspicuous projects would have had more impact on welfare. It is also not surprising

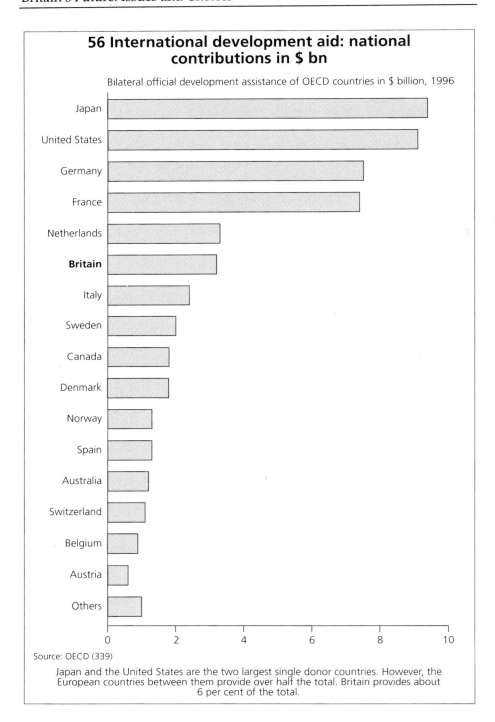

56 International development aid: national contributions in $ bn

Bilateral official development assistance of OECD countries in $ billion, 1996

Source: OECD (339)

Japan and the United States are the two largest single donor countries. However, the European countries between them provide over half the total. Britain provides about 6 per cent of the total.

57 International development aid as a percentage of GDP

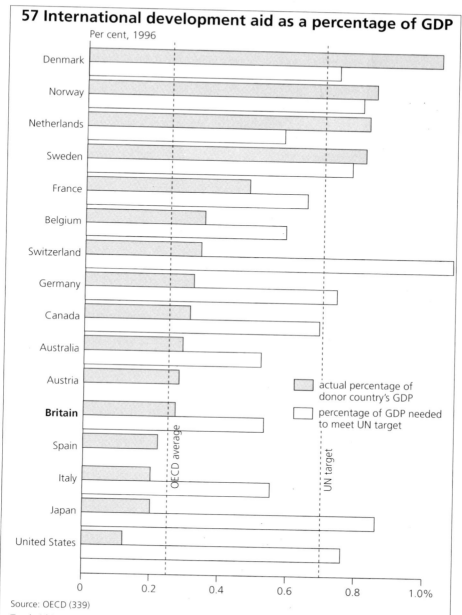

Per cent, 1996

Source: OECD (339)

Total aid in 1996 was equivalent to only about 0.25 per cent of the combined GDP of the donor countries – far short of the UN target of 0.7 per cent of GDP. Britain provided about the OECD average, the Nordic countries and the Netherlands far more, and Japan and the United States far less. To meet the UN target (on a mildly progressive basis) Britain would have to provide twice as much, Italy and Germany more than twice as much, Switzerland three times, Japan four times and the United States six times as much.

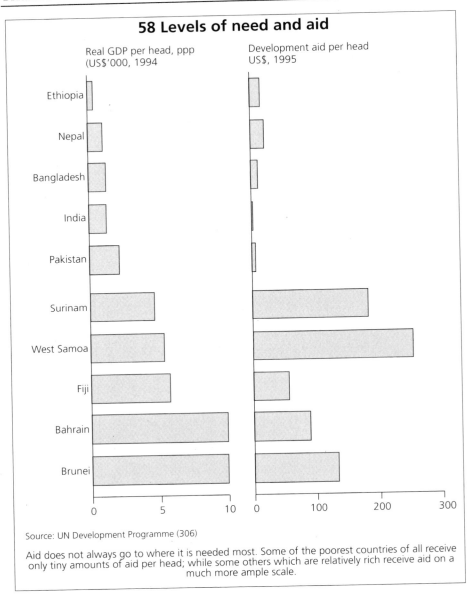

58 Levels of need and aid

Real GDP per head, ppp
(US$'000, 1994

Development aid per head
US$, 1995

Ethiopia

Nepal

Bangladesh

India

Pakistan

Surinam

West Samoa

Fiji

Bahrain

Brunei

0   5   10   0   100   200   300

Source: UN Development Programme (306)

Aid does not always go to where it is needed most. Some of the poorest countries of all receive only tiny amounts of aid per head; while some others which are relatively rich receive aid on a much more ample scale.

that some aid is wasted on governments that are corrupt, incompetent or extravagant in military expenditure.

However, some donor countries already allocate a much higher proportion of their aid to relevant projects. There is growing awareness that if aid programmes were targeted more purposefully, they could make a much bigger impact. In 1995, the World Summit for Social Development adopted a 20:20 strategy under which 20 per cent of donor countries' aid programmes and 20 per cent of recipient countries' national budgets were to be devoted to social development. In 1996, donor countries agreed to aim by 2015 to reduce the numbers in poverty by half, to reduce child and infant mortality by two-thirds, to reduce maternal mortality by three-quarters, and to ensure universal access to primary education and to family planning. In 1997, in Britain, the new government produced a white paper on international development[358] that put the emphasis firmly on the promotion of human welfare; and provision has been made to increase spending by a quarter in the last three years of the parliament.

Rising world population is the cause of, and is caused by, enormous and intractable problems in developing countries, which potentially could damage Britain and bring catastrophe to other parts of the world. They will not be solved overnight. General economic development will take time – probably too much time. Meanwhile, a targeted programme of investment in four key areas of human development should make a decisive difference. Fortunately, the resources required for this are not impossibly large. A manageable increase in the scale of aid and a decisive shift in its direction should be enough. What is needed is clarity of understanding and firmness of purpose. The stakes are high.

8 Security

What will be the threats to security in the twenty-first century, and will there be scope for a peace dividend?

The cold war is over and there is no way it could be restarted. Britain currently faces no risk at all of external attack and is more secure than at any time since the war. This provides a window of opportunity for pre-empting longer-term threats that could arise from the proliferation of both nuclear and conventional weapons.

In the coming post-cold war decades, Britain's main military need will be for the capability to intervene effectively in conflicts in eastern Europe and to take part in peace-making and peace-keeping operations in other parts of the world. For this, the forces required will be relatively small in number, but will need to be highly trained, highly mobile and increasingly closely integrated with the forces of other EU countries.

This will mean giving up the scaled-down cold war defence posture of the past few years, and restructuring the defence effort to meet the needs of future decades instead of past ones. It will give Britain more clout for less cash, releasing substantial resources for better uses.

The end of the cold war

For four decades after the end of the Second World War, western military dispositions and strategic thinking were dominated by the threat of a Soviet invasion of western Europe. The *potential* threat was real enough. East German army documents found after reunification show that the armoured divisions in East Germany were ready for action at 24 hours' notice and there were plans for a blitz to overrun western Europe in a matter of days, using nuclear and chemical weapons from the start.[359]

The likelihood of such plans being put into effect steadily receded as the years went by. But the Soviet Union's capability to launch a massive invasion at short notice compelled NATO (North Atlantic Treaty Organisation) countries to keep substantial and heavily equipped forces deployed in West Germany, and to build up a nuclear arsenal with an awesome 'overkill' to ensure a second-strike capability and MAD (mutually assured destruction.) The ending of the war has completely transformed this situation.

With the collapse of communism, the clash between the opposing ideologies ended and, as long ago as 1990, the NATO summit agreed that the Soviet Union should no longer be seen as an adversary.[360] However, democracy in Russia is neither perfect nor secure. There were attempted coups seeking to restore the old system in 1991 and 1993, and the results were close in the elections of 1993 and 1997. Economic decline, social disruption and a weaker role in the world have brought widespread hardship, disillusion and discontent. While the balance of probability is that democracy will survive and improve in Russia, there is a chance, particularly in the next few years, that a less friendly, or even actively hostile, government will come to power.

Military planners have to provide for worst-case eventualities. However, even with an unfriendly government, Russia would not be a threat because since 1989 the balance of military power has changed fundamentally and irreversibly.

The satellite countries of eastern Europe have left the Warsaw Pact and some have joined NATO. The Soviet Union itself has broken up. Of the newly separated republics, only one, Belarus, has remained close to Russia. The others are concerned to maintain their independence and are suspicious of Russian intentions towards them, particularly as some have large Russian minorities. None of them would be likely to join Russia in any attack on western Europe, and some could actually find themselves in conflict with Russia.

Russia itself, which accounts for only about half the former Soviet Union and about one-third the former Warsaw Pact forces, has had its military capabilities further reduced by a succession of defence cuts. The army is down to less than a third of its 1988 size,[361] and is being cut further. This shrunken force, weakened by officers left unpaid and conscripts failing to report, lacks the morale and effectiveness it once had, as the fighting in Chechnya demonstrated. The Red Army is also 1000 kilometres further away than it was.

The CFE (Conventional Forces in Europe) treaty provided for rough parity between NATO and Warsaw Pact forces in Europe by November 1995. This required more Warsaw Pact than NATO cuts. Now that the Warsaw Pact no longer exists, under the terms of the treaty Russia is allowed only half the former Warsaw pact total.

The balance of forces in Europe has been reversed. Whereas previously, the Warsaw Pact had a strong superiority in conventional forces, those of

59 Cold War 1985

NATO countries
Warsaw Pact countries

Iceland

Norway
Sweden   Finland

United
Kingdom
Ireland
Denmark
The
Netherlands
Belgium
Luxembourg   West
France   Germany
Switzerland   Austria   Hungary
Portugal
Spain
Italy   Albania
Greece   Turkey
Malta
Cyprus

East
Germany Poland
Czechoslovakia
Romania
Yugoslavia
Bulgaria

S o v i e t

U n i o n

Powerful Soviet forces confront NATO face to face in Germany. Soviet and Warsaw Pact armies outnumber and outgun NATO in Europe. Red Army tanks and bombers within 200 km of Bonn, within 600 km of Paris. Iron Curtain, confrontation, tensions, capability for sudden massive attack on Western Europe.

Russia alone are now substantially *weaker* than those of the NATO countries. There is thus now no conceivable way in which Russia could invade western Europe.

This fundamental shift in the military balance was already acknowledged in the 1993 defence white paper;[362] and, in 1998, *The Strategic Defence Review*

60 Post-Cold War 1995

Major Russian and NATO force reductions in Europe, Warsaw Pact disbanded, Soviet Union broken up. Former satellites now democracies, several·seeking to join NATO, effective buffer between Russia and Western Europe. Red Army now 1,000 km further east, busy with 'near abroad' problems. Open borders, friendly relations, economic assistance, no capability for invasion of Western Europe.

confirmed that: 'The collapse of Communism and the emergence of demo-cratic states throughout Eastern Europe means that there is today no direct military threat to the United Kingdom or Western Europe. Nor do we foresee the re-emergence of such a threat.'[363]

The disappearance of the threat of invasion by the Soviet Union, or by

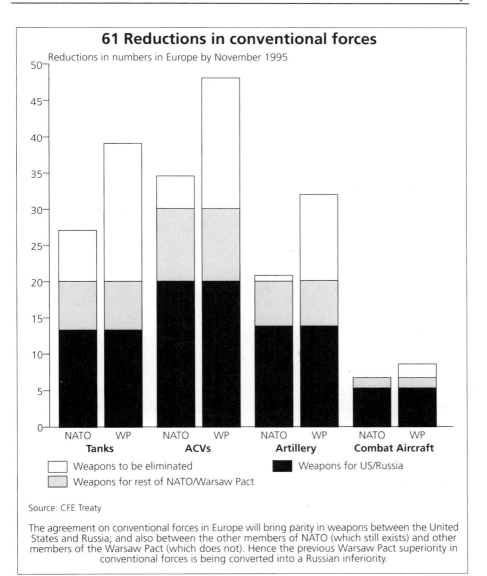

61 Reductions in conventional forces

Reductions in numbers in Europe by November 1995

Weapons to be eliminated | Weapons for US/Russia
Weapons for rest of NATO/Warsaw Pact

Source: CFE Treaty

The agreement on conventional forces in Europe will bring parity in weapons between the United States and Russia; and also between the other members of NATO (which still exists) and other members of the Warsaw Pact (which does not). Hence the previous Warsaw Pact superiority in conventional forces is being converted into a Russian inferiority.

anyone else, has left Britain with more real security than at any time in the past 50 years. It also means that the onerous defence dispositions in readiness for all-out war with a superpower are no longer appropriate. In particular, it will no longer be necessary to maintain in Germany the major forces once needed to repel an attack that will now never come.

The end of the cold war has also put an end to the superpower rivalry, which had been a major factor in causing and exacerbating conflicts in other parts of the world. It *cannot*, however, be expected to end the many conflicts around the world that arise from other causes. In some areas – for example eastern Europe and the new Asian republics of the former Soviet Union – the departure of Soviet power is resulting in instability and new causes of conflict.

And finally, while the ending of the cold war has removed the threat of Soviet invasion, it has not entirely removed the threat posed by the massive Russian arsenal of nuclear weapons.

Weapons of mass destruction

The size and circumstances of the remaining Russian nuclear stockpile still present serious problems. In the longer term, the wider proliferation of nuclear weapons and other weapons of mass destruction represent the greatest single threat to Britain's security. The present international situation provides a favourable window of opportunity for removing it.

Nuclear arms reduction treaties

Valuable progress has been made in reducing the size of nuclear stockpiles and in modifying the form of their deployment. Under START (Strategic Arms Reduction Talks) agreements, the Russians have accepted a 95 per cent reduction in the number of warheads in their land-based intercontinental missiles, a cut of one-third in their submarine-based missiles, and a smaller reduction in warheads carried by their aircraft – together with procedures for monitoring that the reductions are in fact carried out. The Americans have also accepted substantial reductions to arrive at a parity in numbers by 2007.

Under previous treaties, intermediate range missiles were completely withdrawn and the number of tactical weapons deployed greatly reduced. The 7000 or more nuclear warheads[364] in Belarus, Ukraine and Kazakhstan at the time of the break-up of the Soviet Union, appear to have been successfully withdrawn to Russia or dismantled. This is progress on a scale far greater than anyone could have dreamed of when the cold war was at its height.

However, even when the START cuts are completed in 2007, the Russians, like the Americans, will still have 3500 nuclear warheads – with an explosive power equivalent to more than 100 times that of all the munitions used in the Second World War.[365–6]

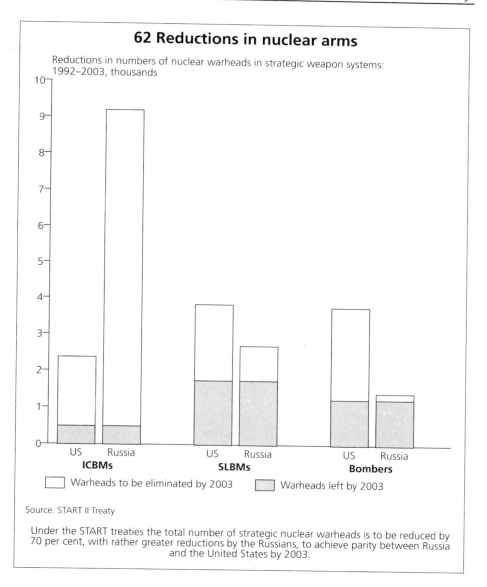

62 Reductions in nuclear arms

Reductions in numbers of nuclear warheads in strategic weapon systems: 1992–2003, thousands

☐ Warheads to be eliminated by 2003   ▨ Warheads left by 2003

Source: START II Treaty

Under the START treaties the total number of strategic nuclear warheads is to be reduced by 70 per cent, with rather greater reductions by the Russians, to achieve parity between Russia and the United States by 2003.

Meanwhile, there are between 10,000 and 20,000 nuclear warheads in Russia awaiting dismantling. Many are stored in conditions where there is a risk of environmental damage or outright loss. Alexander Lebed, former head of Russia's Security Council, has warned that some warheads, including more than 100 suitcase-sized bombs, are missing and could have fallen into the hands of foreign powers or terrorist groups.[367] Even the warheads that are still in service are in the uncertain control of army units demoralised by pay delays and lack of resources. As Russia's defence minister, Igor Rodionov, has warned: 'No-one today can guarantee the reliability of our control systems. Russia might soon approach the threshold beyond which its missiles and nuclear systems cannot be controlled.'[68]

There are three risks in this situation. First, the size of the nuclear arsenal allowed to remain under present treaties is so large that it would present a grave threat to humanity if at some time in the future the government of Russia came into the hands of an aggressive or unstable leader. Second, the increasingly precarious system of control over the arsenal heightens the risk of 'catastrophe by accident'. Even when control was close and secure at the height of the cold war, there were a number of occasions when disaster nearly occurred through errors of judgement (as in the Cuba missiles crisis), misinterpretation of intentions (as in a NATO exercise in 1993), aircraft crashes, submarine fires, computer malfunctions and other systems errors.[369-71] Third, the insecure storage arrangements for the large number of missiles awaiting dismantling add materially to the risks of nuclear proliferation.

Nuclear proliferation

At the height of the cold war, the balance of terror between the two super-powers provided some degree of security. It was assumed that neither side would be so foolish as to unleash nuclear devastation on the other if the certain consequence would be the complete destruction of its own country as well. However, even that degree of security could be neither fully reliable nor permanently durable: it could have broken down if either superpower had had a leader who was unstable, irrational or prepared to take risks.

As nuclear weapons become more widely spread, the risks of their use multiply greatly. With more countries involved, the consequences of any action become harder to assess and the risk of misjudgement increases. It is worrying that among those who acquire nuclear weapons will be leaders who are known to be unstable, irrational and willing to take excessive risks; and even worse – leaders with unresolved disputes with other countries who are driven by such passionate hatreds that they would be prepared to initiate any form of aggression, including suicidal attacks. And if nuclear weapons get into the hands of international terrorist groups, with extreme aims and fanatical leaders, the prospect is more worrying still.

In a world of general nuclear proliferation, there can be no effective defence against the threat of nuclear attack. Anti-ballistic missile systems offer inadequate protection. The US Patriot system installed during the Gulf War succeeded in intercepting only 28 per cent[372] of the old-technology scud missiles launched against Israel and Saudi Arabia. Against nuclear warheads, nothing less than 100 per cent effectiveness is enough; and there is no prospect of this for many years to come.

There is no prospect *at any time* of effective defence against bombs that are smuggled into cities for detonation later at some time of crisis. A nuclear device the size of a grapefruit would be enough to destroy London's West End or Manhattan.[373] The ultimate horror scenario is of a terrorist group announcing that it has placed nuclear bombs in London and other major cities and will detonate them unless its demands are met; whereupon another terrorist group announces that it too has already placed bombs in London and other cities and will not hesitate to detonate them if *its* opposite and incompatible demands are not met. What then?

Are such scenarios too fanciful to worry about? In the next few years – yes. But in the next few decades – they are not merely possible, but probable, if nuclear proliferation is allowed to get out of hand. The only sure defence is to *prevent* proliferation before it happens.

Britain, France and China already have nuclear weapons and the ability to deliver them. Israel, which has unresolved disputes with its Arab neighbours, probably has them. India and Pakistan, countries that have already had three wars with each other and are still in bitter dispute over Kashmir, have now both definitely got them.

North Korea may already have acquired a nuclear capability. Libya and Iran have for years been trying to build or buy nuclear weapons. Iraq would have succeeded in doing so within two or three years[374] if the programme had not been interrupted by the Gulf War – which would have taken a very different form had it come a few years later. The CIA (Central Intelligence Agency) estimates that 15 developing countries may be producing ballistic missiles by the end of the century.[375]

A number of countries with erratic and potentially aggressive regimes will probably be capable of developing nuclear weapons systems out of their own resources within a decade or two. They might be able to develop them more quickly as a result of leaks from Russia. Their main difficulty is getting sufficient quantities of weapons-grade plutonium or enriched uranium; they need five to ten kilograms to make an effective bomb. In Russia, there are about 1000 tons of surplus weapons-grade materials.[376] Much of it is poorly guarded and accounted for and is an attractive target for the Mafia. Plutonium is valuable and easy to smuggle in the small quantities required. Already illicit shipments of weapons-grade plutonium have been intercepted in Germany, larger quantities are believed to be leaking out through Afghanistan, and a market has grown up in 'red mercury', which, it is claimed, can be used for making much more compact nuclear weapons.[377]

Foreign governments may be able to strengthen their nuclear programmes by recruiting scientists from among Russia's thousands of unemployed weapons specialists. Most alarming of all, governments or terrorist groups could acquire an instant nuclear capability through theft of some of the thousands of insecurely held weapons awaiting dismantling. The head of the FBI (Federal Bureau of Investigation) has described the risks of leaks from a disintegrating Russia as 'the greatest long-term threat to the security of the US', and a major study headed by the former US assistant defence secretary[373] has elaborated the gravity of the threat and pressed for urgent action to deal with it.

There is a real threat that, within the next decade or two, nuclear weapons may come into the hands of irresponsible governments, ruthless terrorists or criminal groups. There can be no defence objective more important for Britain and other countries than to prevent this happening. Russia needs to be offered more help to speed up the process of dismantling surplus weapons; to improve control of stocks of fissile material; to combat the Mafia; and to introduce global measures to prevent proliferation.

There have already been some successes in this respect. Belarus, Ukraine, Kazakhstan, Argentina, Brazil and South Africa have all given up their actual or potential nuclear capability. North Korea has been persuaded to accept international inspection of its facilities – just. And Iraq has been obliged to accept effective inspection – albeit only under the imminent threat of renewed military force.

The biggest success has been with the renewal, without time limit, of the nuclear test ban treaty, which by prohibiting tests makes it difficult for a country to develop weapons to the point of proven reliability. However, several countries have declined to sign the treaty. A number of others have made it clear that their support is conditional on implementation of the clauses in the treaty that require *existing* nuclear powers to proceed urgently towards the complete elimination of *their* nuclear weapons. Is this demand reasonable? Or practicable?

Superpower nuclear disarmament

For Russia and the US, the central issue is what purpose do their nuclear arsenals serve in a post-cold-war world? With the end of the cold war their original purpose has gone. Now that there is no longer any threat of invasion, the only threat comes from the weapons themselves.

They have no role in the modern world. It is no accident that nuclear weapons were never used anywhere during the cold war, not even when the superpowers were faced with humiliating defeat, as the Americans were in Korea and Vietnam, and the Russians were in Afghanistan. Nuclear weapons are so powerful, so horrific and unlimitable in their effects, that there were no circumstances in which the superpowers were willing to use them against other countries in the past, or would be prepared to in the future. Every military role can be performed more flexibly, reliably and efficiently by conventional forces.

The power of both Russia and the US depends, not on their nuclear forces, which in practice can never be used, but on *conventional* forces. The US, in particular, has forces that are not only large but are pre-eminent in technology-based conventional weaponry. These include stealth bombers, tomahawk missiles, smart bombs, helicopter gunships, aircraft carriers, AWACS (airborne warning and control system) control aircraft, satellite surveillance systems, hypersonic spy planes, antiballistic missile systems and advanced radar and computer control systems. Other countries have neither the technology nor the financial resources to match these forces. In a nuclear-free world, the dominance of the US would be even more marked than it is today.

By retaining their nuclear arsenals, the US and Russia not only add nothing to their effective power, but create threats to their own future security. They not only risk a disastrous accidental nuclear exchange, but provide a continuing impetus to other countries to achieve nuclear capability – together with a possible means of achieving it as a result of insecure control systems in Russia. In a post-cold war world, nuclear weapons are not the superpower's means of domination. They are the little guy's equaliser. They provide a small country, or even a terrorist group, with the potential to hold a major power to ransom by posing a threat against which even a super-power has no reliable defence.

The US and Russia have no need of nuclear weapons and no conceivable role for them, and their future security would be greater if there were no nuclear weapons anywhere. Complete nuclear disarmament is now a realistic objective *because it is in the military interests of both the US and Russia.*

Are there practical ways of bringing this about? The Henry L. Stimson Center in Washington and the Canberra Commission set up by the Australian prime minister have worked out a systematic rationale for superpower nuclear disarmament and businesslike procedures for putting it into effect.

They propose that a start should be made with a declaration of intent to proceed as expeditiously as possible to complete nuclear disarmament, followed by steps to reduce the risk of accidental conflict by taking forces off alert, detargeting missiles and removing warheads from them, and ending deployment of tactical weapons.

Disarmament would then proceed in a series of careful stages, each preceded by exchange of information and negotiation of the next stage of reduction, and followed by agreed rigorous verification measures in order to build up mutual confidence before proceeding to the next stage. After the final stage, providing for the dismantling of the last of the nuclear weapons, there would be provision for secure control of stocks of fissile material, and close monitoring of civilian nuclear plants, of facilities that could be used in renewed weapons production, and of the development of missiles and other potential means of delivery. Similar provisions would naturally be applied to other countries.

Reliable means of verification would, of course, be crucial to success. These could build on measures already successfully used in implementing the START treaties. These have been found to be workable, even in the tense and suspicious context of the cold war. They should be easier to apply in the atmosphere of confidence and goodwill that would accompany a programme of disarmament.

No system can ever be 100 per cent safe and risk free, but a programme of general nuclear disarmament would present much fewer risks than carrying on as at present – when it is only a matter of time before there is a major accident or wider proliferation of nuclear weapons. The present, while there are sympathetic governments in both Russia and the US, offers a unique window of opportunity to release the world from the nuclear threat. Later it may be too late.

The conclusion that complete nuclear disarmament is the most rational and practical course to follow has come, not from the feelings of predisposed pacifists or sentimental visionaries, but from the analyses of hardened professionals who are deeply involved in the practical realities of nuclear weapons.

The Stimson Center study was chaired by former Supreme Allied Commander in Europe Andrew Goodpaster, and included three senior retired generals, as well as former US Secretary of Defense Robert McNamara, and former US chief arms control negotiator Paul Nitze.

The Canberra report[378] represented the considered opinion of a Commission, which included:

1. Lee Butler, former commander in chief of the US Strategic Air Command, and subsequently the US Strategic Command, responsible for all US Air Force and Navy nuclear deterrent forces.
2. Field Marshal Lord Carver, former Chief of Defence Staff in Britain.
3. Jayantha Dhanapala, UN undersecretary-general for disarmament, chair of the 1995 Nuclear Non-Proliferation Treaty review and Extension Conference.
4. Rolf Ekeus, executive chairman of UNSCOM, the UN commission charged with identifying and eliminating Iraq's weapons of mass destruction.
5. Robert McNamara, former US Secretary of Defense, president of Ford and of the World Bank.
6. Professor Robert O'Neill, former director, International Institute of Strategic Studies, London.
7. Quin Jiadong, member of China's National Committee and vice-chairman of the Foreign Affairs Committee, former ambassador for disarmament affairs and representative to disarmament conference.
8. Joseph Rotblat, president of the Pugwash conferences on science and world affairs, and former physicist working on the atom bomb in the Second World War.
9. Roald Sagdeev, former science adviser to President Gorbachev, director of the Space Research Institute and chairman of the Committee of Soviet Scientists for Global Security.

Russia and the US are only likely to agree to proceed towards total nuclear disarmament as part of a wider arrangement that includes all other actual and prospective nuclear powers. Minor nuclear powers, such as Israel, India and Pakistan, can probably be persuaded to collaborate, as part of a global process, if they are subjected to external pressures and offered appropriate guarantees for their security.

China, large, powerful and prickly, might be expected to be less amenable. However, it too has no need or use for nuclear weapons. Building up a strategic nuclear capability absorbs substantial resources that are badly needed elsewhere. In any case, China is likely to remain permanently inferior to Russia and the US in the number and reach of its nuclear weapons. And, like Russia, it has powerful conventional forces. Hence, if without loss of face and as part of a wider process it were to give up its nuclear weapons, its relative strength in a non-nuclear world would probably be greater than it is now. Hence, as with the US and Russia, it is in China's military interest to take part in general nuclear disarmament. Enquiries by the Canberra Commission suggest that China would indeed be likely to cooperate.

That leaves Britain and France as the other two nuclear powers whose participation would be required.

Trident

Until now, SALT and START (negotiations on strategic arms limitation and reduction) have involved only Russia and the US. British nuclear forces were too small compared with those of the two superpowers to be considered worth bothering about. However, this may no longer be so when further substantial reductions are contemplated and it is therefore improbable that Britain's nuclear weapons could be left out of the next round of negotiations.

Since the withdrawal of nuclear artillery shells, bombs and depth charges, Britain's nuclear forces have consisted of four Polaris submarines carrying a total of 192 warheads, though some estimates put the total actually deployed as low as 40.[379] They are currently being replaced by four Trident submarines capable of carrying a total of 512 warheads, each of which (unlike in Polaris) can be independently targeted.[380] However, the full potential capacity will not be used. The previous government announced that the number of warheads actually deployed would be limited to a maximum of 384,[381] and *The Strategic Defence Review* envisages a maximum of only 200.[363]

Even at the proposed sub-capacity level, the new Trident system will be able to deploy as many warheads as the previous Polaris one, and can strike three times the number of targets, at nearly three times the maximum range and with much greater accuracy and reliability. It is anomalous that Britain should see fit to deploy a significant *increase* in its nuclear striking power at a time when the Americans and Russians are making such massive *reductions* in theirs. It is described in the new defence review as merely the 'minimum necessary to deter'; but, with 200 warheads of 100 kilotonnes each, its total explosive power is 1000 times as great as the bomb that destroyed Hiroshima. It took only two bombs to end a world war. For what do we need so much more now? What exactly is Trident *for*?

What is the purpose of this nuclear force in the post-cold war world? In what circumstances could it conceivably be used? Or even credibly threatened to be used? Against whom? With what effect? Would it be the most cost-effective instrument for the purpose intended?

No specific answer has yet been given to any of these questions. It is strange that in times when public expenditure in all other areas has to be justified on the basis of clear, certain and important need, a programme as expensive and potent as Trident should be pursued for objectives so distant, nebulous or improbable that they cannot even be identified.

For Britain, as for the US, nuclear weapons are too powerful and too indiscriminate for their use to be contemplated in any situation that can realistically be envisaged. They were not even used in the Falklands. Any military needs that Britain may have in the future will be met more effectively by conventional forces – indeed, will *have* to be met by conventional forces, because the consequences of using nuclear weapons would be so drastic and counterproductive.

In so far as any justification is given for Britain's retention of Trident in the post-cold war world, it is usually expressed in vague generalities, such as the need to be able independently to 'defend our essential national interests' or to have an 'ultimate deterrent at a time of supreme national crisis'; or even vaguer generalities that in some way it gives Britain the status of a great power, entitled to a seat at the top table in the councils of the world.

In these protestations of nuclear need, we probably deceive ourselves more than we impress others. What if other countries take us at face value? If our own nuclear weapons are 'essential' to preserve our national interests or save us at a time of crisis, why only Britain? Why not Germany and Italy, which are more exposed than Britain to possible threats? Do they not also need their own nuclear weapons? If Germany and Italy, why not Canada and Australia? Brazil and Argentina? India and Pakistan? South Korea and North Korea? Israel and Egypt? Iran, Iraq, Syria and Libya? If nuclear weapons are deemed to be 'essential' for Britain, then the same arguments apply to all countries, including many with very unstable governments. A world in which they all had nuclear weapons would be very dangerous.

Nuclear weapons are no more essential for Britain's security than they are for the security of most other countries. The pretence that they are essential for security, or even the claim that they bring more power, prestige and influence in the world, provides a constant provocation and stimulus to other countries to seek their own nuclear capability. Our insistence on maintaining Trident is dangerous, expensive and seriously irresponsible. It makes it more difficult to get the superpowers to give up nuclear weapons and other powers to stop trying to acquire them.

Britain's real security interests will best be served, not by clinging to an unusable deterrent to meet an unidentifiable threat, but by recognising that nuclear proliferation is the most dangerous threat to Britain in the post-cold war world. Britain can play a constructive role by declaring a willingness in principle to join in general nuclear disarmament, and by using its existing nuclear capability as a bargaining factor in negotiations to bring a safer nuclear-free world while the window of opportunity is still open.

If the arguments for giving up the independent deterrent are accepted in Britain, they are likely to carry weight also in France, where the issues are similar, thus completing the circle of cooperation needed finally to get rid of the nuclear threat.

Chemical and biological weapons

The world's attention has been focused mainly on nuclear weapons, but chemical and biological ones also pose a deadly threat. New nerve gases are many times more toxic than the poison gases that inflicted such horrific casualties in the First World War. Some biological agents are more potent still. Both can kill millions within hours.

In two respects, chemical and biological weapons are an even more dangerous threat than nuclear weapons. First, they can be made without large plants and expensive facilities, using substances and processes that are used for other, legitimate purposes. They are within the means of most countries, not just technologically advanced ones, and it is difficult to detect and stop their secret development and production. Second, they are highly concentrated and so can be used in very small quantities, which are easy to transport and conceal. It is impossible to prevent their being smuggled into centres of population and clandestinely released.

There are large stockpiles of chemical weapons in Russia and the US; and smaller, but still menacing, amounts in other countries. These are believed to include North Korea, Iran, Iraq, Syria, Libya, Egypt, India and Pakistan. Poison gas was used by Iraq against the Iranians and the Kurds; and the particularly deadly sarin gas was used by the Aum Shinrikyo sect in Japan.

In 1990, Russia and the US signed a bilateral treaty, which provided for both countries to reduce their stocks to 5000 tons by 2002. In 1993, Britain, Russia, the US and more than 150 other countries signed the more comprehensive Chemical Weapons Convention.[382] This not only outlaws the use of chemical weapons, but prohibits the development, production and stockpiling of them; requires any existing stocks and production facilities to be destroyed; and provides for rigorous verification procedures, including permanent surveillance and snap inspections.

Two problems remain. One is the cost of destroying the US stockpile of 40,000 tons, estimated at $12 billion, and the Russian stockpile of 30,000 tons, estimated at more than $10 billion. The Russian government will have difficulty finding such a large sum of money and may need financial and technical help from the US.

The other problem is that several countries, most notably Iraq, have not signed the convention and are believed to be actively pursuing chemical weapons programmes. It is thus in Britain's interest to maintain pressure on suspect countries to ensure that they sign the convention; to press for effective application of the agreed verification procedures; and to join in any endeavours needed to enforce compliance with the convention's provisions.

With biological weapons, international progress has much further to go. The Biological and Toxin Weapons Convention was agreed in 1972, but, unlike the Chemical Weapons Convention, it includes no provisions for verification and enforcement. Biological weapons were given a lower priority than chemical ones because it was thought that they did not offer much scope for effective military use. This perception has proved to be mistaken, mainly because developments in biotechnology have made it possible to develop more toxic, quicker acting, more contagious, less treatable, longer lasting and more predictable biological agents. It is also now possible to produce large quantities much more quickly, without the need for long lead times and hazardous storage, and in plants that are small enough to be mobile.[383] There are also now techniques for greatly increased effectiveness of offensive use.

Biological weapons are now a feasible proposition for any developing country, and even for terrorist groups – a poor man's weapon of mass destruction. And, even with intrusive inspections, it is extremely difficult to detect illicit production, as witnessed by the uncertain results achieved by the UNSCOM team in Iraq. Programmes to develop biological weapons are believed to be under way in a number of other countries, including China, Taiwan, Iran, Syria, Libya and Egypt.

Biological weapons pose an even more serious threat than chemical ones. It is therefore very important to strengthen the convention by adding effective verification and enforcement procedures, and to press all the countries still outside it to join. During Britain's presidency of the EU in 1998, an agreement was reached to pursue this at a special conference to be held early in 1999.

Proliferation of conventional weapons

It is not only world wars or weapons of mass destruction that kill people. In the four decades from 1950 to 1989, there were more than 100 wars around the world. None involved the use of nuclear weapons, but they took the lives of more than 19 million people, injured many others, caused widespread destruction, and impeded economic and social development.[384] So long as there are conflicts in the world, people will be killed in them. And, as was shown in Rwanda, knives and axes can kill people just as dead as bombs and bullets. Modern conventional weapons hugely escalate the impact of conflicts because of their greater range, greater destructiveness and greater expense. The proliferation around the world of the most modern, sophisticated and powerful conventional weapons is therefore a matter of concern.

In 1987, world arms sales totalled $85 billion. By 1994, with the ending of the cold war, this had fallen sharply to $33 billion. Since then it has been rising again, in 1995 to $37 billion and in 1996 to $40 billion.[385] There are several reasons for this.

During the cold war, the forces driving arms supplies were mainly political. By 1996, they had become mainly economic. When the cold war ended, the US, France and Britain all reduced their defence spending. Companies supplying defence equipment faced a declining home market for their products. Instead of diversifying into other lines, they sought to make good the loss by selling more abroad. In this, they were actively encouraged by defence departments, which hoped that export sales would spread development costs, reduce the cost of procurement for national forces, and help maintain a defence industry of sufficient size and diversity to meet whatever needs might arise in the future. They also received more general government support because export earnings from arms were seen as helping solve balance of payments problems.

In Russia, the same considerations applied, only more strongly. Defence cuts were sharper, balance of payments problems were more acute and modern arms, such as fighter aircraft, were among the few world-class products Russia had available for export. Both the government and the newly-privatised companies were desperate. State-of-the-art weapons from the main high-tech companies have been augmented by existing older or surplus weapons, some sold officially at very low prices, and some sold illicitly at even lower prices by the Mafia, after having been 'liberated' from military depots by the underpaid officers in charge of them.

International arms fairs have had no shortage of sellers from the main exporting countries – some of them eager to sell to almost anyone interested in buying and able to pay, even to some who in the event were not able to pay. In each of the five years up to 1995, Britain's Export Credits Guarantee Department had to pay out £250 million for unpaid arms sales.[386]

In theory, arms from Britain are supplied only to countries deemed to be friendly, or that appear to present no 'threat' to Britain. However, as the Scott Inquiry[387] revealed, there are plenty of loopholes in 'dual use' products (ones that also have civilian applications), components and production equipment (as opposed to complete, ready-to-use weapons), selling on to third countries, and lax application of export controls – all within a culture lacking transparency and accountability to a degree that would never be acceptable in a country such as the US.

Among the major arms buyers in recent years have been Greece, Turkey, Cyprus, Chile, Argentina, India, Pakistan, Bangladesh, North Korea, South Korea, Israel, Egypt, Syria, Saudi Arabia, Kuwait, Bahrein, United Arab Emirates, Iran, Singapore, Malaysia, Myanmar, Thailand, Indonesia and China.[306] There are a number of reasons why arms sales to many of them are undesirable.

First, some of them have dictatorships with very poor records on suppression of minority rights or on human rights more generally. The acquisition of modern arms strengthens their prestige and authority and provides the means, directly or indirectly, for internal suppression and denial of democracy.

Second, for poor countries, the purchase of arms can be a heavy burden and a serious obstacle to economic development – and an even more crippling burden if the arms are actually used in civil wars or conflicts with neighbouring countries. In 1995, total military spending by developing countries amounted to $153 billion[306] – only 18 per cent less than ten years before and nearly three times as much as the total they received in international development aid. Lower military spending would bring faster economic growth, slower population growth, and reduced need for international aid (see Chapter 7).

Third, many international arms sales are to countries with unresolved conflicts with other countries – such as Greece and Turkey; India and Pakistan; Israel and the Arab countries and Iran; China and the ASEAN countries and Taiwan. The arms build-up in such areas raises tensions, deepens suspicions, heightens perceptions of threat, and increases the likelihood of conflicts of interest and attitude turning into actual war. It also ensures that, if war comes, it is on a much bigger and more destructive scale than it would otherwise have been.

Fourth, there is the boomerang effect, where weapons are used against the forces of the country that supplied them – as in the Gulf War, when British and US troops came under fire from weapons previously supplied by Britain and the US.

And fifth, there is the general escalation of arms levels, and with it the general erosion of security and the need for higher defence expenditure by the arms supplying countries themselves. When increasing quantities of arms are supplied to the countries most likely to be in violent dispute, any outside military intervention that may become necessary has to be on a much greater scale and at much greater risk. For example, because Saddam Hussein had been able to obtain thousands of tanks and other heavy weapons from abroad and build up the fourth strongest army in the world, it required a campaign of Second World War proportions to remove him from Kuwait. The total cost to the allies was more than \$80 billion[388] – many times the value of the earlier arms exports that had made it necessary.

It used to be argued that an arms build-up in other countries could be offset by the technical superiority of the armed forces of countries such as Britain, France and the US. Nowadays, competition in the international arms trade is so keen that customer countries are being offered the very latest state-of-the-art weapons systems[389] – often under contracts providing for training, maintenance and upgrading as well. In future conflicts, our forces will no longer be able to count on a technical edge to make up for an inferiority in numbers. The only way to keep ahead will be to develop yet more sophisticated weapons systems – which, in turn, will be sold around the world, generating a need to develop systems more advanced still. This escalating circularity is costly and dangerous. It may benefit the arms companies, but makes little sense for anyone else.

A particularly expensive example of this is the Eurofighter, an advanced aircraft being developed for the air forces of Britain, Germany, Italy and Spain. Its total cost is expected to be at least £42 billion, of which Britain's share will be at least £15 billion. It was originally intended to be able to match the equivalent generation of advanced Soviet fighters in the great air battles expected to take place above the great land battles in Germany in the event of a Soviet invasion.

Now that the cold war is over, there will be no invasion and no great air battles. For what then is it intended? Apparently, to ensure our air superiority against a strategic threat too remote and improbable to be identified; or, more realistically, to ensure air superiority in any military interventions that may be required in other parts of the world. Why should such an advanced machine be required for that? Because many Third World air forces have very modern aircraft, and something even better will be needed to ensure superiority. How is it that they have such good aircraft? Because we (or the French, or the Americans or the Russians) sold them to them. For how long will we be able to keep the edge through having the Eurofighter? Not very long because we are already trying very hard to sell them the Eurofighter too[390] – several years before our own air forces have even taken delivery of their machines, indeed before development work is even complete. If they also have Eurofighters, what will we do then? Develop an even more advanced, potent and expensive machine. . . .

Similarly with other advanced weapons systems. By operating a largely free market in arms exports, we create an upwardly spiralling escalation in both the numbers and sophistication of the arms sold, bringing heavy costs and increasing dangers to the countries of the developing world and also to the countries supplying the arms.

It is often said that, damaging as arms sales may be, 'If we do not supply a customer, someone else will.' This argument is not accepted as justification for drugs sales, and it should not be accepted for arms sales either. The constructive approach is not passively to accept the operation of market forces, but to seek to control the market so as to reduce the scale of supply. What are the chances of bringing about a *general* reduction in arms sales?

At present the US, Britain, Russia and France dominate the arms trade, accounting between them for 87 per cent of the total.[385] With the cold war over, they no longer *need* to compete in the world arms market. On the contrary, they have a strong *common military interest* in collaborating to cut back the flow of arms to other countries. All four may need to intervene militarily in disputes beyond their borders. They will be able to do this with less risk if potential antagonists are not armed with the latest equipment. They have a *common economic interest* in slowing the proliferation of the most advanced weapons systems. It would reduce the pressure on their defence budgets of having to develop ever more advanced weapons to deal with them.

A start on curbing the arms trade has already been made with landmines. More than 100 million mines have been laid in more than 60 different countries.[391] They kill and maim thousands of people a month, most of them civilians. The numbers have been growing. In 1994, between two and five million new mines were laid, at a cost of only about $3 each. Of these, only 100,000 were cleared, at a cost of between $300 and $1000 each.[392] For many years, Britain opposed a ban on landmines. However, a global ban was finally agreed in 1997, with active support from the new government, which has also been pressing for greater efforts to clear the mines already laid.[391]

More general international restrictions on arms exports have been proposed at various times by Britain, France, the US, Russia, Italy, Canada,

Norway and other countries. A United Nations Register of Conventional Arms has been established, and the Wassenaar Arrangement makes provision for some restrictions. Recently, on Britain's initiative, the EU has agreed to common standards for arms exports, and a provision to prevent 'undercutting'. If one country rejects an arms deal, another one wishing to take it up must first inform (privately) the country that turned it down. This is a useful start, but should be extended to provide that *all* arms deals are made public and are subject to *prior* parliamentary scrutiny (as they are in Sweden), to cover international brokers and controls over end-use, and to include follow-up monitoring and enforcement. It needs to be followed by a more ambitious deal with the US and Russia to bring about a drastic reduction in the scale of the arms trade. This is an area in which Britain, as the world's second largest supplier, should be in a position to play a leading role.

Future defence needs

While Britain no longer faces a threat of direct attack, there are still likely to be conflicts between and within other nations as a result of political differences, religious intolerance, nationalist fervour and disputes over economic and environmental resources. These are most likely to affect Britain in the form of military intervention to contain conflicts in eastern Europe and participation in UN peace-keeping exercises in other parts of the world. There may also be an increasing security threat from international terrorist groups and crime syndicates, which will need a different kind of response from that appropriate for more conventional military threats.

Conflicts in Europe

The collapse of communism and of Soviet power has brought independence to the countries of eastern Europe. To some, it has also brought dangerous instability, with shaky economies, fractured social systems and insecure democracies. Others have seen a resurgence of ancient enmities directed against neighbouring countries or internal minorities. The tragedy in Bosnia may not be the last one.

Accordingly, it is important for Britain to retain its capability to intervene in a limited war in Europe, but the requirements for this would be different in scale and kind from those of the cold war.

First, the forces to be confronted would be smaller and less sophisticated – Serbia is not in the same league as the Soviet Union. Second, Britain would always be acting in alliance with other EU countries – fewer forces are needed for an effort shared with up to 14 other countries than for a solo venture. And third, without a direct threat to national survival, participation would be largely discretionary. The decision about whether to take part and, if so, in what form and on what scale, could be made in the light of the circumstances of the time.

Although heavy battle tanks, attack helicopters and so on may be relevant, they will not need to be provided by Britain on anything near the scale considered necessary for repelling an all-out assault by the Soviet armoured divisions in East Germany.

In practice, the scope for preventing or containing potential conflicts in Europe will probably depend less on the strength of the military forces available than on the cohesion of the countries providing them. The Bosnian tragedy could have been averted by firm, purposive intervention in the early stages. Dithering, division and delay by western European countries allowed the situation to worsen, so that the eventual intervention had to be on a much larger scale than would have been needed earlier.

If closer union in Europe included developing a common foreign policy, it would become possible to formulate joint initiatives to give effect to it. If it also included developing a common defence policy, any joint military operations would become more effective. There have already been steps towards closer military integration in the EU with a bigger role for the Western European Union (NATO's European pillar) and the setting up of a number of international military formations, such as Eurocorps (a French and German armoured division with units from Spain and Belgium), the Multinational Division (Belgian, British, Dutch and German air-mobile forces), and the UK/Netherlands Amphibious Force of marines. Eventually, there should be advantages in developing a 'European Army' to complement rather than replace national forces. A unified force would be able to respond quickly and decisively to crises in eastern Europe, without the various impediments inherent in separate national military arrangements and political processes.

International peace-keeping

With its overseas dependencies reduced to a scattering of tiny places with a total population of only 200,000, Britain no longer has 'vital interests' outside Europe in need of military protection. Television coverage of disturbing events in faraway places has, however, increased public willingness to contemplate British participation, under UN auspices, in international operations to monitor peace arrangements between countries previously at war, to *make*

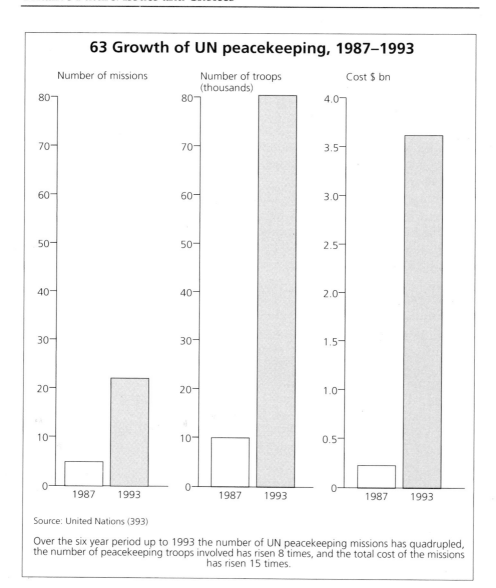

63 Growth of UN peacekeeping, 1987–1993

Number of missions

Number of troops (thousands)

Cost $ bn

Source: United Nations (393)

Over the six year period up to 1993 the number of UN peacekeeping missions has quadrupled, the number of peacekeeping troops involved has risen 8 times, and the total cost of the missions has risen 15 times.

peace when hostilities take place, and to intervene *within* countries where civil wars are in progress, minorities are being repressed, law and order has broken down, or there are extreme abuses of human rights.

The continuing frequency of conflicts and a growing sense of the value of international intervention have led to a steady increase in UN peace missions.

Between 1987 and 1993, the number of missions doubled, the number of troops involved increased eightfold, and the total cost of the operations increased fifteenfold.[393] Unfortunately, the arrears in financial contributions to pay for them have risen to more than $600 million, and some of the operations have been less than fully successful.

It seems likely there will be a continuing series of UN operations and a continuing succession of requests for British participation in them. For this role, Britain's forces will need to be well organised and disciplined, trained and equipped, highly mobile and instantly available. They will need a plentiful supply of transport aircraft and helicopters, but not much, if any, of the heavy weaponry assembled to repel a Soviet invasion of western Europe.

As with conflicts in Europe, participation will be discretionary, since no vital national interests will be involved; and operations will almost always be undertaken in partnership with other countries. There is no need for Britain to maintain a capability for mounting major distant operations on its own.

Weapons and equipment

Britain spends about 40 per cent of its defence budget, about £9 billion a year, on equipment.[363] Modern weapons systems are becoming increasingly sophisticated and expensive to develop and produce. With reduced arms expenditure since the end of the cold war, unit costs have tended to rise because development costs have to be spread over smaller production runs. They will rise further still if production volumes are reduced as a result of closer control over exports.

In the US, defence purchases fell by more than a half between 1985 and 1996. The response to this has been a drastic consolidation of the defence industry and in the range of items ordered. Now there are far fewer companies making a very much narrower range of equipment.

There has been some progress towards defence integration in Europe in recent years. To establish a viable basis for the defence industries of the future, further consolidation will be necessary, as will far more joint procurement of equipment specified to a common standard. It will also probably be necessary to purchase more from the US. Defence analysts have estimated that Britain could save £3 billion of its defence budget each year by adopting a single European procurement programme and that buying American would save even more.[394]

While the future structure of defence procurement will be important, a realistic assessment of future *needs* will be even more so. Modern weapons systems have long lead times and many on order were originally conceived during the cold war to meet a different type of threat. Some of them are very expensive and, at a time when all public expenditure is under scrutiny, it is reasonable to ask whether they all still represent good value for money.

The two most expensive items are Trident and Eurofighter. The cost of acquiring Trident submarines, missiles and warheads (£12.5 billion) has already been incurred or committed. The further cost of operating the system is expected to be £680 million a year.[363] Some of this could be saved if Trident were included in the next round of nuclear disarmament negotiations.

Britain's share of the cost of Eurofighter is currently put at £15 billion (it has already doubled and could rise further). Most of the R&D costs have been incurred, so it is probably too late to buy cheaper, and arguably better, planes from the US, or even Russia. But there is still time to question whether we need so many of them. Britain is currently planning to buy 232 at £39 million each. Why does Britain need more planes than Germany (180), Italy (121) and Spain (87)?

There are also a number of other very expensive projects whose relevance to future needs is open to question, among them:[95,396-7]

£1.8 bn	Nimrod replacement aircraft for hunting Soviet nuclear submarines threatening vital North Atlantic life-lines
£4.3 bn	Merlin helicopters, also for hunting Soviet nuclear submarines
£2.0 bn	Three nuclear submarines, additional to the existing 12, also for attacking Soviet submarines and surface ships
£1.7 bn	Spearfish heavy torpedo, also for attacking the Soviet fleet
£4.0 bn	12 Horizon Eurofrigates for protecting the rest of the British fleet from Soviet air, missile and submarine attack
£2.5 bn	67 Apache helicopters for attacking massed formations of Soviet tanks advancing across Germany
£600 m	Brimstone airborne missile; also for attacking massed Soviet tanks
£2.1 bn	386 Challenger heavy battle tanks for attacking any Soviet tanks surviving Apache and Brimstone

There was a time when Soviet submarines posed a mortal threat in the Atlantic sea lanes, when thousands of Red Army tanks were poised to sweep across Germany, and when hundreds of Migs were ready to do battle over Germany – but no more. In the post-cold war world, where the threats are smaller in scale and different in kind, what are these weapons systems actually *for*?

It is not that, like Trident, it is hard to think of *any* situation in which such weapons might be used – some of them might be handy to have in some circumstance, some place, some time. But the idea that systems of such power, in such numbers, are *essential* for Britain's security in the twenty-first century is difficult to sustain. Much of Britain's military procurement programme has been frozen in a scaled-down cold war posture, which does not fit well the actual needs of the future. And, because it is so enormously expensive, it has not left enough funds over for the kinds of equipment that *will* be required to meet the real, but different, needs in prospect.

The new government has recently undertaken a strategic defence review,[363] which represents an advance on past policies in a number of important ways. It recognises that, with the end of the cold war, Britain no longer faces any threat of attack, and goes on to draw the logical conclusion that Britain's forces need to be restructured to equip them for the tasks of the future: mainly intervention in limited wars in and around Europe and peace-keeping operations further afield. It sees that, with more combined operations overseas, there will be a need for a different balance of equipment (in particular better air and sea transport) and for inter-service integration in special joint rapid reaction forces.

However, it still fails to explain why Trident is needed or in what circumstances it could conceivably be used (though it does propose further reducing the number of warheads to be deployed). It proposes only marginal reductions in some expensive areas – attack submarines cut only from 12 to 10, destroyers and frigates from 35 to 32, minehunters from 25 to 22 – and no cuts at all in the 386 new battle tanks on order, or the 44 antisubmarine helicopters, or the 232 Eurofighters. Later, it envisages buying two new large aircraft carriers at about £4 billion each.

It is often claimed that some extravagance in defence spending is justifiable on account of all the jobs it provides. Eurofighter, for example, is estimated to give employment to 14,000 people. However, on a project costing £15 billion, this works out at more than £1 million a job – more than *a hundred times* as much per job as the welfare to work scheme. If job creation is the object, there are other ways of achieving it that are better, safer and very much cheaper (see Chapter 4).

Peace dividend

With the ending of the cold war, Britain's security is now greater than at any time in the past 50 years. There is no risk of attack by Russia, or by anyone else. Compared with the cold war period, the security outlook for the future is far less menacing. Instead of the threat of a struggle for national survival in all-out war with a superpower, the threats of the future involve more limited military operations, always in partnership with other countries, and with discretion to choose whether or not to take part.

Greatly reduced threats imply greatly reduced capabilities for meeting them – and greatly reduced expenditure needed to provide those capabilities. At present, Britain's defence expenditure is only about 30 per cent lower than it was at the height of the cold war. If the level of spending *then* was about right, then the level appropriate for *now* must be a great deal less.

The Strategic Defence Review contemplates defence spending continuing at around the present high level indefinitely. This is because, while getting right the new tasks of the armed forces, it sets much too high a level for their *objective*: to be able to respond to *two* major international crises (say a Gulf War and a Bosnia) *at the same time*.

To be able to do this *alone* is manifestly beyond the range of any country except the US. It has not been thought practicable or necessary for Britain in the past and will not be necessary for Britain in the future. The kinds of military operations envisaged are limited and are undertaken in partnership with other countries. So we can share the tasks and we can choose to what extent we wish to become involved.

The capabilities provided for in the review are not merely far greater than are needed to protect our vital national interests; they are far greater than are needed for any reasonable contribution to international peace-keeping; and far greater than are contemplated by other countries such as Germany, Italy, Spain, Canada, Australia or Japan.

Nowadays, Britain's defence needs are similar to those of other NATO countries in western Europe. Yet, their expenditure on defence is, on average, about a third lower than Britain's[398] and is falling. If Britain's expenditure were to match theirs, it would need to be reduced by about £7 billion a year. There is no obvious reason why a reduction of this order should not be feasible and safe, and achievable within the next few years. It would leave Britain with at least as much security as any other country in western Europe, and at least as well able to take part in peace-keeping missions.

Why then should Britain go far beyond this and aspire to be a go-it-alone semi-superpower, a role it does not need and cannot afford? The unspoken rationale appears to be that by punching above our weight we can somehow acquire the status of a great power. But is this really so? If it were, what would be the benefit? Is it really worth paying £7 billion a year for a seat at the top table?

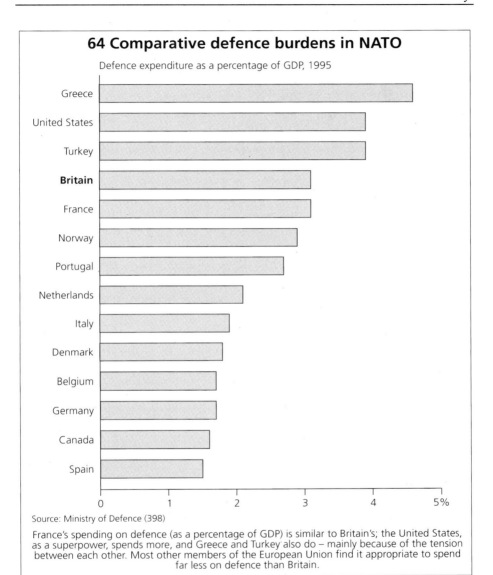

64 Comparative defence burdens in NATO

Defence expenditure as a percentage of GDP, 1995

Source: Ministry of Defence (398)

France's spending on defence (as a percentage of GDP) is similar to Britain's; the United States, as a superpower, spends more, and Greece and Turkey also do – mainly because of the tension between each other. Most other members of the European Union find it appropriate to spend far less on defence than Britain.

But *The Strategic Defence Review* says: 'We British are, by instinct, an internationalist people. We believe that as well as defending our rights, we should discharge our responsibilities in the world. ... We want to give a lead, we want to be a force for good.'[63]

This could be taken to mean that spending far more on defence than other countries is not actually a matter of *realpolitik*, but of altogether loftier considerations. It implies that the British are uniquely idealistic among nations, that we are willing to forgo all kinds of things we would like in Britain in order to do far more than other countries to make the world a better place. If so, spending more than our share on peace-keeping would be one possible way. But it is not the only way, or the most useful, way.

If, instead of spending £7 billion a year more than we need on defence, we put the same resources into international development aid, it would make us the world superpower in international development; it would make our contribution far bigger than those of either the US or Japan, it would enable us, on our own, to provide the poor people of the whole world with safe water and sanitation[309,339] (see Chapter 7). It would do more than make a useful difference – it would make *all* the difference. If we really wanted to win respect as the world's best citizens, we should at least put the resources where they will be most cost-effective – we should think less about getting ourselves a seat at the top table and more about getting a decent dinner for everyone.

9 The Way Forward

Will building a better future require a new approach to the role of the market?

For nearly two decades, the prevailing view in Britain has been a strong belief in the merits of the market system. Government policies have been directed towards freeing the economy from any remaining constraints on the operation of free market forces, and market-based systems have been extended to as many areas of life as possible.

While the New Labour government made a fresh start in many areas, it has not questioned the underlying assumption that, in general, it should continue to rely on the market system. Its 'Third Way' is presented as replacing some of the old ideological drive with a more pragmatic approach – acceptance of market-based systems on their merits where they work best; but also a willingness, at least in principle, to regulate, adapt, override or replace the market where that seems likely to bring better results.

It is therefore timely to reassess the role of the market. What changes will be needed to meet the challenges facing Britain in the next century?

As a way of running a modern economy, the market system has many important advantages and, in general, market economies have out-performed the others. But this does not mean that the adoption of extreme *laissez-faire* policies across the board will automatically bring unlimited benefits in all areas. The success of the market mechanism has been mainly in manufacturing production and trade, but far less in other areas. Some of the countries with the greatest economic and social success have in fact run highly *managed* market economies – far removed from the *laissez-faire* one established in Britain. The wisest proponents of free market systems, from Adam Smith onwards, have stressed the importance of an appropriate degree of *regulation* to ensure that a market system works to the greatest general benefit.

For best results, market forces need to be used sensibly, rather than indiscriminately, and selectively, rather than universally. In each of the seven main areas in which Britain will face major challenges in the next century, there are important ways in which it will be necessary to modify the operation of the market, adapting the policies of the past to meet the needs of the future.

Ageing population

The first challenge is an ageing population (see Chapter 2). In Britain, this will give rise to real problems. Older people cost more in health care and pensions, and there will be many more of them – by 2041 the number of people over 65 will have increased by a half and the number over 75 will have doubled.[3]

It is estimated that an ageing population will on its own require an increase in health-care spending of about 30 per cent over the next 40 years.[30] This will be serious and unavoidable, but not unaffordable – a similar increase as a result of ageing over the *past* 40 years has already been accommodated. With increases in costs from other causes, total spending on health will need to be more than doubled. Spread over 40 years, however, the total is likely to rise no faster than the rate of economic growth, and will still leave Britain spending a smaller percentage of GDP on health care than most other OECD countries.

The attempt to avert these increases in costs by introducing an 'internal market' into the NHS has been a failure. It has brought a two-tier service, with inequity between the patients of fundholding and non-fundholding doctors. The 'efficiency savings' achieved have been more than offset by higher administrative costs.[14] The scheme has brought a mountain of new paperwork, with thousands of separate contracts each year and millions of items to be costed, billed, paid for and accounted for. Altogether, the internal market has increased NHS management costs from 6 per cent to 10.5 per cent – by about £1.8 billion a year;[16] it has brought a 400 per cent increase in the number of NHS managers,[17] together with drastic falls in the recruitment and morale of nurses and doctors.[18–19]

A more thoroughgoing market solution, with full private medicine instead of a quasi-market system within the NHS, would create worse problems. Medical needs would be the same, but the cost of meeting them would be greater, not smaller, because of the considerable extra administrative costs involved in collecting contributions from patients, checking entitlements, processing bills and vetting hospitals. There would be problems of under-treatment of anyone left out of adequate insurance schemes and *over*-treatment of people in more generous schemes. Other countries with market-based health-care systems have much higher health-care costs than Britain, and much more uneven access to treatment.

The best way of meeting our future needs would be not to look for something different but to develop the NHS we already have. It is the fairest way, and also the most efficient and economical way of providing health care for all. It is the envy of people in many other countries and the most popular institution for many people in this country. What it needs is not restructuring, but more money to bring resourcing up to the levels of other comparable countries.

In health care, there is no magic way round the basic fact that you only get what you pay for, and taxation is the fairest and most practical way of paying for it. Health is one area in which some informal hypothecation (linking specific taxes directly with specific benefits) might be useful. The NHS is so popular that the great majority of people would be prepared to pay higher taxes to give it the extra resources it needed.[34]

The increase in the number of old people will also bring a large and unavoidable increase in the cost of pensions. Relying on the market for provision in the form of occupational schemes and individual pension plans would bring worse provision at a *higher*, not lower, cost.

Occupational schemes have the disadvantage that half the population is not covered, including most people in smaller companies, most short-term and casual workers, people who take time off work to look after small children, and people who are unemployed or made redundant. A change of job normally involves reduced entitlements, penalising and discouraging labour mobility at a time when more frequent job changes are becoming more desirable for the economy and less avoidable for the individual. Many schemes provide inadequate pensions that are not indexed for inflation.[38] Employers set the levels and conditions and control the assets – which carries the risk of occasional Maxwell-type misappropriations. Also, occupational schemes involve a disguised subsidy from taxpayers in the form of tax relief on contributions, which costs the exchequer £7 billion a year.[39]

The newer individual personal pension plans do not impede labour mobility but have other serious disadvantages. They do not cover people who have to drop out if they cannot afford to keep up fixed regular contributions – for example, if they are made redundant, or have to take a worse paid job. They provide no guarantee of final pension level because that depends on a triple lottery – the size of the long-term rise in the stock market, the skill of the fund's investment manager, and the rate of interest at the time the fund is converted into an annuity to provide the pension. The worst-managed funds provide only half the return of the best ones,[42] and many do not provide an adequate pension at the end.

All schemes are burdened with high charges to cover promotion, administration and profits. These average about 25 per cent,[35] compared with administration costs of only 1.2 per cent for national insurance. Contracts are complex and difficult for ordinary people to understand and compare, and many people get talked into unsuitable schemes. A survey[44] of people who had been persuaded to move from occupational schemes to personal plans found that 91 per cent had made the change on the basis of suspect advice or insufficient information. It is estimated that 2.4 million people have been talked into disadvantageous schemes, at a total cost that may reach £11 billion.[45] Personal pension plans also involve a heavy public subsidy in the form of income tax relief on contributions.

Circumstances in Britain have changed greatly since Beveridge wrote his report in the 1940s. Divorce has become more common; more women are at work; there are more frequent changes in people's jobs and earnings (for example, there is more self-employment and casual and part-time work); there is greater variety in life styles and aspirations; and a wider range of ages for retirement. Britain needs a *modernised* national scheme to provide for the circumstances not of 50 years ago, but of the 50 years ahead.

It needs to be *inclusive*, covering everyone. It needs to be funded by *contributions* from everyone, with provisions for credit for time when contributions cannot be made because, for example, of time spent on education, training, looking after young children, sickness, disability or unemployment. It needs to provide *guaranteed benefits* so that everyone can be assured a decent standard of living in retirement. It needs to be *individualised,* with contributions and benefits for women in their own right, not just as appendages to their husbands. And it needs to be *flexible*, allowing for variations in individual preferences for higher/lower contributions in return for higher/lower pension levels in retirement, or with earlier/later retirement ages, and provision for adjustment of entitlements for people who want to change the age at which they decide to give up work, or who want to go over to part-time working, or to phase-in their retirement over a period of years.

For such a scheme, contributions would inevitably have to be high – but not nearly as high as would be needed for private schemes providing far less attractive benefits. The government would need to top it up to cover people not in a position to pay their own contributions at various stages – but it would be far less expensive than the present cost of giving tax relief to private schemes and paying income support to all those who for various reasons are not properly covered by them.

In a modern, prosperous, caring and cohesive society, it is reasonable to expect a system that provides decent incomes for all in old age. Only a new public scheme could provide coverage that is sufficiently inclusive, individual, flexible, fair, economical and affordable to meet the needs of retirement in the circumstances of the next century. No market-based arrangements can come near to meeting future needs so well. In this area, state provision is manifestly the most practical way ahead; it should not be ruled out of the agenda by the dogma that the market must provide everything, even when it does not offer the best solution.

Social division

A second challenge for Britain in the next century is the threat to social cohesion presented by sharply rising inequality (see Chapter 3). Britain used to be renowned for its stability and social cohesion, the result largely of changes made during two world wars, consolidated subsequently by full employment, the welfare state and a system of progressive taxation. However, between 1979 and 1993/4, the gap between the richest tenth of the population and the poorest tenth almost doubled,[54] the number of people in poverty more than doubled,[54] and the number of children in poverty trebled.[54] If these trends towards greater inequality and poverty continued, the whole future social cohesion of Britain would be put in jeopardy.

A greater reliance on market forces would provide no solution to this problem. Indeed, the market-oriented policies adopted in recent years are the main *cause* of the problem. The policies responsible are in the areas of the labour market, taxation and social security.

After 1979, measures were introduced to end labour market 'distortions' at the bottom by ending incomes policies, abolishing wages councils, cutting back trade union powers, encouraging low-paid part-time and casual work, and putting out council services to low-paying private contractors. At the same time, 'distortions' at the top were removed by ending any inhibitions over disproportionate pay increases for top managers and directors.

The consequent release of market forces has not improved economic performance (see Chapter 5), but it *has* brought the widest spread of earnings since Victorian times.[83] At the bottom, more and more people are working for pay too low to live on and need to have their incomes topped up by family credit. At the top, directors of major companies reward themselves with very high pay when things go really well, with very high pay regardless when things go badly, and with very generous compensation packages when things go so badly that they have to be put out to rest. Remuneration for directors of privatised utilities, for example, has risen sixfold since privatisation, largely to the same people as before, without any commensurate improvement in their capabilities or performance.[93]

High tax rates were seen as reducing incentives and thus distort the best operation of the market system. Accordingly, a range of tax changes were introduced, and these have predominantly benefited people with high incomes. For example, cuts in income tax alone have amounted to £32 billion (equivalent to 40 per cent of the social security budget), and of this, half has gone to the top 10 per cent of incomes and 30 per cent to the top 1 per cent of incomes.[110] These changes have had no measurable effect on incentives or economic performance, but they have added significantly to the inequality of distribution of post-tax incomes.

Social security expenditure was seen as a 'burden' on the market economy, and the aim of policy was to reduce it by limiting benefit increases to the rate of inflation (instead of increasing them, as before, in line with average national earnings), and by moving as far as possible from universal benefits to means-tested ones. The result of the former change has been to freeze the real level of benefits, and thus widen the gap between benefits and other incomes. The effect of the latter change has been to lock more unemployed people into the poverty trap, where returning to work is not worthwhile because almost all the earnings are clawed back in reduced benefit entitlements.

If benefits are confined to those in greatest need, so that better-off people get no benefit from the system and feel that they have no stake in it, in the long run, it will foster a division in society between 'us' who pay and 'them' who benefit, thus putting pressure on the government to lower benefits to minimal levels, which in turn will cause even greater social exclusion.

If these free market policies for earnings, taxation and social security were maintained, they would bring further increases in inequality and poverty. According to UNDP figures, Britain's income distribution has already become the most unequal in western Europe.[59] By 2010, it would become as unequal as Brazil.

The trend towards increasing inequality and social division can, however, be reversed. The widening gap in earnings is going to be checked at the bottom by the introduction of a statutory minimum wage to provide a floor for low earnings. At the top it could be offset by a fairer tax structure with a higher tax rate for very large incomes.

The twenty-first century thus requires a new, inclusive social security system, in which universal contributions bring universal benefits to all, provide a decent standard of living and ensure that everybody enjoys the benefits of future improvements in national prosperity. A scheme of this sort would have important advantages over present arrangements. It would provide genuine security for everyone, not just the most needy few; it would end the friction of the means test and the waste of the poverty trap; it would be cheaper to administer; and it would foster social cohesion. It would, however, be expensive, and so would need to be built up over a period of years.

Employment

Britain's third challenge in the next century will be jobs – the need to end persistent mass unemployment and the economic waste, social damage and personal hardship that results from it (see Chapter 4). The currently fashionable market-based solution to unemployment – labour market flexibility – usually means flexibility *downwards* of wages, conditions, legal rights and general standards, and flexibility *upwards* of top salaries. The argument is that, if labour markets are made more flexible, some of the less eligible workers, who would otherwise be unemployed, will be able to price themselves into a job by accepting lower pay. The US is cited as a model of the success of this approach.

Economic growth and rising employment in the US have, however, had less to do with labour-market flexibility than with rising population, low interest rates and expansionary macroeconomic policies. Moreover, the lower unemployment rate in the US needs to be seen in combination with the higher rates of non-employment for other reasons – for example, the prison population equivalent to 1.9 per cent of the workforce, with a further 1.5 per cent guarding them at an average cost of $30,000 a year per head.[150]

The high level of new job creation in the US has been accompanied by a sharp increase in inequality, insecurity and crime. Many of the new jobs are low-skill, low-pay, insecure ones, providing limited prospects for the future and inadequate support for the present. Many do not even cover the basic needs of subsistence, and 60 per cent of US households in poverty have someone who is in work but earning too little to support a family.[148] Between 1990 and 1996, when real wages rose by 60 per cent in Europe, they *fell* by 1 per cent in the US.[170] The benefit of the rise in GDP in the US has gone predominantly in higher profits, share values and dividends – three-quarters of which went to only 2.5 per cent of households.[149]

More relevant for increasing employment than low pay will be vocational training to equip people for the high-skill, high-pay jobs of the future. But here market forces in Britain have failed to deliver. While in some other countries firms have seen a competitive advantage in building up long-term, highly-skilled, highly-motivated workforces by offering job security and opportunities for training and advancement, in too many British firms, a short-term market advantage has been sought through low pay, short contracts, 'downsizing' and neglect of training.

Though the new welfare-to-work scheme will help by providing training opportunities and other measures to help people find jobs, on their own they will not be enough to end unemployment. In the 1970s, Edward Heath's government provided a massive increase in training through the Manpower Services Commission, but it did not end unemployment because it did not generate new jobs to go with the new skills. Germany has the best industrial training and highest level of skills of any country in Europe, but that has not prevented a large increase in unemployment.

The key factor in the level of unemployment is the level of demand for jobs. When economies are run at a high level of demand, economic growth is rapid and enough jobs are created for all, even those with fewer skills – as in Britain in the 1950s and 1960s, when unemployment was mostly below 2 per cent, and as in some other countries subsequently. The world has changed since the 1950s and 1960s. There are difficulties in running economies at a higher level of demand, but these can be overcome (see Chapter 4). It is a matter of priorities, of giving higher priority to economic growth and full employment than to other objectives which, although desirable, are of less central importance.

Mass unemployment has involved huge costs in personal suffering and economic loss. A market system that keeps so many people out of work when so much work needs to be done makes no sense, economically or socially. For a good society in the twenty-first century, we should settle for nothing short of full employment. This *can* be achieved – but only by intervening positively in the market system.

The global economy

The fourth challenge facing Britain in the next century is the economy (see Chapter 5). How are we to secure faster economic growth in an increasingly globalised market system? The emergence of a global market offers enormous potential benefits, but it also poses serious problems. There are three main areas of concern.

First, while the globalisation of investment gives multinational companies the freedom to choose the most profitable location in which to expand their operations, it also means that national governments have to compete to attract the investment flows, which are the basis of future development. This puts them under constant pressure to keep wages low; to keep down taxes and social security contributions (and to trim social services and other public expenditure to make this possible); to relax labour regulations and legal and accounting requirements; and to reduce standards of safety and of environmental and consumer protection.

Second, the growing interdependence of modern economies, as a result of the increasing flows of trade and investment between them, means that the effects of macroeconomic policies adopted by one country spill over into other countries and are diluted. Conversely, economies can be severely hit by shocks resulting from changes taking place in other economies. Consequently, governments find it difficult, acting alone, to pursue national policies designed to bring economic expansion and full employment.

Finally, and most worryingly, the most striking feature of the global economy has been the astronomic growth of international financial movements. Current annual turnover in the world's foreign exchange markets is ten times the world's annual GDP.[190] Movements on this scale are far too great for national central banks to be able to control, and this leaves them vulnerable to international movements of speculative funds.

These global developments impose serious constraints on the freedom of any national government to manage its own independent economic policy if it acts alone. However, if governments act together, they can do much to regulate the global market.

Since multinationals can locate their investment anywhere in the world, investment will tend to flow to countries that offer the most favourable terms. For a country the size of Britain it is not practicable to stand out against this – the investment will simply go elsewhere.

It is another matter for the EU as a whole. It is too big a market to be bypassed. It also generates enough investment of its own not to be dependent on investment from outside. It is therefore feasible for the member countries to keep control of their affairs by setting common standards and insisting on keeping to them. Already a start is being made with an agreement to prevent countries bidding against each other with higher financial incentives to attract inward investment.

If one lone government decided to introduce expansionary economic policies to bring higher employment and faster growth, the effects would tend to leak away to other countries. This would not happen if the EU countries coordinated their actions and all reflated their economies together. This is what was proposed with the Delors expansion plan a few years ago, and has been proposed again more recently by Jospin.

National governments on their own cannot withstand global speculative movements, as the collapse of sterling on 'Black Monday' demonstrated. With the euro it will be another matter. Joining together in a common currency automatically ends the possibility of currency speculation within the euro group of countries. As a new, strong and widely used currency, with pooled reserves many times greater than those of any one participant country, the euro will be better placed than sterling to see off speculation relative to other currencies.

Moreover, because the EU is the world's biggest single market and is largely self-sufficient, it is not vulnerable to serious damage from speculation against the euro. Extra-EU imports and exports are each equivalent to only about 10 per cent of the EU's GDP, and in most years the EU has a net trade surplus with the rest of the world.[195] It has little need to fear speculation in global currency markets.

Ultimately, an international currency regulatory regime will be needed to replace the Bretton Woods system set up after the war. This will take time to set up. Meanwhile, there may be scope for a scheme to reduce the scale of speculative movements. It is estimated[202] that between 90 and 95 per cent of international financial transactions are speculative, seeking quick gains from very small margins on very large volumes, often on borrowed money. It follows that a very small levy on all international transactions would be enough to make the majority of speculative deals much less attractive, while not being enough to make any significant difference to normal commercial business. Such a levy would dampen speculation and reduce volatility, while at the same time yield substantial revenue – even a levy of 0.01 per cent could yield as much as $30 billion a year,[190] part of which could provide a useful addition to funds available for international development.

Using the computer systems already employed by the major banks for internal monitoring and control would make it technically feasible to introduce such a levy. The databases generated in this way could provide information on global financial movements that would be of great value to those engaged in international trade and investment, to governments and to the foreign exchange market itself.

The key requirement will be to get the political agreement of the main financial countries, the G8 group. A few years ago, such agreement would have looked unrealistic to expect. But now, after the shocks of the past year, the prospects are much stronger.

The environment

The fifth challenge facing Britain in the next century is the environment (see Chapter 6), which is increasingly threatened by congestion, pollution and global warming. In these, and also in almost every other area of environmental concern, market forces are pulling strongly in unhelpful directions.

Market forces encourage developers to put houses, shops, offices, factories and recreational developments on cheaper greenfield sites, even though this undermines existing city centres, erodes green belts around towns, destroys areas of natural beauty, and adds to car traffic, air pollution and emissions of greenhouse gases.

Market forces encourage ever increasing use of private cars, which discourages walking, cycling and public transport and increases air pollution, greenhouse gas emissions and self-defeating traffic jams. They encourage oil companies to seek to sell more fuel rather than to encourage economy or develop cleaner fuels, and car manufacturers to promote cars that are bigger and faster rather than ones that are more economical and cleaner.

And market forces make it more difficult to reduce greenhouse gas emissions to prevent global warming. They encourage the suppliers of fossil fuels to try to sell more, not less, and to set their tariffs and marketing strategies to favour larger users, and give incentives to higher consumption, rather than to promote economy, efficiency and substitution. They encourage the use of existing fossil fuels if they are at present cheaper, rather than the development of alternative renewable energy sources, many of which will become cheaper only after investment in their further development. At the global level, they encourage each country to pursue its own national advantage, allowing its greenhouse gas emissions to go on rising, even though if other countries do the same the total will rise to unacceptable levels.

To get a better quality of environment in our towns and countryside in the next century, and better means of getting around in them, it will be necessary to moderate the working of market forces to take account of wider considerations – in particular by getting a better balance between the use of cars and other forms of transport.

To make city centres easier to get to and more attractive to arrive in, it will be necessary to change the present balance in a number of different ways. These would include:

- a shift in development, with investment in city centre renewal rather than out-of-town centres in the countryside;

- a change in use of space, with more bus lanes, cycleways, traffic restrictions in residential areas and pedestrian precincts in town centres;
- improvements in public transport with lower fares and investment in more modern facilities;
- reduced pollution through promotion of cleaner and more economical vehicles and restrictions on use of dirty ones; and
- reduced use of cars through dearer petrol, road-use pricing, higher charges for parking, car sharing and park-and-ride schemes.

By a range of interventions to modify the working of the market it should be possible to ensure in the next century both more effective mobility and a higher quality and more sustainable environment.

The threat of global climate change can only be dealt with by overriding market forces through international agreement on targets for reducing greenhouse gas emissions; and through action by national governments to develop renewable energy sources, to reduce consumption of fossil fuels, and to promote energy efficiency and conservation through information, regulation and a range of financial incentives and penalties.

This is one area in which it is widely recognised that the free operation of market forces offers no solution. That is why it was possible to get international agreement at Kyoto on national targets for reduced greenhouse gas emissions. That agreement marked an important start, but a limited and inadequate one. Internationally, the agreement still needs to be ratified by the US and extended to the developing countries, targets need to be made more stringent and their effective implementation ensured. Domestically, measures will need to be introduced to ensure reductions in greenhouse gas emissions – eventually by margins far greater than those currently contemplated.

World population

The sixth challenge is the continuing rise in world population (see Chapter 7). This poses a threat to supplies of food, water and other resources, giving rise to new sources of conflict and distress, and is making it more difficult to close the gap in living standards between industrial and developed countries, and to end the extreme poverty which many people still suffer. It is the poorest countries that are the most threatened by rising population, but Britain and other European countries will also be affected, for example by increasing pressures for immigration.

World population increases will eventually be checked by the lower fertility rates that inevitably accompany higher standards of living. Waiting for market forces to bring general economic development will, however, take too long. Private investment can be valuable, but on its own will not be enough. Most private international investment from developed countries goes to other developed countries. What little private investment does go to developing countries goes mostly to a handful of the more developed ones,[314] which are not the ones with the worst population problems. In many developing countries, the inward flow of investment from developed countries has been offset by an outward flow of flight capital *to* developed countries.[338]

According to the World Bank,[309,342] to avert unsustainable population increases it will be necessary to invest in four areas of human development – family planning, education for girls, water and sanitation, and primary health. The resources required are not enormous but, because they offer no scope for commercial profit, there is no prospect of their being provided by market forces.

The required investment in human development will therefore need to come from international aid programmes funded by governments. In the past, these programmes have often been used to help promote exports, secure arms deals, or gain political or strategic advantages for the donor country. However, the change of government has brought a radical change in Britain's international development policy,[358] with the future emphasis firmly on the kinds of human development required, and a commitment also to increased resources in the future.

Security

The seventh challenge to face Britain as it enters the next century is how to reshape its defence policy to take account of the fundamentally changed security situation in the post-cold war world (see Chapter 8).

Defence is one area in which market forces are clearly *not* the key factor in future developments. But, even in defence, market forces have become an important, and for the most part unhelpful, factor, not just in meeting requirements, but in determining the form and scale of the threats for which we need to provide.

With the end of the cold war, Britain no longer faces any risk of an attack posing a threat to national survival. Future requirements are likely to be for means of effective participation in limited wars and peace-keeping operations, normally in cooperation with allied countries and with discretion about the extent of involvement. Hence, there will be a need for forces with quality, flexibility and mobility; but not for the large quantities of advanced weapons systems that were thought necessary during the cold war to deter or defeat an all-out invasion by a superpower.

However, in Britain and other leading arms producing countries, the defence industries, faced with falling demand in their home countries, have sought to make up for this by selling their weapons – even the most advanced ones – to other countries around the world. And defence ministries, hoping to contain their expenditure by spreading development and procurement costs over a larger output, have encouraged this. The consequence of this is that other countries have acquired formidable weapons systems, which could, as in the Gulf War, be used against ourselves. To ensure superiority over these higher level threats, it has then been considered necessary to develop and procure even more advanced systems; which are then sold on to other countries, which then makes it necessary to develop still more advanced systems, and so on.

With defence industries trying to expand sales and defence ministries trying to keep down unit costs, market forces are creating a pernicious circularity, with a steady escalation of external threats and, hence, of requirements for meeting them, making conflicts more destructive and defence budgets more expensive.

International agreement to a drastic reduction in arms exports is needed to secure a scaling down of defence budgets and the realisation of a 'peace dividend'. A start has been made with the worldwide ban on landmines and with a British-initiated agreement between EU countries to toughen controls on arms exports. The criteria for appropriate destination countries are now defined more tightly. When one country refuses to supply arms to another, there is now a commitment for any third country planning to take up the order to notify (privately) the one that initially refused it. This is a crucial start, but much remains to be done to make arms deals and refusals public, to make controls more stringent; and to extend the scheme to the other main arms exporting countries.

There is a long way to go in this, but there are grounds for optimism. Only four countries (the US, Britain, France and Russia) between them account for 87 per cent of world arms exports;[385] and all of them have a common interest in a world with fewer and smaller armed conflicts, less demanding defence capability requirements, and less expensive budgets.

Limitations of the market

In each of the areas in which Britain faces major challenges in the twenty-first century, greater use of market forces does not offer a promising way forward. Indeed, in many areas a key need will be to regulate, redirect or replace market forces in order to secure socially desirable outcomes.

The three main reasons why the unrestrained operation of market forces will be unlikely to provide a solution to most of the problems of the future is that they do not take account of externalities, they bring increasing inequalities, and they generate instabilities that threaten world economic development.

Externalities

By its nature, the market takes account only of those factors that operate in it. But life is wider than that. Many of the things left out are important; giving weight only to those that figure in the market is too narrow a basis on which to provide a rich and varied future. Outcomes that may be 'efficient' within the narrow definition of the market are often less efficient, or less desirable, if account is taken of the various externalities beyond the market.

Car manufacturers, oil companies, bus operators, housebuilders, shopkeepers and commuters may each pursue their own interests in the market in ways that result in an 'efficient' outcome in terms of the market forces involved. But the interplay of these forces on their own does not take account of wider social and environmental considerations. It is therefore unlikely to bring an optimum outcome in terms of traffic jams, accidents, noise and air pollution, or even of quick, cheap and easy journeys.

Coal, oil, gas and electricity producers' interactions with consumers in the market encourage neither conservation and efficient use of energy nor the development of non-fossil sources of energy to reduce global warming.

A similar logic applies to incomes. In a free labour market each firm may pay its employees at rates that seem sensible in relation to its business needs. However, the market takes no account of differences in social needs, for example as a result of different family circumstances or health; still less does it take account of the overall income distribution that results from all the separate company decisions, or of the consequences of income inequalities on social cohesion and poverty.

The same goes for employment. A firm may decide it is profitable to 'downsize', reducing its costs by making people redundant. What the firm does not take into account in its calculations is that if the people made redundant become unemployed and draw benefits, taxpayers will have to pay more to cover the costs and the economy as a whole may be worse off. And if the total of all the jobs provided by all the employers is less than the total number of people seeking a job, the market provides no mechanism for boosting aggregate demand in order to reduce unemployment.

Leaving things to be settled by market forces implies a built-in distortion, with permanent pressures to narrow the range of provision to things that can profitably be provided on a commercial basis, and to cut down on things that are not profitable in narrow commercial terms – such as public health services, public education, public libraries, public transport, public parks, public service broadcasting.

The narrowness of the market is a matter not merely of economic costs and benefits, but of attitudes to people, how they behave and what they value in life. Extreme *laissez-faire* economics, like Marxist economics, pre-supposes that economic considerations are virtually the only ones that matter. But life is broader than that, and so also are people. People need money to live, but they do not value only the things that have a price in the market. Other quite different things are also important, such as friendships and families, sunsets and socialising, work satisfaction and recreation. Indeed, many people find fulfilment in work that is poorly paid, or not paid at all, but is creative or provides service to others.

With market forces setting the agenda, the numbers and talents going into different occupations will increasingly come to reflect market values – better pay in business and financial services, worse pay in teaching and social services; expensively trained physicists and engineers seeking new careers as bankers and accountants; and expensively trained teachers and nurses having a struggle to survive or giving up in despair.

The introduction of market practices and attitudes into unsuitable areas also involves distortions in what people do within particular occupations. For example, the introduction of business methods and attitudes into social services involves professional staff spending more time on business tasks and less on the professional work they have been trained to do. The result is likely to be increased tension, frustration and waste of time – and ultimately higher costs when people in the caring occupations come to accept the business ethos and demand the highest pay they can get.

The inability of market forces to take account of externalities means that giving undue prominence to them will bring a narrowing of choices and a distortion of values, which will limit the scope for making the most of the opportunities of the future.

Inequalities

The second general objection to over-reliance on the market is that market forces, when given free rein, bring increasing inequality. In the postwar decades this tendency was largely offset by Keynesian economic management policies that brought full employment and economic growth, and by redistributive taxation and the welfare state that reduced disparities in income and wealth and ensured that the rise in living standards was broadly spread. But in the past two decades the return to a more *laissez-faire* kind of economic system, together with the extension of market-based systems to new areas, has reduced these moderating influences and brought an inexorable rise in inequality, poverty and social division.

In Britain and the US the current concentration on maximising shareholder value is bringing higher dividends and capital gains, resulting in a redistribution in favour of those who hold wealth and a diminution of concerns for employees, consumers, the wider environment and society in general. And, for employees, it is bringing enormous increases in remuneration for those at the top, while those lower down are subject to 'downsizing', 'delayering', restructuring, cost-cutting, casualisation and redundancy. The result is a steady increase in inequality in the distribution of incomes as a whole and, for earned incomes, a widening of the gap between top and bottom until it is now the greatest since records were first kept over a hundred years ago.

Market forces, on their own, do not ensure full employment or economic growth. And economic policies designed to please the preferences of market sentiment have brought deflation and high unemployment. Unemployment in turn brings further inequalities between those in a job and those out of work with low incomes and poor prospects. And even for those who have a job, the persistence of high unemployment brings further inequalities between those whose job is secure and those who are on short contracts or at risk of redundancy, or who have to accept low pay, long hours or poor conditions in order to keep a job at all.

When global market forces are paramount, and countries feel a need to make themselves attractive to footloose international investment, governments are under constant pressure to improve 'incentives' by cutting taxes, specially for companies and top incomes, and to reduce the 'burden' of the welfare state by cutting benefits. But redistributive taxes and social security benefits are two of the principal mechanisms for offsetting inequalities in original incomes. When they are eroded their impact is reduced and inequalities grow unchecked.

And when the market is extended into the welfare system itself, it brings still further inequalities. National social security schemes normally provide basic cover for everyone and often include some redistribution between people with different income levels. But company pension schemes give the best terms to the most senior people, commercial personal pensions give the best terms to those with the highest and steadiest incomes, and both kinds of market provision leave many people out altogether – and these are often the very people who are in greatest need. So the inequalities in people's working lives are extended to, and amplified in, their old age.

And in health care the 'internal market' has brought a two-tier standard of provision, while private medicine would bring even greater inequalities.

And similarly at the international level, the global market system, in its present form, does not provide a level playing field for developing countries seeking to improve their economic situation, and it does not provide the investment in human development needed to bring an early improvement in living standards. Hence, with development depending mainly on market forces, international inequalities persist – indeed the enormous gap between the richer industrialised countries and the poorest of the developing countries, so far from narrowing, is widening further.

Market forces generate inequalities, unless specific measures are taken to counterbalance their effects. Hence giving free rein to them implies a future with a more unequal Britain in a more unequal world; greater poverty in Britain, and desperate privation in much of the Third World; sharper social division in Britain, and greater gaps and possible conflicts between the richer countries and the poor ones. *Laissez-faire* is bringing a harder, meaner, unfairer world.

Instabilities

The third general objection to relying too much on the free play of market forces for meeting the needs of the future is that they do not provide a sound basis for steady future economic progress. The global market system has evolved in a way that has brought great increases in international trade and investment flows, increasing interdependence of different national economies, and astronomic increases in international financial movements. The last of these, in particular, is giving rise to increasing problems.

It used to be claimed that the global market provided a neutral and rational 'hidden hand', with a steady, soundly-based natural equilibrium, and a reliable mechanism for smooth, automatic adjustments to take account of longer-term changes. Instead, market forces have become erratic, volatile and destabil-ising; they are immensely powerful and out of control, and pose an increasingly unacceptable threat to future economic development. Recently, a run on Thailand's currency has led to crises and disruption in other Southeast Asian countries, Russia, Brazil and a number of other countries, and has rocked stockmarkets in Europe and the US. The market system, so far from damping down fluctuations, has amplified local difficulties into a global crisis.

The scale of financial movements has become so great that they are beyond the power of national governments to handle. For example, on the day that the run on the pound forced Britain out of the ERM, turnover on the London market was about $450 billion – more in a single day than the value of imports and exports over the whole year, and more than ten times the total value of the national foreign exchange reserves.[200-3] More recently, a single American hedge fund built up a speculative exposure totalling $200 billion and had to be rescued from collapse because it was so large that its failure would have threatened the whole US banking system.

Some money movements are needed to cover normal trade and investment, and some are hedges against possible future changes in exchange rates. The vast majority of movements, however, are speculative[190,202] – buying and selling with a view to making a profit on future changes. This means speculating not just on real future events, but on the reactions of the market to them – that is, speculating on the speculations of other speculators. This makes the currency markets extremely volatile, with enormous sums moving suddenly as a result of changes in sentiment. The result is to produce huge and unpredictable swings, which national governments cannot easily foresee, prevent or provide for. All national economies are therefore exposed to the risk of instant destabilisation.

It used to be said that 'you cannot buck the market', and that this could be an advantage, providing a necessary and healthy corrective to the follies of fallible national governments. But with the way that money markets work at present, this is manifestly not so.

At the time of the attack on the pound, sterling was overvalued and the enforced adoption of a more realistic exchange rate proved beneficial in helping the economy out of recession. However, on other occasions, speculative currency movements have been less justifiable or useful. For example, a year later, the French franc was attacked, even though it was *not* overvalued, and this attack resulted in the disruption of the whole of the narrow-band ERM. More recently, in the Far East, speculative attacks on currencies have destabilised a succession of economies that were previously regarded, by the market itself, as particularly successful in their internal growth and in their performance in the global market.

Market forces at one point regarded half a dozen Asian economies as soundly based and a model of how things should be run. Only a few months later, these same economies were regarded as hopelessly mismanaged and in need of complete overhaul – even though little had changed in them except the assessment of the market and its consequences. The assessment of global market forces may have been right at the earlier date or it may have been right a few months later; but it is not credible to suppose it could have been equally right, or even approximately right, on *both* occasions.

At the same time, market forces brought sudden falls of as much as 50 per cent in the exchange rates of these countries' currencies. Again, it is not credible to suppose that the valuation of the market was equally right both before and after the falls, that the real value of several currencies fell by as much as a half in a matter of weeks.

Similarly, one stock market's prices can fall by as much as 30 per cent in a day or two, and the fall can then be reflected in similar changes in other stock markets around the world. It is possible to believe that the market value of a particular share at a particular time reflects the earning power of the factories and other assets of the company that issued the share, and that this value will vary over time in line with the changing fortunes of the company. What is *not* credible is that when there is a stock market crash, and the average value of shares in all the world's major stock markets fall within hours, that this means there has been a substantial fall in the real value of the factories of thousands of different companies all over the world – all in a matter of hours.

Clearly, market forces are in no sense the ultimate objective indicator of reality. They are, of course, related to reality, like bookies are to horse races, but the link is imprecise, unclear, changeable and unreliable. Market changes are based more on sentiment than on substance, the result of speculation piled on speculation, a great global casino chimera, with the solidity of a hologram and the validity of a roulette ball – but with a punch that can rock the strongest economy.

The objection to global market forces, then, is not that they represent a wicked conspiracy by greedy men, but rather that they constitute blind, impersonal forces that work in a capricious and damaging way, with no claim to objective validity and no justification in functional merit. They do not deserve to be revered and they do not need to be deferred to. The time is ripe for governments to get together to tame the mindless mischief of the markets and assert the human purpose of bringing stability to the global economy.

New Labour, new hope?

The previous government had an ideologically driven conviction of the need for market-based solutions to nearly all problems – TINA ('There Is No Alternative'). There *are* alternatives, and in some areas they are preferable. Does the arrival of a new government mean that they will now be pursued?

New Labour offers a fresh, new, more pragmatic attitude, an emancipation from old dogmas, a willingness to try new approaches, an eagerness to go for whatever works best. Does this mean that there is now a more balanced approach to the market, that there is a readiness to regulate or modify the operation of market forces where this is necessary for achieving better social outcomes? More specifically, will it undertake the particular interventions with the market system needed to ensure we are on course for dealing with the main challenges of the next century?

New Labour's new start

The new government has made a fresh start in many areas, and already in the first year or so there have been a number of relevant initiatives.

The health-care problems resulting from an ageing population are to be met through an improved NHS, and substantial additional funding is to be provided to make a start on this. The creeping privatisation of health care has been halted with the ending of the tax concession for private care and major changes to the internal market to remove its worst features.

With the other problem arising from an ageing population – the increased cost of pensions – no firm new proposals have yet been put forward, although there is at least an awareness of the drawbacks of personal pensions in their present form, and a tougher attitude towards getting redress for the victims of mis-selling.

The problem of social division as a result of rising inequality has been given recognition in the setting up of the Social Exclusion Unit with a broad remit to identify problems and find new solutions to them. And there is to be an annual report on poverty trends. A floor is being provided for low earnings through the national minimum wage, and more money is to be paid to people who have only their national insurance pensions to live on. More is to be spent on social housing, and on the multiple problems of some of the worst housing estates. The child allowance is being increased and a Sure Start scheme is being introduced to ensure that all children are well cared for in their first three years. The first two budgets have included a useful degree of redistribution in favour of the poorer members of the community.

The reduction of unemployment is being given much higher priority than hitherto, and considerable resources are being put into the 'welfare-to-work' scheme, with counselling, training, new job subsidies for previously unemployed people, help with child care costs for single parents going out to work, a new working families tax credit, and other changes to reduce the severity of the poverty trap. The employability and earnings prospects of young people should be improved by the funding of more than 400,000 additional places in further education.

Longer-term environmental issues are also being addressed, with increased investment in public transport, better coordination of services, more priority for bus and cycle lanes, reduced concessions for company cars and lower tax for smaller cars, the introduction of charges for office parking space and for use of congested road space, a higher rate of landfill tax and a lower rate of VAT on insulating materials. Internationally, the government has played an active role in getting the Kyoto agreement on greenhouse gas emissions, and has announced a determination to ensure that Britain's commitments are honoured.

In international development, the government has produced a white paper that sets out a fundamental change of approach in favour of the kinds of investment needed in human welfare. Funding for the international development programme is being increased by a quarter over three years, with further increases envisaged later.

Finally, in defence, the strategic review has begun the process of restructuring the forces for future roles. The importance of the international trade in arms has been recognised, with a crucial first European agreement on arms exports, which is the result of an initiative by Britain.

These measures only go a limited way towards meeting the needs of the future; but they are a start, and they are a clear improvement on what would have been likely had the previous government continued in power. Since the problems are longer-term ones, it is not necessary to put in place all the measures for dealing with them in the course of the first year or so of the new government.

New Labour's old inheritance

However, there are grounds for concern, not so much about the gaps in the new as in the residue from the old. New Labour appears to have inherited from the previous government a number of old attitudes to the market, which seem prejudicial to its declared social purposes.

The fresh start is supposed to be founded on clear-sighted pragmatism.

The tired old divisive dichotomies of traditional political ideologies are supposed to have been swept aside in favour of a new 'Third Way' based on common purpose and common sense. But, although the rhetoric is new and looking towards the future, some of the policies and attitudes look suspiciously like the old ones that have failed in the past. In particular, the central dichotomy of TINA – private good/public bad – seems to linger on.

By this criterion, top people's pay rises in the private sector are a natural part of the working of the free market, but public sector wage claims have to be blocked to prevent inflation. Private welfare arrangements bring security through self reliance, but the public welfare state is a burden bringing dependency. Private expenditure on personal consumption is inherently good and to be expanded by cutting taxes, but public expenditure on public services is inherently bad and has to be kept under rigorous control to avoid the need for higher taxes. Private productive investment creates wealth and should be applauded and encouraged to grow, but public productive investment is suspect and a burden, needing to be firmly held within the fixed limits of the PSBR (public sector borrowing requirement) – or converted into private investment through the PFI (private finance initiative), even though this will increase total costs, reduce social control and shift the burden to future generations. And following from this is the more general policy implication: market forces are beneficial and should be accepted without question, but social forces are suspect and must be constrained with firmness.

Of course New Labour does not subscribe to such an extreme ideological position, but there appear to be elements of it in its approach to many areas of market regulation and, in particular, to its view of the role of government and the public sector.

For example, the comprehensive spending review was introduced as 'all based on a clear understanding that government should only do what it has to do'. It provided for a sharp increase in spending on health and education, but much smaller increases in other areas, leaving total government current spending at the end of the parliament projected to be lower, as a percentage of GDP, than it was at the beginning.[32]

It provided for public capital expenditure to be doubled – but from a very low level, and with the increase offset twice over by further sales of public assets, and also by increasing numbers of projects under the PFI.[32]

It provided for the functions of government departments and agencies to be reviewed every five years to assess whether they would be better privatised – but not for any equivalent reviews of functions already privatised, such as water and railways, to assess whether they would be better *de*-privatised.

This does not appear to be an even-handed pragmatism, using public agencies or private, whichever works best, but rather an expression of the inherited ideology that government's role should be kept as small as possible and private solutions should be preferred except where a special case can be made for public ones.

The drawback with this built-in bias is that it restricts policy choices by ruling out potentially attractive new options and even putting at risk existing ones. For example, a new, modern public pension scheme could provide much better value than commercial alternatives, and prove highly popular. It should be examined on its merits, not ruled out of discussion simply because it would involve increased public spending and contributions. Higher spending on health and education is much needed and will be highly popular – to the extent that people would be prepared to accept higher taxes to pay for them. If it has to be contained within a fixed maximum of public spending, it means that now it can only be accommodated by making cuts in other areas, asset sales and PFI deals; and if economic circumstances become more difficult later, there could come a time when even these priority areas have to be cut – unless the possibility of higher taxes for better services is considered on its merits.

The government's reticence in public spending is designed to produce budget surpluses, year after year, and declines in public debt, year after year, on a scale unmatched by previous governments or other countries. These heroically painful objectives are sought not because they will bring a stronger economy or a better society, but apparently as ends in themselves – or as symbols to impress the markets that Britain's policies are 'sound' according to the conventional wisdom of the day.

But, as Ramsay MacDonald discovered, impressing the markets by showing that a Labour government can be even more rigorous than its predecessors in holding to 'sound' financial policies brings little lasting joy if those policies do not happen to work. The policies currently in fashion are *not* working.

In the short term, making the Bank of England independent with a remit to focus only on inflation has brought high interest rates and a hugely overvalued pound, which is throwing the balance of payments into deficit and doing great damage to British industry. It is being done to try to get stable prices in the longer term; but if it goes on, for many firms there will be no longer term. Exporting companies need not only stable home prices but, even more, a stable and realistic exchange rate for sterling. They can live with an extra 1 or 2 per cent inflation, but a 30 per cent overvaluation of sterling is devastating – enough to make even highly efficient companies uncompetitive at a stroke.

More generally, the economic policies in fashion with the markets in the past two decades have not worked well. They have brought slower growth, higher unemployment, and mounting instability. Abdicating to global market forces, instead of joining with other countries to regulate them, is making it more difficult to secure full employment and faster growth, and impossible to avoid the risk of a sudden crisis as a result of speculative financial movements.

The residue of the old ideology with its bias towards the market puts New Labour's social objectives doubly at risk: first by arbitrarily restricting the means available for carrying them out to predominantly market-based, private sector, low tax ones, even though other alternatives might be preferable; and second by prejudicing the attainment of the improved economic performance on which everything else depends by clinging to the traditional macroeconomic policies that have produced such poor results over the past two decades.

There will be much better prospects with a genuinely pragmatic approach, using public or private instruments, whichever work best for particular tasks, and trying new macroeconomic policies that work, in place of the present ones that do not.

This seems consistent with New Labour's 'Third Way', which, on some interpretations,[399-400] clearly distinguishes itself from the *laissez-faire* 'New Right' in that, while accepting a mainly market-based system, it stresses the need to intervene in a variety of ways to regulate market forces to the benefit of social ends. Many of the market modifications advocated in previous chapters would fit well with other principles of 'Third Way' thinking, such as building a closer community, ending social exclusion, improving equality of opportunity, increasing investment in human capital, reducing unemployment and balancing rights with responsibilities. More generally, they fit the 'Third Way' emphasis on pragmatism, going for what works best without being constrained by the sterile dichotomies of the past.

Thus, even if New Labour in some important ways still appears to be imprisoned by legacies of the previous government's attitudes and policies, this does not seem to be inevitable, and it may not turn out to be enduring. It is too early to conclude that New Labour is simply old hat with pretty new ribbons. There is still everything to hope for, and to argue for.

The way forward

The present is not as good as it could be and the future can only get better – if we make it so; if we don't, it won't. The longer-term developments expected in the first half of the next century will bring exciting new opportunities for Britain, but also serious new problems. It is therefore important to analyse likely developments and the factors underlying them so as to make the best of the prospects available. By thinking clearly and acting early we can make the future much better than it would have been otherwise.

The previous chapters have examined seven of the most important issues to be faced in the decades ahead, analysing how past policies will not meet the needs of the future, and proposing new policy approaches to meet the challenges ahead. The present chapter has highlighted an aspect common to most of them – the market.

Over most of the past two decades, the orthodoxy in fashion has been that the market provides the best solution to almost all problems; and that, accordingly, market forces should be allowed to work with minimum constraint, and their operation should be extended to as many new areas as possible. This *laissez-faire* approach has given rise to many of the problems of the present; and it is unlikely to solve many of the problems of the future. On the contrary, the dogmatic insistence on market-oriented policies has proved to be too narrow and lopsided, and leaves out of account much that matters – there is more to life than the bottom line. Leaving everything to the market allows no active purpose and abdicates the chance of choice.

To meet the future's challenges successfully, we must abandon dogma and adopt a more balanced approach, examining issues objectively, assessing policies on their merits, subjecting alternatives to the pragmatic test of which works best. In some cases, the best outcomes are likely to ensue from giving market forces as free a rein as possible. But in many others, better outcomes are likely to result if market forces are regulated to prevent abuses or to reconcile conflicts; if their operation is modified to take account of wider economic, social or environmental considerations; or if they are replaced altogether by various kinds of social provision.

The need will be for a radical pragmatism, not just a token one, because the dogmas of *laissez-faire* are deeply entrenched in current policies and attitudes. Thatcher raw and strident may be gone; but merely moving on to Thatcherism with a softer voice will not be enough. What we need is not just less abrasiveness, but more effectiveness; not just finding better ways of meeting the needs of the market, but new ways of making market systems meet the needs of the community; not just accepting the consequences of impersonal market forces, but reasserting the primacy of human values.

Settling for *laissez-faire* means letting go of the future: it cannot care and it does not work. It has no purpose or values beyond the basic calculus of profit and loss; it is too narrow to take account of the full range of human needs and aspirations; and it brings slow growth and insecurity at home, and instability and havoc in the economies of the world.

And yet the market system can be enormously productive and useful if it is managed with economic skill and social purpose. The challenge, then, is not to try to minimise the mess while the forces of the global market roll over us, but to find new ways of harnessing the forces of the market to the needs of the future. There is no need to 'think the unthinkable', merely to recognise the obvious: that the purpose of market systems is to serve the needs of people, not the other way about.

The future is what we make it, for it will be shaped largely by the policy choices we make along the way. In the seven key issues for future choice, the market system will be a good servant but a poor master. If we use it sensibly, selectively and firmly, it will make a useful contribution to a better Britain. But if we allow the market to run out of control, market forces will damage our economy and our environment, and market values will take over our lives and our society.

References

1 Introduction

1. Jim Northcott, *Britain in 2010*, Policy Studies Institute, London, 1991.

2. Jim Northcott, *The Future of Britain and Europe*, Policy Studies Institute, London, 1995.

2 Ageing Population

3. Office of Population Censuses and Surveys, *1994-based National Population Projections*, Government Statistical Service, HMSO, London, 1996.

4. HM Treasury and Department of Health, (unpublished figures), London, 1989.

5. Nuttall et al, 'Financing Long-Term Care in Britain', *Journal of the Institute of Actuaries*, London, 1994.

6. House of Commons Health Committee, First Report, Session 1995–96: Long Term Care: NHS responsibilities for meeting continuing health care needs, vol 3, HMSO, London, 1995.

7. CIPFA, *Personal Social Services Statistics, 1994/95, Actuals*, Chartered Institute of Public Finance and Accountancy, London, 1994.

8. Office of Population Censuses and Surveys, *General Household Survey: carers in 1990*, Government Statistical Service, HMSO, London, 1992.

9. Richard Best and Janet Lewis (eds), *Meeting the Costs of Continuing Care: report of the Inquiry*, Joseph Rowntree Foundation, York, 1996.

10. Laing and Buisson Ltd, *Care of Elderly People: marketing survey 1996*, Laing and Buisson, London, 1996.

11. R.Young and G.Wistow, *Domiciliary Care Markets: growth and stability*, Nuffield Institute for Health, Leeds University, Leeds, 1996.

12. Norman Warner, *Better Tomorrows: Report of a national study of carers and the community care changes*, Carers National Association, London, 1995.

13. Audit Commission, *Practices Make Perfect: the role of the Family Health Services Authority*, HMSO, London, 1993.

14. Audit Commission, *What the Doctor Ordered*, HMSO, London,1996.

15. Nicholas Timmins, 'NHS wastes £1bn on ineffective treatments', *Independent*, London, 2 January 1996.

16. Nicholas Timmins, 'Trusts spending 10% on managers', *Independent*, London, 7 June 1995.

17. David Brindle, 'Boom in NHS top staff', *Guardian*, London, 11 October 1995.

18. David Brindle, 'Too few new nurses for hospitals', *Guardian*, London, 22 April 1996.

19. Sarah Boseley, 'NHS set to run out of doctors by 2010', *Guardian*, London, 18 June 1998.

20. Eleanor Mills, 'Oral cancer rise blamed on dental cutbacks', *Observer*, London, 29 October 1995.

21. *Laing's Review of Private Healthcare 1995*, Laing and Buisson, London, 1995.

22. *The Fitzhugh Directory of Independent Healthcare 1996–97*, William Fitzhugh, London, 1996.

23. *Laing's Review of Private Health Care 1997*, Laing and Buisson, London, 1997.

24. Sir Duncan Nichol (chairman), *UK Health and Healthcare Services: challenges and policy options,* Healthcare 2000, London, 1995.

25. Chris Mihill, 'Privatising the NHS could destroy it', *Guardian*, London, 24 June 1996.

26. *The Distribution of Wealth in the UK*, Institute for Fiscal Studies, London, 1994.

27. Jean Shaoul, *NHS Trusts: a capital way of operating*, Department of Accounting and Finance, University of Manchester, 1996.

28. Jean-Marie Robine, 'Espérance de santé: concepts, théories et objectifs', *Risques*, No 26, Les Cahiers de l'Assurance, Geneva, April–June 1996.

29. Karen Dunnell, 'Population Review (2): are we healthier?', *Population Trends 82,* HMSO, London, winter 1995–96.

30. John Hills, *The Future of Welfare: a guide to the debate*, Joseph Rowntree Foundation, York, 1993.

31. Andrew Adonis, 'Cash-starved NHS sinking like the Titanic', *Financial Times*, London, 25 June 1996.

32. *Comprehensive Spending Review: new public spending plans 1999–2002,* Modern Services for Britain: Investing in reform, Treasury, HMSO, London, 1998.

33. OECD in Figures: Statistics on the Member Countries, supplement to the *OECD Observer*, June/July 1997, Paris.

34. Lindsay Brook, John Hall and Ian Preston, 'Public Spending and Taxation', in *British Social Attitudes, the 13th Report*, Social and Community Planning Research, London, 1996.

35. Barbara Castle and Peter Townsend, *We CAN Afford the Welfare State: security in Retirement for everyone*, London, 1996.

36. Richard Disney and Paul Johnson, 'The strange death of a pension scheme', *Financial Times*, London, 3 February 1995.

37. Bryn Davies, *Locking the Stable Door: the ownership and control of occupational pension funds*, Institute for Public Policy Research, London, 1992.

38. Richard Miles, 'Five million face shortfall in pensions', *Guardian*, 18 September 1996.

39. *Inland Revenue Statistics 1997*, Inland Revenue, HMSO, London, 1997.

40. 'Pensions: the facts', *Independent*, London, 5 April 1997.

41. Personal Investment Authority figures quoted by Christopher Brown-Humes, 'Personal pension lapse rate high', *Financial Times*, London, 5 November 1997.

42. 'Survey of Personal Pension Plans', *Money Management*, London, October 1996.

43. Annuity Digest figures quoted by Paul Nuki, 'Pensioners exploited on annuities', *Sunday Times*, 24 April 1994.

44. Paul Durman, 'Nine in 10 pension deals suspect', *Independent*, London, 17 December 1993.

45. Christopher Brown-Humes, 'Pensions mis-selling costs may reach £11bn warns FSA', *Financial Times*, London, 13 March 1998.

46. Christopher Brown-Humes, 'Quarter of pension cases settled', *Financial Times*, London, 19 September 1997.

47. Anne Ashworth, 'Personal finance', *Times*, London, 9 March 1996.

48. *New Ambitions for our Country: a new contract for welfare*, Green Paper on welfare reform, HMSO, London, 1998.

49. Sir Gordon Borrie (chairman), *Social Justice: strategies for national renewal*, Commission on Social Justice, Vintage, London, 1994.

50. Ralf Dahrendorf (chairman), *Report on Wealth Creation and Social Cohesion in a Free Society*, Commission on Wealth Creation and Social Cohesion, London, 1995.

51. Frank Field, *How to Pay for the Future: building a stakeholders' welfare*, Institute of Community Studies, London, 1996.

52. Sir John Anson (chairman), *Pensions 2000 and Beyond*, The Retirement Income Inquiry, London, 1996.

53. Eurostat, *Demographic Statistics*, Commission of the European Communities, Brussels, 1997.

3 Social Divison

54. *Households below Average Income: a statistical analysis, 1979–1993/94*, Government Statistical Service, HMSO, London, 1997.

55. Alissa Goodman, Paul Johnson and Steven Webb, *Inequality in the UK*, Oxford University Press, Oxford, 1997.

56. Sarah Jarvis and Stephen Jenkins, *Changing Places: income mobility and poverty dynamics in Britain*, Working Paper No 96–16, ESRC Research Centre on Micro-Social Change, University of Essex, Colchester, 1996.

57. Alissa Goodman and Steven Webb, *For Richer, for Poorer: the changing distribution of income in the United Kingdom, 1961–1991*, Institute for Fiscal Studies, London, 1994.

58. A.B. Atkinson, 'Income Distribution in Europe and the United States', *Oxford Review of Economic Policy*, Vol 12, No 1, Oxford, 1996.

59. *Human Development Report 1996*, United Nations Development Programme, Oxford University Press, Oxford, 1996.

60. Adam Smith, *The Wealth of Nations*, 1776.

61. *Low Income Statistics: low income families, 1979–1989*, First Report of Social Security Committee, HMSO, London, 1993.

62. *Low Income Statistics: low income families, 1989–1992*, Second Report of Social Security Committee, HMSO, London, 1995.

63. Eurostat poverty survey, Commission of the European Communities, Brussels, 1997.

64. Carey Oppenheim and Lisa Harker, *Poverty: the facts*, 3rd edition, Child Poverty Action Group, London, 1996.

65. Janet Ford, *Consuming Credit: debt and poverty in the UK*, Child Poverty Action Group, London, 1991.

66. Richard Berthoud and Elaine Kempson, *Credit and Debt: the PSI report*, Policy Studies Institute, London, 1992.

67. Sally Holtermann, *All Our Futures: the impact of public expenditure and fiscal policies on children and young people*, Barnardos, London, 1995.

68. *The Hunger Within*, The School Milk Campaign, Stafford, 1997.

69. Nicholas Timmins, 'Suicide-poverty link is reinforced in new study', *Independent*, London, 24 July 1995.

70. Chris Mihill, 'Poor suffer more illness than rich', *Guardian*, London, 24 October 1995.

71. British Heart Foundation figures quoted by Chris Mihill, 'Heart illness risk for poor', *Guardian*, London, 24 July 1997.

72. Alison Quick and Richard Wilkinson, *Income and Health*, Socialist Health Association, London, 1991.

73. Jillian Smith, 'The OPCS Longitudinal Study', special paper in *Social Trends 26*, Government Statistical Service, HMSO, London, 1996.

74. Figures from Royal Geographical Society survey for Department of Health and Social Security quoted by Paul Brown, 'NHS plea over homelessness deaths', *Guardian*, London, 9 January 1998.

75. *Tackling Health Inequalities: an agenda for action*, King's Fund, London, 1995

76. *Health Inequalities*, HMSO, London, 1997.

77. J.A. Bishop, J.P. Formby and W.J. Smith, *International Comparisons of Income Inequality: Luxembourg income study*, working paper 26, 1989.

78. C. Marsh, *Exploring Data*, Polity Press, Cambridge, 1988.

79. Richard Wilkinson, *Unhealthy Societies: the afflictions of inequality*, Routledge, London, 1996.

80. *Human Development Report, 1993*, United Nations Development Programme, Oxford University Press, Oxford, 1993.

81. Dan Corry and Andrew Glyn, 'The macroeconomics of equality, stability and growth', in Andrew Glyn and David Miliband (eds), *Paying for Inequality: the economic cost of social injustice*, IPPR/ Rivers Oram, London, 1994.

82. *World Development Report 1991: the challenge of development*, the International Bank for Reconstruction and Development, Oxford University Press, Oxford, 1991.

83. *New Earnings Survey, 1997* (and earlier years), Government Statistical Service, HMSO, London, 1997.

84. Jonathan Haskell, *Why have Economic Fortunes Turned Against the Unskilled?*, Centre for Economic Policy Research, London, 4 October 1996.

85. Philip Pearson and Matilda Quiney, *Poor Britain: poverty, inequality and low pay in the nineties*, Low Pay Unit, London, 1992.

86. *The New Review*, No 42, Low Pay Unit, London, November/December, 1996.

87. *Employment Outlook, 1996*, Organisation for Economic Cooperation and Development, Paris, 1996.

88. Daniel Feenberg and James Poterba, *Income Inequality and the Incomes of Very High Income Taxpayers*, Working Paper No 4229, National Bureau of Economic Research, December 1992.

89. Stephen Machin, 'Wage inequality in the UK', *Oxford Review of Economic Policy*, Vol 12, No 1, Oxford, 1995.

90 *Priced into Poverty*, Low Pay Network, Manchester, 1995.

91. Richard Donkin, 'Top directors' pay packages rise by more than 12 per cent', *Financial Times*, 17 September 1996.

92. Paul Gregg, Stephen Machin and Stefan Szymanski, 'The disappearing relationship between directors' pay and corporate performance', *British Journal of Industrial Relations*, Vol 31, London, 1993.

93. Chris Blackhurst, 'Pay bonanza for privatised utilities bosses', *Independent*, London, 21 October 1996.

94 Robert Frank and Philip Cook, *The Winner-Take-All Society*, The Free Press (Simon and Schuster), New York, 1995.

95. Paul Clegg, Stephen Machin and Alan Manning, 'High pay, low pay and labour market efficiency', in Andrew Glyn and David Miliband (eds), *Paying for Inequality: the economic cost of social injustice*, IPPR/Rivers Oram Press, London, 1994.

96. Alan Manning, 'Minimum wages: the European experience', *Economic Policy*, No 23, Blackwell, Oxford, 1996.

97. Richard Layard, *What Labour Can Do*, Warner, London, 1997.

98. Richard Freeman, *Minimum Wages: again!*, conference on Economic Analysis of Low Pay and Effects of Minimum Wages, Arles, 1993.

99. Gary Burtless, 'Minimum wages in the USA', *New Economy*, London, Winter 1995.

100. Stephen Bazen, 'Part of the furniture: the minimum wage is a non-controversial part of the labour market scene on the Continent', *New Economy*, London, Winter 1995.

101. *Out of Poverty, towards Prosperity*, Low Pay Unit, London, 1996.

102. John Hills, *Income and Wealth: the latest evidence*, Joseph Rowntree Foundation, York, 1998.

103. *Department of Social Security Statistics, 1996/97*, HMSO, London, 1996.

104. David Wighton, 'Benefit agency paid out nearly £635m "wrongly"', *Financial Times*, London, 13 December 1996.

105. *Housing Benefit Fraud: third report of the Social Security Committee, 1995–96*, HMSO, London, 1996.

106. Sir Gordon Borrie (chairman), *Report of the Commission on Social Justice*, Vintage, London, 1996.

107. *The New Review, No 35*, Low Pay Unit, London, September/October 1995.

108. A.B. Atkinson, *The Welfare State and Economic Performance*, Welfare State Programme, London School of Economics, London, 1995.

109. J. Banks, A. Dilnot and H. Low, *The Distribution of Wealth in the UK*, Institute of Fiscal Studies, London, London, 1994.

110. John Hills, 'Tax policy: are there still choices?', in David Halpern, Stewart Wood, Stuart White and Gavin Cameron (eds), *Options for Britain: a strategic policy review*, Dartmouth, Aldershot, 1996.

111. Christopher Giles and Paul Johnson, *Taxes Down, Taxes Up: the effects of a decade of tax changes*, Institute for Fiscal Studies, London, 1994.

112. John Hills, *Changing Tax: how the tax system works and how to change it*, Child Poverty Action Group, London, 1988.

113. Gavyn Davies, Andrew Dilnot, Christopher Giles and David Walton, *Options for 1997: the green budget*, Institute for Fiscal Studies, London, 1996.

114. Paul Johnson, 'Taxes, Benefits, Equality and Efficiency', in Andrew Glyn and David Miliband (eds), *Paying for Inequality: the economic cost of social injustice*, IPPR/Rivers Oram Press, London, 1994.

115. Tony Atkinson, 'Targeting Poverty', *New Economy*, Blackwell, Oxford, March 1998.

4 Employment

116. 'Unemployment statistics from 1881 to the present day', *Labour Market Trends*, January 1996, Department of Employment, London.

117. Peter Spencer, 'Reactions to a flexible labour market', in Roger Jowell, John Curtice, Alison Park, Lindsay Brook and Katarina Thomson (eds), *British Social Attitudes: the 13th report*, Social and Community Planning Research, Dartmouth, Aldershot, 1996.

118. 'Ethnic groups and the labour market: analysis from the Spring 1994 Labour Force Survey', *Employment Gazette*, June 1995, Department of Employment, London.

119. *European Labour Force Survey*, Eurostat, Commission of the European Communities, Luxembourg, 1995.

120. *Report of the Working Party on the Measurement of Unemployment in the UK*, Royal Statistical Society, London, 1995.

121. *Living in Britain: results from the 1995 General Household Survey*, Government Statistical Office, HMSO, London, 1997.

122. *Labour Force Survey*, Autumn 1996, Department of Employment, London.

123. Paul Convery, 'How many people are unemployed?, *Working Brief*, Unemployment Unit, October 1996, London.

124. Paul Convery, 'Claimant count down by a third of a million', *Working Brief*, April 1997, Unemployment Unit, London.

125. John Philpott, 'The incidence and cost of unemployment', in Andrew Glyn and David Miliband (eds), *Paying for Inequality*, IPPR/Rivers Oram Press, London, 1994.

126. Michael White, *Against Unemployment*, Policy Studies Institute, London, 1991.

127. *Abstract of Statistics for Index of: retail prices, average earnings, social security benefits and contributions*, Department of Social Security, London, 1994.

128. *The OECD Jobs Study: facts, analysis, strategies*, Organisation for Economic Cooperation and Development, Paris, 1994.

129. Balbir Chatrik and Paul Convery, 'Nine out of ten young people have no income', *Working Brief*, February 1997, Unemployment Unit, London.

130. M. Clark, 'The unemployed on supplementary benefit: living standards and making ends meet on a low income', *Journal of Social Policy*, vol 7, 1978.

131. S. Moylan, J. Millar and B. Davies, *For Richer, for Poorer? DHSS cohort study of unemployed men*, research report 11, Department of Health and Social Security, HMSO, London, 1984.

132. J. Bradshaw and J. Morgan, *Budgeting on Benefit: the consumption of families on social security*, Family Policy Studies Centre, London, 1987.

133. *Households below Average Income: a statistical analysis 1979–1993/94*, Department of Social Security, Government Statistical Service, HMSO, London, 1996.

134. Council of Mortgage Lenders, press release, London, February 1991.

135. W.W. Daniel, *The Unemployed Flow*, Policy Studies Institute, London, 1990.

136. *The Health of the Population in North West Thames*, North West Thames Regional Health Authority, 1990.

137. Steve Platt and Neil Kreitman, 'Trends in parasuicide and unemployment among men in Edinburgh, 1962–1982', *British Medical Journal*, London, 1984.

138. *Social Trends 26*, Office of Population Censuses and Surveys, HMSO, London, 1996.

139. Margaret Whitehead, *The Health Divide*, 1987.

140. Michael Benzeval, Ken Judge and Margaret Whitehead, *Tackling Inequalities in Health*, King's Fund, London, 1995.

141. Ruth Kelly and Larry Elliott, 'Study links crime to jobless rise', *Guardian*, 7 January 1994, London.

142. Terry Kirby, '70 per cent of convicted offenders are found to be unemployed', *Independent*, 9 April 1994, London.

143. Matthew Nimmo, 'Welfare myths challenged by Government's own research', *Working Brief*, January 1997, Unemployment Unit, London.

144. Mark Atkinson, 'Flexible workforce fails to boost jobs market', *Observer*, 15 December 1996, London.

145. *Transition and Transformation: employee satisfaction in the 1990s*, ISR International Survey Research, London, 1996.

146. *Employment Outlook*, Organisation for Economic Cooperation and Development, Paris, 1996.

147. Richard Layard, *What Labour Can Do*, Warner, London, 1997.

148. Douglas McWilliams (former chief adviser to the Confederation of British Industry) quoted by Magnus Grimond in 'Harsh US capitalism heading for UK', *Independent*, 28 April 1997.

149. Will Hutton, 'Shock that threatens downtown America', *Guardian*, 24 January 1996, London.

150. R.B. Freeman, 'The limits of wage flexibility to curing unemployment', *Oxford Review of Economic Policy*, Spring 1995, Oxford.

151. R.B. Freeman, 'Crime and the labour market', in J.Q. Wilson and J. Petersilia (eds), *Crime*, ICS Press, San Francisco, 1994.

152. Jim Northcott and Petra Rogers, *Microelectronics in British Industry: what's happening in Britain*, Policy Studies Institute, London, 1992.

153. Jim Northcott and Petra Rogers, *Microelectronics in British Industry: the pattern of change*, Policy Studies Institute, London, 1994.

154. Jim Northcott, *Microelectronics in British Industry: promise and performance*, Policy Studies Institute, London, 1986.

155. Jim Northcott and Annette Walling, *The Impact of Microelectronics: diffusion, benefits and problems in British industry*, Policy Studies Institute, London, 1988.

156. Ian Christie, Jim Northcott and Annette Walling, *Employment Effects of New Technology in Manufacturing*, PSI, London, 1990.

157. Jim Northcott, 'La micro-électronique, menace pour l'emploi?', *Futuribles*, April 1993, Paris.

158. Bérengère de Lestapis, *'Diffusion de la Micro-Electronique dans l'Industrie*, Bureau d'Informations at de Prévisions Economiques (BIPE), Paris, 1985.

159. Werner Knetsch and Mario Kliche, *Die Industrielle Mikroelektronik-Anwendung in Verarbeitenden Gewerbe der Bundesrepublik Deutschland*, VDI–VDE Technologiezentrum, Berlin, 1986.

160. ASSESS Group, *The Social and Economic Implications of New Technology*, First Biennial Report to the President of the European Parliament, Forecasting and Assessment in Science and Technology (FAST), Commission of the European Communities, Brussels, 1991.

161. Jim Northcott and Graham Vickery, 'Surveys of the diffusion of microelectronics and advanced information technology', *STI Review*, April 1993, Organisation for Economic Cooperation and Development, Paris.

162. Jim Northcott, Colin Brown, Ian Christie, Michael Sweeney and Annette Walling, *Robots in British Industry: expectations and experience*, Policy Studies Institute, London, 1986.

163. S. Prais and K. Wagner, 'Productivity and management: the training of foremen in Britain and Germany', *National Institute Economic Review*, no. 123, February 1988, London.

164. M. Rigg, *Training in Britain: individuals' perspectives*, PSI, HMSO, London, 1989.

165. *Skills Audit*, DFEE and Cabinet Office, HMSO, 1996.

166. *Education Statistics for the UK 194*, Department of Education, HMSO, London, 1995.

167. Alan Smithers and Pamela Robinson, *Post–18 Education: growth, change, prospect*, Council for Industry and Higher Education, London, 1995.

168. *Education at a Glance: OECD indicators*, Organisation for Economic Cooperation and Development, Paris, 1995.

169. *Learning to Succeed*, Report of the National Commission on Education, Heinemann, London, 1993.

170. Paul Gregg and Jonathan Wadsworth, *Employment Audit*, Employment Policy Institute, London, 1997.

171. O. Marchand, 'Une comparaison internationale des temps de travail', *Futuribles*, May–June 1992, Paris, and J.-Y. Boulin, 'L'évolution du temps de travail en Europe', *Futuribles*, April 1992, Paris, quoted by E. Fontela, *The Long-term Outlook for Growth and Employment*, University of Madrid and Geneva, Madrid, 1993.

172. Paul Gregg, 'Share and share alike', *New Economy*, Spring 1994, London.

173. 'Labour market survey among employees', *European Economy*, Commission of the European Communities, Brussels, October 1994.

174. John Grieve Smith, *Full Employment: a pledge betrayed*, Macmillan, London, 1997.

175. Paul Krugman, 'Cycles of conventional wisdom on economic development', *International Affairs*, October 1995, Royal Institute of International Affairs, London.

176. Paul Ormerod, 'The western employment policy is going round in circles', *Demos Quarterly*, 2 1994, Demos, London.

177. M. Kitson, J. Michie and H. Sutherland, 'The fiscal and distributional implications of job generation', *Cambridge Journal of Economics*, 1997, 21, Cambridge.

178. *Budget Red Book*, HMSO, London, 1996.

179. Robert Rowthorn, 'Capital formation and unemployment', *Oxford Review of Economic Policy*, Spring 1995, Oxford University Press, Oxford.

180. Andrew Glyn, 'The assessment: unemployment and equality', *Oxford Review of Economic Policy*, Spring 1995, Oxford University Press, Oxford.

181. Leonard Nakamura, *Is US Economic Performance Really that Bad?*, working paper no. 95–21, Reserve Bank of Philadelpia, US.

182. Peter Robinson, 'Is there a pay problem?, in J. Michie and J. Grieve Smith (eds), *Employment and Economic Performance: jobs, inflation and growth*, Oxford University Press, Oxford, 1997.

5 The Economy

183. 'The GATT deal', *Financial Times*, London, 24 September 1993.

184. OECD figures quoted by Frances Williams in 'Global trade growth slips back', *Financial Times*, London, 10 December 1996.

185. GATT Secretariat Background Paper, *An Analysis of the Proposed Uruguay Round Agreement with Particular Emphasis of Aspects of Interest to Developing Countries*, GATT, Geneva, 1993.

186. World Trade Organisation figures quoted by Martin Wolf in 'A vision for world trade', *Financial Times*, London, 27 February 1996.

187. *World Development Report 1993*, World Bank, Washington DC, Oxford University Press, Oxford, 1993.

188. D. Felix, 'The Tobin tax proposal', *FUTURES*, London, March 1995.

189. BIS and IMF estimates quoted in 'Survey: the world economy', *Economist*, London, 7 October 1995.

190. Hazel Henderson and Alan F. Kay, 'Introducing competition to the global capital markets', *FUTURES*, London, May 1996.

191. Krishna Guha, 'Making the right choices', *Financial Times*, London, July 1997.

192. *World Investment Report 1993: transnational corporations and integrated international production*, UN Conference on Trade and Development, United Nations, New York, 1993.

193. Tony Walker, 'China's economy keeps up rapid rate of growth', *Financial Times*, London, 19 April 1997.

194. William H. Wetherell, 'An agreement on investment', *OECD Observer*, Paris, October/November 1996.

195. Directorate-General for Economic and Financial Affairs, *European Economy*, No. 58, 1994, Commmission of the European Communities, Brussels, 1994.

196. P. Cecchini, *The European Challenge 1992: the benefits of a single market*, Wildwood House, London, 1988.

197. Samuel Brittan, 'Where GATT's $200bn really comes from', *Financial Times*, London, 4 October 1993.

198. UNCTAD figures quoted by J.P. Agarwal, in 'European Integration and German FDI: Implications for Domestic Investment and Central European Economies', *National Institute Economic Review*, 2/1997, London, 1997.

199. Ray Barrell and Nigel Pain, 'The growth of foreign direct investment in Europe', *National Institute Economic Review*, 2/1997, London, 1997.

200. Bank of England figures quoted by Philip Gawith in 'Forex market growth startles exchanges', *Financial Times*, London, 20 September 1995.

201. Matthew Crabbe, 'Cashing in on the cash', *Sunday Times*, London, 27 September 1992.

202. James Blitz and Emma Tucker, 'Pointing a finger is pure speculation', *Financial Times*, London, 25 September 1992.

203. Figures from IMF and central banks quoted in 'Foreign Exchange Survey', *Financial Times*, London, 26 May 1993.

204. N. Crafts and G. Toniolo, *Post-war Growth: an overview*, Centre for Economic Policy Research, London, 1995.

205. *Economic Trends*, 1997 (and earlier), Office for National Statistics, HMSO, London, 1997.

206. John Mills, *Tackling Britain's False Economy*, Macmillan, London, 1997.

207. *UK Balance of Payments: the pink book 1997*, Government Statistical Service, HMSO, London, 1998.

208. *United Kingdom National Accounts Blue Book 1997* (and earlier), Government Statistical Service, HMSO, London, 1997.

209. John Grieve Smith, *Full Employment: a pledge betrayed*, Macmillan, London, 1997.

210. Robert Rowthorn, 'Capital formation and unemployment', *Oxford Review of Economic Policy*, Oxford, spring 1996.

211. Nick Crafts, 'Post-neoclassical endogenous growth theory: what are its policy implications?', *Oxford Review of Economic Policy*, Oxford, Spring 1996.

212. Will Hutton, *The State We're In*, Jonathan Cape, London, 1995.

213. *Share Ownership: the share survey register report end 1993*, HMSO, London, 1994.

214. Stephen R. Bond, Michael P. Devereux and Malcolm J. Gammie, 'Tax reform to promote investment', *Oxford Review of Economic Policy*, Oxford, Spring 1996.

215. Jim Northcott with Annette Walling, *The Impact of Microelectronics: diffusion, benefits and problems in British industry*, Policy Studies Institute, London, 1988.

216. Jim Northcott with Colin Brown, Ian Christie, Michael Sweeney and Annette Walling, *Robots in British Industry: expectations and experience*, Policy Studies Institute, London, 1986.

217. Jean Guinet and Hiroko Kamata, 'Do tax-incentives promote innovation?', *OECD Observer*, Paris, October/November 1996.

218. David Henderson, 'International economic integration: progress, prospects and implications', *International Affairs*, Royal Institute of International Affairs, London, October 1992.

219. Will Hutton, *The State to Come*, Vintage, London, 1997.

220. Paul Hirst and Grahame Thompson, *Globalisation in Question: the international economy and the possibilities of governance*, Polity, Cambridge, 1996.

221. Paul Krugman, *Pop Internationalisation*, MIT Press, Cambridge MA, 1996.

222. OECD figures quoted by Margaret Sharp in 'Industrial policy and gobalisation: what role for the nation state', in Kirsty Hughes (ed), *The Future of UK Competitiveness and the Role of Industrial Policy*, Policy Studies Institute, London, 1993.

223. George Soros, *Soros on Soros: staying ahead of the curve*, John Wiley, New York, 1995.

224. James Tobin, 'A proposal for international monetary reform', Presidential Address to the Eastern Economic Association, published in *Eastern Economic Journal*, 4, 1978.

225. *Economist*, London, 3 October 1992.

226. *World Development Report 1995*, The World Bank, Washington, Oxford University Press, Oxford, 1995.

227. José Vinals, *Building Monetary Union in Europe: is it worthwhile, where do we stand, and where are we going?*, Centre for Economic Policy Research, London, 1994.

228. P. De Grauve and W. Vanhaverbeke, 'Labour markets and European monetary unification', in P.R. Masson and M.P. Taylor (eds), *Policy Issues in the European Community*, Cambridge University Press, Cambridge, 1993.

229. J. Sachs and X. Sala-i-Martin, 'Fiscal federalism and optimum currency areas: evidence for Europe and the United States', in M. Canzonieri, V. Grilli and P.R. Masson (eds), *Establishing a Central Bank: issues in Europe and lessons from the US*, Cambridge University Press, Cambridge, 1992.

6 The Environment

230. *Living in Britain 1995*, report on the 1995 General Household Survey, General Statistical Office, HMSO, London, 1996.

231. *Transport Statistics 1997* (and earlier), Department of Transport, HMSO, London, 1997.

232. David Black, 'London speeds up 3mph since 1912', *Independent*, London, 30 November 1989.

233. *A New Deal for Transport: better for everyone*, white paper on the future of transport, HMSO, London, 1998.

234. Fred Pearce, 'How green is your golf course?', *New Scientist*, London, 25 September 1993.

235. Simon London, 'A longer shopping list', *Financial Times*, London, 2 June 1995.

236. Stuart Hampson, *Planning for Shopping*, paper given at conference on 'Britain in 2010: future patterns in shopping', Royal Society of Arts, London, 22 June 1989.

237. Neil Buckley and Simon London, 'Back to where they once belonged', *Financial Times*, London, 15 May, 1995.

238. Simon London, 'Planners fail to halt out-of-town retailing exodus', *Financial Times*, London, 15 May 1996.

239. John Roberts, *The European Experience*, paper given at conference on 'Britain in 2010: future patterns in shopping', Royal Society of Arts, London, 22 June 1989.

240. Mayer Hillman and Stephen Plowden, *Speed Control and Transport Policy*, Policy Studies Institute, London, 1996.

241. Parliamentary Advisory Council for Transport Safety, *Taking Action on Speeding*, London, 1996.

242. *The National Cycle Network*, Sustrans, Bristol, 1996.

243. Sir John Houghton (chairman), *Royal Commission on Environmental Pollution, Twentieth Report: transport and the environment - developments since 1994*, HMSO, London, 1997.

244. Christian Wolmar, 'Can £42m make Britain a nation of cyclists?', *Independent*, London, 12 September 1995.

245. 'On to the buses', *Financial Times*, London, 30 June 1997.

246. Association of London Authorities, London, 1995.

247. Sir John Houghton (chairman), *Royal Commission on Environmental Pollution, Eighteenth Report: transport and the environment*, HMSO, London, 1994.

248. David Pearce, *Blueprint 3: measuring sustainable development*, Earthscan, London, 1993.

249. *Myths and Facts: transport trends and transport policies*, Transport 2000, London, 1994.

250. Austin, *Road Pricing in London for Congestion and Emissions*, 1995; Royal Commission on Environmental Pollution, *Twentieth Report: transport and the environment - developments since 1994*, HMSO, London, 1997.

251. Roger Stokes and Bridget Taylor, 'Where next for transport policy?', in Roger Jowell, John Curtice, Lindsay Brook and Daphne Ahrendt (eds), *British Social Attitudes, 11th Report 1994/95*, Social and Community Planning Research, London, 1994.

252. United Nations Environment Programme, *Environmental Data Report, 1993–94*, United Nations, Blackwell, Oxford, 1993.

253. *Digest of Environmental Statistics, No 19, 1997*, Department of the Environment, Transport and the Regions, HMSO, London, 1997.

254. Christopher Parkes, 'Fuels for the future: US breathes more easily', *Financial Times*, London, 17 April 1997.

255. Keith Howard, 'Air-powered car goes into production in 99', *Autocar*, London, 20 May 1998.

256. Scott Morrison, 'Clean-air technology, blue-sky profits, *Financial Times*, London, 3 June 1997.

257. Sir John Houghton et al (eds), *Climate Change 1995: the science of climate change*, Second Report of the International Panel on Climate Change, United Nations Environment Programme and World Meteorological Organisation, Cambridge University Press, Cambridge, 1995.

258. Worldwatch Institute figures quoted by Geoffrey Lean, 'It's true: there really are more disasters than there used to be', *Independent*, London, 30 June 1996.

259. *Report of the Intergovernmental Panel on Climate Change*, United Nations Enviroment Programme and World Meteorological Organisation, 1990.

260. *Review of the Potential Effects of Climate Change in the United Kingdom*, Department of the Environment, HMSO, London, 1996.

261. Leyla Boulton, 'Debate warms up', *Financial Times*, London, 29 May 1996.

262. Jan Sinclair, 'Global warming may distort carbon cycle', *New Scientist*, London, 26 May 1990.

263. Mark E. Fernau, William J. Makofske and David W. South, 'Review and impacts of climate change uncertainties', *FUTURES*, London, October 1993.

264. John Gribbin, 'Methane may amplify climate change', *New Scientist*, London, 2 June 1990.

265. Geoffrey Lean, 'Deep under the ice a chilling secret lies', *Independent*, London, 18 February 1996.

266. Fred Pearce, *Turning up the Heat*, Paladin, London, 1989.

267. Michael Grubb and Christiaan Vrolijk, *The Kyoto Protocol: specific commitments and flexibility mechanisms*, Energy and Environmental Programme Climate Change Briefing Paper No 11, Royal Institute of International Affairs, London, April 1998.

268. Dean Anderson, Duncan Brack and Michael Grubb, *Emissions Trading and the Control of Greenhouse Gases*, Energy and Environmental Programme Briefing Paper No. 37, Royal Institute of International Affairs, London, May 1997.

269. James Harding, 'China emerging as bad boy in pollution stakes', *Financial Times*, London, 9 December 1997.

270. *World Development Report 1992: development and the environment*, The International Bank for Reconstruction and Development, Washington DC, Oxford University Press, Oxford, 1992.

271. World Resources Institute, Washington DC, quoted in 'Disappearing forests fan fears over tropical action plan', *New Scientist*, London, 23 January 1990.

272. Norman Myers, *Biodiversity and Biodepletion*, Green College Centre for Environmental Policy and Understanding, Oxford University, Oxford, 1993.

273. Paul Ehrlich and Edward Wilson, 'Biodiversity studies: science and policy', *Science*, 16 August 1991.

274. *Digest of United Kingdom Energy Statistics, 1997*, Department of Trade and Industry, London, 1997.

275 Walt Patterson and Michael Grubb, *Liberalising European Electricity: impacts on generation and environment*, Energy and Environment Briefing paper No. 34, Royal Institute of International Affairs, London, November 1996.

276. Pierre Tanguy, chief inspector for nuclear safety of Electricité de France, quoted by Paul Brown in 'One in 20 chance of nuclear accident', *Guardian*, London, 19 March 1990.

277. Robert Peston, 'Ex-nuclear director warns of sell-off safety risk', *Financial Times*, London, 18 October 1995.

278. Harold Bolter, *Inside Sellafield*, Quartet, London, 1996.

279. David Lascelles, 'Construction of N-plants axed', *Financial Times*, London, 12 December 1995.

280. David Lascelles, 'Ministers in climbdown over British energy debt', *Financial Times*, London, 29 March 1996.

281. David Lascelles, 'Generating profits for investors', *Financial Times*, London, 5 March 1996.

282. David Lascelles, 'Nuclear clean-up fund may need £200m', *Financial Times*, London, 29 December 1995.

283. Patrick Tooher, 'Nuclear sale goes through at half price', *Guardian*, London, 15 July 1996.

284. *Energy for the Future: renewable sources of energy*, White Paper for a Community Strategy and Action Plan, Commission of the European Communities, Brussels, 1997.

285. *1996 Annual Energy Review*, Commission of the European Communities, Brussels, 1996.

286. Michael Grubb, 'Wind energy', in Michael Grubb and John Walker (eds) *Emerging Energy Technologies*, Royal Institute of Interntional Affairs, London, 1992.

287. Pat Brown, 'Wavepower undercuts nuclear cost', *Guardian*, London, 19 March 1990.

288. Bob Hill, 'Solar electricity from photovoltaics', in Michael Grubb and John Walker (eds), *Emerging Energy Technologies*, Royal Institute of International Affairs, London, 1992.

289. Michael Peel, 'Solar power cost could be cut by 80%', *Financial Times*, London, 25 August 1997.

290. *The Impact of Transport on the Environment*, Commission of the European Communities, Brussels, 1992.

291. John Griffiths, 'Motor vehicles: global race for fuel efficiency', *Financial Times*, London, 28 November 1997.

292. Claire Holman, 'Clean and efficient cars', *Emerging Energy Technologies*, Royal Institute of International Affairs, London, 1992.

293. Leonie J. Archer, *Aircraft Emissions and the Environment: CO_2, SO_2, HO_2, NO_x*, Papers on Energy and the Environment, Oxford Institute for Energy Studies, Oxford, 1994.

294. Association for the Conservation of Energy, memorandum to Energy Committee of the House of Commons, Memoranda of Evidence, Volume II, *Energy Implications of the Greenhouse Effect, Sixth Report, Energy Committee of the House of Commons*, HMSO, London, 1989.

295. March Consulting Group, *Energy Efficiency in Domestic Appliances*, report for the Energy Efficiency Office, Department of Energy, HMSO, London, 1990.

296. 'Most and least efficient appliances', *Which?*, Consumers' Association, London, August, 1994.

297. Department of Science, Technology and Society, Utrecht University, *Policies and Measures to Reduce CO_2 Emissions by Efficiency and Renewables*, Worldwide Fund for Nature, Utrecht, Netherlands, 1996.

298. J. Goldenberg, T. Johansson, A. Reddy and R. Williams, *Energy for a Sustainable World*, World Resources Institute, Washington DC, 1987.

299. Terry Barker, *Full Employment in Europe*, paper at Cambridge Econometrics conference on Full Employment in Europe, Robinson College, Cambridge, 7–8 July 1994.

300. Tim Jackson and Michael Jacobs, 'Carbon taxes and the assumptions of environmental economics', in Terry Barker (ed), *Green Futures for Economic Growth: Britain in 2010*, Cambridge Econometrics, Cambridge, 1991.

301. Ian Christie and Heather Rolfe with Robin Legard, *Cleaner Production in Industry: integrating business goals and environmental management*, Policy Studies Institute, London, 1995.

302. ECOTEC, *The UK Environmental Industry: succeeding in the changing global market*, Department of Trade and Industry/Department of the Environment, HMSO, London, 1994.

302. Stephen Tindale and Gerald Holtham, *Green Tax Reform*, Institute for Public Policy Research, London, 1996.

7 World Population

304. *World Population Prospects 1950–2050*, Population Division, United Nations, New York, 1996.

305. *Long-Range World Population Projections: two centuries of population growth 1950–2150*, Department of International Economic and Social Affairs, United Nations, New York, 1992.

306. *Human Development Report 1997*, United Nations Development Programme, New York, Oxford University Press, Oxford, 1997.

307. 'Global trends of age distribution, 1950–1990', *Changing Population Age Structures*, Population Division, United Nations, New, York 1992.

308. T.R. Malthus, *An Essay on the Principle of Population as it Affects the Future of Mankind*, 1798, reprinted Macmillan, London, 1926.

309. *World Development Report 1992: development and the environment*, World Bank, Washington DC, Oxford University Press, Oxford, 1992.

310. D. Gale Johnson, 'World food and agriculture', in Julian Simon and Herman Kahn (eds), *The Resourceful Earth*, Basil Blackwell, Oxford, 1984.

311. *Agrostat PC*, United Nations Food and Agriculture Organisation, Rome, 1991.

312. Gerald Barney, *Global 2000 Revisited*, The Millennium Institute, Arlington, Virginia, 1993.

313. *World Grain Database* (unpublished printouts) and *World Grain Situation and Outlook*, US Department of Agriculture, Washington DC, March 1993.

314. *World Development Report 1997*, World Bank, Washington DC, Oxford University Press, Oxford, 1997.

315. L.R. Oldeman, V.W.P. van Engelen and J.H.M. Pulles, 'The extent of human-induced soil degradation', annex 5 of L.R. Oldeman, R.T.A. Hackeling and W.G. Sombroek, *World Map of the Status of Human-Induced Soil Degradation: an explanatory note*, revised 2nd edition, International Soil Reference and Information Centre, Wageningen, Netherlands, 1990.

316. H.E. Dregne, *Desertification of Arid Land*, Harvard Academic Publishers, New York, 1993.

317. Michael Carley and Ian Christie, *Managing Sustainable Development*, Earthscan, London, 1992.

318. *Fertiliser Yearbook 1993*, United Nations Food and Agriculture Organisation, Rome, 1991.

319. V.W. Ruttan (ed), *Agriculture, Environment and Health: toward sustainable development into the 21st century*, University of Minnesota Press, Minneapolis, 1990.

320. *Review of the State of World Fishery Resources*, UN Food and Agriculture Organisation, Rome, 1990.

321. *World Resources 1996–97*, The World Resources Institute, New York, Oxford University Press, Oxford, 1997.

322. *Environmental Data Report 1993–94*, United Nations Environment Programme, New York, Blackwell, Oxford, 1993.

323. Lester Brown, Hal Kane and Ed Ayres (eds), *Vital Signs 1993–94*, Worldwatch Institute, Earthscan, London, 1993.

324. *Resources and Man*, Committee on Resources and Man, National Research Council, US Academy of Sciences, W.H. Freeman, San Francisco, 1969.

325. Donella Meadows, Dennis Meadows and Jørgen Randers, *Beyond the Limits*, Earthscan, London, 1992.

326. Peter Vitouseh et al, 'Human appropriation of the products of photosynthesis', *Bioscience*, 363, 1986.

327. *Water Development and Management*, Proceedings of UN Water Conference, 1977, Mar del Plata, Argentina, Pergamon Press, Oxford, 1977.

328. 'European energy to 2020', *Energy in Europe*, Commission of the European Communities, Brussels, 1996.

329. *Human Development Report 1992*, United Nations Development Programme, New York, 1993.

330. *The State of World Population 1993*, United Nations Population Fund, New York, 1993.

331. *The State of the World's Children 1998*, United Nations Children's Fund, New York, Oxford University Press, Oxford, 1997.

332. *Bridging the Gaps: world health report 1995*, World Health Organisation, Geneva, 1995.

333. *World Development Report 1991: the challenge of development*, World Bank, Washington DC, Oxford University Press, Oxford, 1991.

334. *Human Development Report 1993*, United Nations Development Programme, New York, Oxford University Press, Oxford, 1993.

335. Sharon Russell and Michael Teitelbaum, *International Migration and International Trade*, World Bank, Washington DC, 1992.

336. 'The World's Refugee Populations', *Population Newsletter*, No. 51, United Nations Population Division, New York, 1991.

337. Didier Blanchet, 'Estimating the relationship between population and aggregate economic growth', in *Consequences of Rapid Population Growth in Developing Countries*, Taylor and Francis, New York, 1991.

338. *Global Economic Prospects and the Developing Countries*, World Bank, Washington DC, 1993.

339. *Financial Flows to Developing Countries in 1996*, press release by Development Assistance Committee, Organisation for Economic Cooperation and Development, Paris, June 1997.

340. OECD figures quoted by Graham Bowley, 'Rich nations make sharp cuts in aid', *Financial Times*, London, 6 February, 1997.

341. Isaiah Frank, *Foreign Enterprise in Developing Countries*, US Committee for Economic Development, Johns Hopkins University Press, Baltimore, 1980.

342. *World Development Report 1993: investing in health*, World Bank, Washington DC, Oxford University Press, Oxford, 1993.

343. *Population Issues Briefing Kit 1993*, United Nations Population Fund, New York, 1993.

344. John Hobcraft, *Child Spacing and Child Mortality*, Proceedings of the Demographic Health Surveys World Conference, Washington DC, 1991, IRO/Macro International, Columbia, MD, 1992.

345. Edy Kogut and Carlos Langoni, 'Income distribution and economic development', *International Labour Review*, 1975.

346. *The State of World Population 1992*, United Nations Population Fund, New York, 1992.

347. *Population and the Labour Force in Rural Economies*, FAO Economic and Social Development Paper 59, United Nations Food and Agriculture Organisation, Rome, 1989.

348. Mahmoud Fathalla, *Reproductive Health in the World: two decades of progress and the challenges ahead*, paper from UN Expert Group Meeting on Population and Women, Gaborone, Botswana, 1992.

349. *Migration and Population Distribution*, International Labour Organisation, Geneva.

350. Hans Lundgren and Carl Wahren, 'Basic education for development', *OECD Observer*, Paris, December 1992/January 1993.

351. *Education de Base et Alphabétisation*, Statistical Office, United Nations Educational, Scientific and Cultural Organisation, Paris, 1991.

352. John Hobcraft, 'Women's education, child welfare and child survival: a review of the evidence', *Health Transition Review 3*, 1993.

353. *Global Outlook 2000*, United Nations, New York, 1990.

354. Lawrence Summers (formerly chief economist, World Bank), 'The most influential investment', *People and the Planet*, Vol. 12, No. 1, 1993, United Nations Population Fund, New York, 1993.

355. Stephen Esray et al, 'Health benefits from improvements in water supply and sanitation: survey and analysis of the literature of selected diseases', *Water and Sanitation for Health Technical Report 66*, United States Agency for International Development, Washington DC, 1990.

356. *Human Development Report 1991*, United Nations Development Programme, New York, Oxford University Press, Oxford, 1991.

357. *The Reality of Aid, 1997–1998*, Eurostep, Brussels, International Council of Voluntary Agencies, Ottawa, and Actionaid, London, Earthscan, London, 1997.

358. *Eliminating World Poverty: a challenge for the 21st century*, White paper on International Development, Cmd 3789, HMSO, Department for International Development, London, November 1997.

8 Security

359. Richard Ingham, 'L'offensive éclair de l'Armée rouge: un plan d'attaque en Occident comprenait l'usage immédiat de l'arme atomique', *Figaro*, Paris, 7 August 1991.

360. Trevor Taylor, 'West European security and defence cooperation: Maastricht and beyond', *International Affairs*, Royal Institute of International Affairs, London, January 1994.

361. Hannes Andomeit, 'Russia as a great power in world affairs: images and reality', *International Affairs*, Royal Institute of International Affairs, London, 1993.

362 *Defending our Future: statement on the defence estimates 1993*, HMSO, London, 1993.

363. *The Strategic Defence Review and Supporting Essays*, Ministry of Defence, HMSO, London, 1998.

364. William Walker, 'Nuclear weapons in the former Soviet republics', *International Affairs*, Royal Institute of International Affairs, London, April 1992.

365. Ruth Leger Sivard, *World Military and Social Expenditures 1993*, World Priorities, Washington, 1993.

366. *The Military Balance 1993–94*, International Institute of Strategic Studies, London, 1993.

367. Phil Reeves, 'Some of our bombs are missing Lebed tells the West', *Independent*, London, 6 September 1997.

368. Phil Reeves, 'Russia raises alarm over nuclear arsenal', *Independent*, London, 8 February 1997.

369. Scott Sagan, *The Limits of Safety: organisations, accidents and nuclear weapons*, Princeton University Press, Princeton, 1993.

370. Michael McGwire, 'Is there a future for nuclear weapons?', *International Affairs*, Royal Institute of International Affairs, April 1994.

371. Bob Flynn, 'Seconds from Armageddon', *Guardian*, London, 22 November 1996.

372. 'Survey of defence in the 21st century', *Economist*, London, 5 September 1992.

373. Graham Allison, Owen R. Cote Jr, Richard A. Falkenrath and Steven E. Miller, *Avoiding Nuclear Anarchy: containing the threat of Russian nuclear weapons and fissile material*, Centre for Science and International Affairs, Kennedy School of Government, Harvard University, 1996.

374. Richard Latter, *The Nuclear Threat to Global Security*, Wilton Park Paper 85, Wilton Park, Steyning, HMSO, 1994.

375. Peter Rudolph, 'Non-proliferation and international export controls', *Aussenpolitik*, IV/91, Hamburg, 1991.

376. Berkhout Albright and Sipri Walker, *Plutonium and Highly Enriched Uranium 1996: world inventories, capabilities and policies*, Oxford University Press, Oxford, 1997.

377. 'Nuclear experts blame Russian Mafia for red mercury demand', *Guardian*, London, 16 August 1994.

378. *Report of the Canberra Commission on the Elimination of Nuclear Weapons*, Department of Foreign Affairs and Trade, Australia, 1996.

379. Caroline Kennedy, Colin McInnes and Len Scott, *Disarmament in a Changing World*, Fabian Society, London, 1991.

380. Malcolm Rifkind, Secretary of State for Defence, statement in House of Commons, London, 16 November 1993.

381. Michael Clarke, 'Reassessing the need for British nuclear weapons', in Jane M.O. Sharp (ed), *About Turn, Forward March with Europe: new directions for defence and security policy*, IPPR/Rivers Oram, London, 1996.

382. Stephen Pullinger, 'Priorities for nuclear, chemical and biological arms control', in Jane M.O. Sharp (ed), *About Turn, Forward March with Europe: new directions for defence and security policy*, IPPR/Rivers Oram, London, 1996.

383. Richard Latter, *Curbing Biological Weapons Proliferation*, Wilton Park Paper 79, Wilton Park, Steyning, HMSO, 1993.

384. *World Development Report 1991: the challenge of development*, World Bank, Washington DC, Oxford University Press, Oxford, 1991.

385. *The Military Balance 1997–98*, International Institute of Strategic Studies, London, 1997.

386. Richard Norton-Taylor, 'The weapons that cost British taxpayers an arm and a leg', *Guardian*, London, 6 January 1996.

387. Sir Richard Scott, *Report on the Sale of Arms to Iraq*, HMSO, London, 1996.

388. Susan Willett, 'Rethinking British arms export policy', in Jane M.O. Sharp (ed), *About Turn, Forward March with Europe: new directions for defence and security policy*, IPPR/Rivers Oram, London, 1996.

389. Richard Latter, *Controlling the Arms Trade*, Wilton Park Paper 68, Wilton Park, Steyning, HMSO, 1992.

390. General Sir Hugh Beach, Field Marshal Lord Carver and Admiral Sir James Eberle, 'Senior officers call for tighter curbs on arms exports', letter to *Independent*, London, 15 February 1997.

391. Michael White, 'Ministers double cash to clear landmines', *Guardian*, London, 3 October 1997.

392. UN figures quoted by Ted Bardache, 'The perfect defensive soldiers who refuse to stop killing', *Financial Times*, London, 6 January 1996.

393. Marrack Goulding, former UN undersecretary-general for peace-keeping operations, 'The Evolution of United Nations peacekeeping', *International Affairs*, Royal Institute of International Affairs, London, July 1993.

394. Paul Vallely, 'How Blair can save billions on defence', *Independent*, London, 10 February 1997.

395. *UK Defence Statistics 1997*, Ministry of Defence, HMSO, London, 1997.

396. Alexander Nicoll, 'Drive to get smart on weapons procurement', *Financial Times*, London, 6 February 1998.

397. Bernard Gray, 'Horizon steers for rough water', *Financial Times*, London, 24 February 1997.

398. *Statement on the Defence Estimates, 1996*, Ministry of Defence, HMSO, London, 1996.

9 The Way Forward

399. Anthony Giddens, *The Third Way: The Renewal of Social Democracy*, Polity Press, Oxford, 1998.

400. David Halpern with David Mikosz (eds), *The Third Way: summary of the NEXUS on-line discussion*, NEXUS, London, 1998.

Further Reading

1 The future in general

Britain in 2010 (Jim Northcott, Policy Studies Institute, 1991) gives a general overview of likely developments over two decades. It includes forward projections by Cambridge Econometrics, with alternative figures to illustrate the implications of different economic policies. It is mainly about Britain, but includes sections on global and regional futures.

The Future of Britain and Europe (Jim Northcott, Policy Studies Institute, 1995) compares expected future developments in Britain with other European countries and assesses how far they will bring underlying long-term pressures towards closer union. It examines likely changes in the shape of the European Union and Britain's place in it.

Towards the Millennium (Yorick Blumenfeld, Chimera, 1997) presents optimistic visions for change; *Into the 21st Century* (Brian Burrows, Alan Mayne and Paul Newbury, 1991) presents a guide to a sustainable future; *The Age of Insecurity* (Larry Elliott and Dan Atkinson, Verso, 1998) argues for an anti-big business radical Keynesian future; and *The Third Way: the renewal of social democracy* (Anthony Giddens, Polity Press/ Blackwell, Oxford, 1998) gives a coherent exposition of his view of the 'third way' to the future.

Studies of the 21st Century (edited by Martha J. Garrett, Institute for 21st Century Studies, 1991) gives an account of national and regional futures studies in 37 different countries, together with studies on particular aspects and on methodologies, and a commentary on lessons from them.

1997 State of the Future (edited by Jerome C. Glenn and Theodore J. Gordon, United Nations University Millennium Project, 1997) gives an assessment of global future prospects in many different areas based on an international survey of people working on futures studies.

The World in 1999 (Economist, 1998) is an annual round-up of short-term future prospects in countries around the world.

The Future is Ours (Graham H. May, Adamantine, 1996) is about why and how to study the future. It raises many interesting issues and provides a good introduction to the MA course on foresight studies at Leeds Metropolitan University.

2 Health care, pensions and the welfare state

The Future of Welfare (John Hills, Joseph Rowntree Foundation, 1993) is a clear, well documented and well presented account of long-term developments and issues in health, pensions and other areas of the welfare state. *Meeting the Costs of Continuing Care* (Joseph Rowntree Foundation, 1996) supplements it with a fuller study of care needs for old people. And *Private Welfare Insurance and Social Security* (Tania Burchardt and John Hills, Joseph Rowntree Foundation, 1997) examines the drawbacks of private insurance for health, long-term care and mortgage protection.

Social Justice: Strategies for National Renewal (Sir Gordon Borrie, Vintage, 1994) is the report of the Labour Party's Commission on Social Justice, the outcome of a wide-ranging study of the future of the welfare state.

New Ambitions for Our Country: a new contract for welfare (HMSO, 1998) is the government's green paper on welfare reform.

We CAN Afford the Welfare State (Barbara Castle and Peter Townsend, 1996) is a call to return to universal benefits.

How to Pay for the Future: building a stakeholders' welfare (Frank Field, Institute of Community Studies, 1996) makes the case for funded individual second pensions.

Report on Wealth Creation and Social Cohesion (Ralf Dahrendorf, 1995) is the findings of an independent commission set up to work out a new basis for the welfare state.

3 Inequality and poverty

Households below Average Income: a statistical analysis, 1979–1994/95 (HMSO, 1997) provides the official basic statistics of inequality and poverty. The government has promised that in future there will be an annual report on poverty trends – hopefully, with more up-to-date figures.

Inequality in the UK (Alissa Goodman, Paul Johnson and Steven Webb, Oxford University Press, 1997) makes a comprehensive analysis of the statistics for income and expenditure distribution and poverty and provides an account of the causes.

Income and Wealth (John Hills, the report of the Joseph Rowntree Foundation inquiry, 1995) and *Income and Wealth: the latest evidence* (Joseph Rowntree Foundation, 1998) give a well presented account of the facts and issues of income distribution and poverty.

Poverty: the facts (Carey Oppenheim and Lisa Parker, Child Poverty Action Group, 1996) spells out what poverty means to those affected, and examines its causes and consequences and ethnic, gender and geographical dimensions.

Unhealthy Societies: the afflictions of inequality (Richard Wilkinson, Routledge, 1996) analyses the effects of inequality on health, welfare and social cohesion.

Paying for Inequality (edited by Andrew Glyn and David Miliband) assesses the costs of inequality in health, education, training, unemployment and crime.

The Winner-Take-All Society (Robert H. Frank and Philip J. Cook, Martin Kessler, 1995) analyses the reasons for the growth of extremely high incomes at the top and the damaging economic, social and cultural consequences.

Taxes Up, Taxes Down: the effects of a decade of tax changes (Christopher Giles and Paul Johnson, Institute for Fiscal Studies, 1994), and a series of other IFS reports, measure the effects of actual and potential changes in taxes.

4 Unemployment

Full Employment: a pledge betrayed (John Grieve Smith, Macmillan, 1997) gives a well documented case for how it should be possible to achieve full employment again through a return to Keynesian economic policies.

What Labour can do (Richard Layard, Warner, 1997) explains the importance of training and social security reform in reducing unemployment.

Against Unemployment (Michael White, Policy Studies Institute, 1991) and *The Unemployed Flow* (W.W. Daniel, Policy Studies Institute, 1990) give the results of research on the form unemployment takes and the effects it has. *Employment Effects of New Technology in Manufacturing* (Ian Christie, Jim Northcott and Annette Walling, Policy Studies Institute, 1990) gives the results of research showing that adoption of new technology does not have the adverse effects on employment that it is commonly believed to have.

The *Labour Force Survey* (HMSO) gives the figures for unemployment in Britain, and the *European Labour Force Survey* (Eurostat 1995) gives figures for all EU countries on a comparable basis. The OECD's *Employment Outlook* each year gives figures for employment and unemployment in all the OECD countries, together with much interesting analysis of trends and characteristics of the labour market.

5 The economy and globalisation

The State We're In (Will Hutton, Jonathan Cape, 1995) and its sequel *The State to Come* (Will Hutton, Vintage, London) give a devastating critique of contemporary capitalism in Britain, with particular emphasis on the damaging impact of financial short-termism on investment and the labour market.

Tackling Britain's False Economy (John Mills, Macmillan, 1997) makes a persuasive case for achieving faster growth through Keynesian demand expansion and a more competitive exchange rate.

The Future of UK Competitiveness and the Role of Industrial Policy (edited by Kirsty Hughes, Policy Studies Institute, 1993) and *Managing the Global Economy* (edited by Jonathan Michie and John Grieve Smith, Oxford University Press, 1995) consider various aspects of national operation in a global economy. Drucker, Ohmae, Porter and Peters (Economist Publication, 1989) give a convenient summary of the prescriptions of four of the leading management gurus.

Introducing Competition to the Global Currency Markets (Hazel Henderson and Alan F. Kay, Futures, May 1996) and *The Tobin Tax Proposal* (David Felix, Futures, March 1995) explain how the international financial markets work and outline the feasibility and likely consequences of a transactions tax.

6 Environment and natural resources

Digest of Environmental Statistics (HMSO), *Digest of United Kingdom Energy Statistics* (HMSO) and *Transport Statistics* (HMSO) give each year the basic environmental statistics for Britain, with a commentary on them; and the *Environmental Data Report* (United Nations, Blackwell) does the same at a global level.

A New Deal for Transport: better for everyone (HMSO, 1998) is the government's white paper on integrated transport. It provides a good analysis of current problems and a wide range of proposals for addressing them – but only limited actions, mostly some years away.

Royal Commission on Environmental Pollution, 18th Report: transport and the environment and *20th Report: transport and the environment - developments since 1994* (Sir John Houghton, HMSO, 1994 and 1997) provide a wealth of information on the environmental problems of road traffic and a useful examination of the scope for various ways of dealing with them.

Speed Control and Transport Policy (Mayer Hillman and Stephen Plowden, Policy Studies Institute, 1996) makes the case for lower speed limits and *The National Cycle Network* (Sustrans, 1996) makes the case for cycleways.

The *Energy and Environmental Change Briefing Papers* (Michael Grubb et al, Royal Institute of International Affairs, 1995–1998) provide a useful summing up of the many complex issues involved in climate change and the measures proposed for dealing with it, including the Kyoto agreement.

Emerging Energy Technologies (Michael Grubb et al, Institute of International Relations, 1992) outlines the scope for the various alternative technologies.

Energy for the Future: renewable sources of energy (Commission of the European Communities, 1997) sets out the Commission's action plan for increasing the share of energy provided by renewables from 5 per cent in 1995 to 12 per cent in 2010.

Green Tax Reform (Stephen Tindale and Gerald Holtham, Institute of Public Policy Research, 1996) makes the case for use of green taxes.

Green Taxes and Charges: policy and practice in Britain and Germany (Stephen Smith, Institute for Fiscal Studies, 1995) measures the effects of green policies adopted so far.

Green Futures for Economic Growth: Britain in 2010 (edited by Terry Barker, Cambridge Econometrics, 1991) examines the scope for a carbon tax and other environmental policy measures.

Cleaner Production in Industry (Ian Christie and Heather Rolfe, Policy Studies Institute, 1995) describes what environmental measures are being, and could be, taken by industry.

World Resources (World Resources Institute, with UN Environment and Development Programmes, Oxford University Press) provides each year a massive review, with statistics, of global use and abuse of natural resources and the problems of sustainability.

Vital Signs (edited by Lester R. Brown, Worldwatch Institute, Earthscan) each year reviews trends in areas where sustainability could be a problem.

Global 2000 Revisited (Gerald Barney, The Millennium Institute, 1993) is an assessment of whether the earth's resources will be sufficient to support the rising population in prospect.

Beyond the Limits (Donella Meadows, Earthscan) is a rerun of the original Club of Rome computer simulation to assess future sustainability with rising population, economic growth, resource use and pollution.

Managing Sustainable Development (Michael Carley and Ian Christie, Earthscan) proposes policies for achieving sustainability.

7 World population and development

The excellent *Human Development Report* (United Nations Development Programme, Oxford Uiversity Press) produced each year by the UNDP gives a wealth of statistics, for all countries, on population, economic growth, employment, energy use, food, water, health, education, social investment, the position of women, trends in human development, military expenditure, aid flows and the gaps between North and South. Each year it also has an in-depth study of a particular aspect of development, such as global inequalities in consumption in 1998, poverty eradication in 1997, growth and human development in 1996, governance in 1993 and economic development and the North–South gap in 1992.

The *World Development Report* (World Bank, Oxford University Press) also provides each year many tables of statistics, mainly of economic indicators, for all countries. It also has an annual in-depth analysis of a particular development issue – for example, health in 1993, the environment in 1992 and the development of human resources in 1991.

The State of World Population (United Nations Population Fund) provides a report each year on the size and conditions of world population, with an appendix of demographic and social indicators.

Development Cooperation (Development Assistance Committee, OECD) provides particulars each year of the international development aid provided by the 21 OECD donor countries.

The Reality of Aid (Actionaid and the International Council of Voluntary Agencies) gives an independent review each year of the size, form and effectiveness of aid programmes.

Eliminating World Poverty (HMSO, 1997) is the white paper signalling a new and more effective course for Britain's international aid policy, with aid targeted firmly on promoting human development.

8 Security

Report of the Canberra Commission on the Elimination of Nuclear Weapons (Department of Foreign Affairs and Trade, Australia, 1996) – some of the former top players at the hard end of the cold war make a considered case for the systematic reduction and complete elimination of nuclear weapons.

The Strategic Defence Review and Supporting Essays (Ministry of Defence, 1998) makes a foreign policy-based reassessment of defence needs after the end of the cold war and proposes a restructuring of defence capabilities for new roles – but on a larger scale than other European countries and keeping Trident.

About Turn, Forward March with Europe: new directions for defence and security policy (edited by Jane M.O. Sharpe, IPPR/Rivers Oram, 1996) is a collection of studies covering nuclear, chemical, biological and conventional weapons and roles, missions and resources in the post-cold war world, and arguing for a restructuring of capabilities with closer European integration.

Index